Doing Identity Labor

Doing Identity Labor

How Mixed-Race Politicians Disrupt Descriptive Representation

Danielle Casarez Lemi

OXFORD UNIVERSITY PRESS

OXFORD
UNIVERSITY PRESS

Oxford University Press is a department of the University of Oxford. It furthers the University's objective of excellence in research, scholarship, and education by publishing worldwide. Oxford is a registered trade mark of Oxford University Press in the UK and in certain other countries.

Published in the United States of America by Oxford University Press 198 Madison Avenue, New York, NY 10016, United States of America.

CIP data is on file at the Library of Congress

ISBN 9780197816820

ISBN 9780197816813 (hbk.)

DOI: 10.1093/9780197816851.001.0001

Paperback printed by Integrated Books International, United States of America

The manufacturer's authorized representative in the EU for product safety is Oxford University Press España S.A. of Parque Empresarial San Fernando de Henares, Avenida de Castilla, 2 – 28830 Madrid (www.oup.es/en or product.safety@oup.com). OUP España S.A. also acts as importer into Spain of products made by the manufacturer.

To Union City, CA

The town and the people that inspired this book.

And to Bernadette.

Contents

Acknowledgments

In December 2019, six months after moving to the midwest and starting a new post-doc, I submitted my two weeks' notice to quit. I was over academic precarity.

So I broke my lease. Sold my furniture on Craigslist. And bought a one-way plane ticket to Dallas, Texas.

When I quit, Nadia Brown shared Zora Neale Hurston's quote with me: "If you are silent about your pain, they'll kill you and say you enjoyed it," and I've lived by it since. I will always remember and appreciate how Nadia and Ryon Cobb encouraged me to use my voice and how Valeria Sinclair-Chapman said what needed to be said.

I have never regretted leaving. I could not stay in that situation and be proud of myself. If your department doesn't recognize your value (see Dr. Monica Cox's work on diversity), save up your "f∗ck you" money and do what you need to do to take care of yourself.

After moving into my new apartment, I treated myself. I went to the spa and got a massage. I got a fresh set of nails. I dressed up in a sparkly, gun-metal jumper with beaded black heels and purple eyeshadow. I took myself out to a New Year's Eve party with The Asociación Puertorriqueña de Dallas-Fort Worth. In the Lyft to the party, I marveled at the lights of the downtown skyline and thought to myself, "I can't believe I did it. I left. I'm here. I did it." After ringing in the new year at midnight, I celebrated with late-night French toast at IHOP. I was ready to start my new life.

The transition was bittersweet in the months that followed. I had way more stability. More free time. Didn't have to worry about peer review or hitting some number of publications per year anymore. Didn't have to go to conferences anymore. I slept. So. Good. But I felt disconnected from the people from my old life. My routine had changed. I would stay in touch, but it wouldn't be the same. I miss everyone.

In those months, I was grateful to peers (including peers a little more senior) who shared kind words and/or were explicit about including me in various academic activities. Thank you for not forgetting about me: Natasha Altema-McNeely, Guillermo Caballero, Polly Calderon, David Cortez, Vanessa Cruz Nichols, Al Fang, Brielle Harbin, Jenn Jackson, Melina Juárez, Ron Kwon, Nazita Lajevardi, Greg Leslie, Maricruz Osorio,

Mara Ostfeldt, Periloux Peay, Ngoc Phan, Alicia Reyes-Barriéntez, Jamil Scott, Shyam Sriram, Fernando Tormos-Aponte, Rachel Torres, Dilara Üsküp, Gabi Vitela, Meghan Wilson, Diane Wong, and Kelly Zvobgo.

My new routine meant I could read more widely. I could produce truly interdisciplinary work. I could write what I wanted. I could grow. I joined a collective, Decolonizing Political Science, and I met beautiful people who showed me a better way. Their influence is reflected in this book's final form.

As I settled into my new routine, I was humbled by the support of close senior colleagues, mentors, and coauthors. At Southern Methodist University's Tower Center, Jim Hollifield, Luisa del Rosal, Ray Rafidi, and Bora Laçi gave me institutional affiliation so I could keep going. And although I learned that I could not carry major grants without employment at a university—even with a faculty sponsor—Marianne Stewart at the University of Texas, Dallas supported my application to a National Science Foundation grant to conduct more data collection for this book.

The Tower Center was the best gig ever and I had so much fun those two years. Dallas changed my life and I'll forever be grateful to this city and the communities that welcomed me. I love Texas. I pity the Coastal Libs who talk down on Texas or the people who live there—bless their hearts. Shoutout to Ryon, Alicia Reyes-Barriéntez, and Aileen Cardona-Arroyo for telling me to apply to and join SMU.

I presented this book to a few venues and received thoughtful comments and engagement. In 2021, thanks to Neil Foley and Ruth Elmore at the Clements Center and Jim Hollifield and Bora Laçi at the Tower Center, I had a virtual book workshop and received invaluable feedback from Lauren Davenport, Natalie Masuoka, and Valeria Sinclair-Chapman. They spent their whole morning and afternoon with me, and I'm incredibly grateful for their support. In 2023, Greg Leslie kindly invited me to share my work at The Racial Frontier: Multiracial or Mixed-Race Research in the Social Sciences at Princeton University, and I got to spend a whole day with creative folks interested in mixed-race identity. In 2024, Ange-Marie Hancock invited me to present my work to the Kirwan Institute at Ohio State University as part of the Kamala Harris Project; I was star-struck and honored to participate in the conversation. Thank you to all of you for making the time and creating the space for me and my work.

Mirya Holman, a wonderful senior mentor, recommended to me Kelly Clancy at Epilogue Editing as a developmental editor, and the experience was transformational. Kelly and Angela Chnapko at Oxford University Press were there throughout all the rounds of revisions, giving me helpful guidance to improve the story. Ashley Beene copyedited the drafts before the drafts, carefully catching all the awkward sentences. Many thanks to the anonymous reviewers for pushing me to make the manuscript better. In this book, I tried to venture a bit into creative non-fiction and was inspired by Anthony Ocampo's, Davin Phoenix's, and Steven Salaita's writing styles. I took creative writing classes with Catapult while I wrote this book. Hope my attempt worked!

I've been thinking about this book for a very long time. Portions of the book were published/built on research published in:

Lemi, Danielle Casarez. 2017. "Identity and Coalitions in a Multiracial era: How State Legislators Navigate Race and Ethnicity." *Politics, Groups, and Identities*, 6(4): 725–742. https://doi.org/10.1080/21565503.2017.1288144, copyright © 2017 Western Political Science Association, reprinted by permission of Taylor & Francis. Ltd, https://www.tandfonline.com on behalf of 2017 Western Political Science Association

Lemi, Danielle Casarez. 2021. "Do Voters Prefer Just Any Descriptive Representative? The Case of Multiracial Candidates." *Perspectives on Politics* 19(4): 1061–81. doi: 10.1017/S1537592720001280. © American Political Science Association 2020, published by Cambridge University Press, Reprinted with permission.

The research in Chapter 3 was funded by the Peter G. Peterson US 2050 Project, and the research in Chapter 5 was funded by the Qualtrics Behavioral Research Grant. Thank you to Grace Reon and Rachel Forster for excellent research assistance in the earlier phases of this project.

Along the way I received encouragement, meaningful support, and helpful feedback on drafts of drafts of drafts. I can't remember everyone (please forgive me if you should be on this list, I haven't seen most of you in years!), but thank you. In addition to the folks already named above, I'd like to also thank: Janni Aragon, Maneesh Arora, Sharon Austin, Nichole Bauer, Tiffany Barnes, Michael Bernhard, Ray Block, Cristina Bodea, Tabitha Bonilla-Silva, Shaun Bowler, John Bretting, David Brunsma, Shantel Buggs, Mary Campbell, Tony Carey Jr., Ivy Cargile, Chinbo Chong, Harold Clarke, Jared Clemons, Allan Colbern, Loren Collingwood, Jonathan Collins, Alex Coppock, Kim Yi Dionne, Kelly Dittmar, Kevin Esterling, Emily Farris, Andrew Flores, Bernard Fraga, Luis Fraga, Lorrie Frasure, Jennifer Garcia, Sarah Gershon, Andra Gillespie, Eric Gonzalez Juenke, Roberto Gallardo, Sergio Garcia-Rios, Farah Godrej, Jake Grumbach, Sarah Hayes, Melissa Herman, Mirya Holman, Jane Junn, Nathan Kalmoe, Augustine Kposowa,

Mona Lena Krook, Pei-te Lien, Val Martinez-Ebers, Yalidy Matos, Jessica Lavariega Monforti, Anna Mahoney, Liz Maltby, Kim Mealy, Jenn Merolla, Melissa Michelson, Ángel Molina, Ben Newman, Angela Ocampo, Anthony Ocampo, Francisco Pedraza, Davin Phoenix, Dianne Pinderhughes, Rebecca Reid, Molly Reynolds, Emmit Riley, Sara Sadhwani, Ani Sarkissian, Kira Sanbonmatsu, Monica Schneider, Paru Shah, Sono Shah, Andrea Silva, Jennifer Sims, Christopher Stout, Logan Strother, Joe Tafoya, Jakana Thomas, Vanessa Tyson, Erika Vallejo, Yamil Velez, Ajay Verghese, Hannah Walker, Julian Wamble, Nick Weller, Tiffany Willoughby-Herard, Ricardo Ramírez, Tye Rush, Gabe Sanchez, Candis Watts Smith, Christina Wolbrecht, and Christina Xydias. I'd also like to thank participants at PRIEC, SPIRE, and IPRG meetings. Thank you to Mo Torres for introducing me to Fields and Fields's *Racecraft*—it helped me figure out what I'd been trying to say for years.

Thank you to digital artist David Maloba (Instagram: @maloba_david) for the beautiful cover art! The cover of the book is based on a photo of Barack Obama and Kamala Harris fist-bumping at the 2021 presidential inauguration, still masked up to protect themselves and others from COVID-19. When I saw that photo, I *knew* I wanted that interaction to be on the cover. I found Maloba's renditions of the Obamas and Joe Biden and Kamala Harris on Instagram and loved that style of drawing. I am thankful that Maloba accepted my commission and supported the vision.

Big shout out to my professors at San Jose State University in San Jose, CA, who showed undergraduate me what was possible: Constantine Danopoulos, Lawrence Quill, Kenneth Peter, Kathryn Wood, and Marianina Olcott. Much love to my McNair family and Jeannine Slater and Nisha Gurbuxani. PROTECT TRIO!!

I must give a big thanks to my glam team that I met in Michigan—Vanitee Nails & Spa (Lansing) and Hair by Renee (Okemos). They made me look good, and they created fun atmospheres for me to talk about all the profiles I swiped left on while I lived there. I miss them.

My family has always helped make whatever I want to happen possible. My mom, dad, and sister are the inspiration for many of my ideas. Everyone in our family is mixed and has a different dad.

My partner has been here for the entire writing process. I wanted to quit many times. I wrote this book while still working through my complicated feelings of leaving academia, the career path that had been my plan for a decade. I wrote while feeling anger towards predatory diversity post-doc programs and disappointment with the faculty who promote them. I wrote while adjusting to the challenges of trying to finish up my research pipeline while working a 9-to-5. I wrote in the early mornings before work and in the evenings til past midnight after work. I wrote on weekends. I used my PTO to write, workshop, or give talks. I wrote without a research budget, conference budget, and access to university funds, major grants, or research leaves. My partner made all of this possible by graciously cleaning, cooking meals, and listening to me work through my ideas. My partner believed in this project even when I considered dropping it. Valar morghulis.

And most importantly, I want to express my sincere gratitude to those who participated in the research presented in this book. To the people who took my surveys, legislative staff who kindly got me on legislators' schedules, and legislators who told me candid stories about their lives—thank you.

1
Introduction

"What are you? . . . are you really?"

–A common question

This book is about ethnoracial identity and representational politics, but it's also about me and my hometown. I grew up in Union City, California, a suburb of San Francisco in the East Bay Area. I am a lighter-skinned Mexican and Filipino American with some maternal ancestry that traces to Poland—though our ancestral origin on that side has long been unclear. Mexipinos are common in California (Guevarra 2012).

I haven't been home in a decade. But when you land at Oakland International Airport (OAK) and enter the jetway, the fresh air and breeze of the bay hit you immediately. Growing up, Union City was over 40 percent Asian American and about a quarter Hispanic[1]—and you could smell the Filipino food in the air. My hometown hosts myriad Filipino stores and restaurants: Seafood City Supermarket, Red Ribbon Bakeshop, Valerio's Tropical Bakeshop, Island Pacific Seafood Market, Gerry's Grill, and of course, Jollibee. On the weekends, when my mom would run errands, she'd take me with her to get foods you could only get somewhere like Seafood City—like fried tilapia, head on, to eat for dinner with chopped white onions, tomatoes, rice, and soy sauce. Sweet Sensations, then a local Filipino bakery and dessert shop, was my favorite. On hot days, we'd head to Sweet Sensations for halo halos, puto, and kutsinta. In the evenings, she taught me how to cook rice in a rice cooker using a line on my finger to measure the water, how to roll lumpia, and how to make pancit, palabok, adobo, and lugaw. Every day, we took our shoes off at the front door when we got home. And while our family was not religious and rarely went to church, I received my first communion at St. Anne Catholic Church, a predominantly Filipino American church (I later dropped out of confirmation classes, to my mom's dismay because she couldn't get a refund on the course fee). I did not fully appreciate any of this until I found myself in a predominantly white setting in graduate school. The

[1] Bay Area Census. 2025. "Union City: Total Population in 2000." https://census.bayareametro.gov/population?year=2000&location=union_city.

Doing Identity Labor. Danielle Casarez Lemi, Oxford University Press. © Oxford University Press (2025).
DOI: 10.1093/9780197816851.003.0001

funny thing about this is that while my mother bore the duty of exposing me to my Filipino heritage, she's not Filipino. My mother grew up in Oakland with a large Asian American community and a Filipino father figure. Marrying my dad meant marrying his culture too.

My middle school, now named after Filipino American labor organizers Larry Itliong and Philip Vera Cruz, is off Fredi St.[2] In middle school, I started to feel like I did not fit in with Filipino Americans specifically.[3] My skin lightened, my nose lengthened, my eyebrows got thicker, and my arms got hairier. Like many other Filipino Americans, I don't speak a Filipino language, ours being Tagalog. I also don't speak Spanish, and I am fourth-generation American on my Mexican American side. When I started middle school, I realized people thought I was white as I slowly changed from looking like my dad to looking like my mom. As I made new friends, I became exposed to Filipino and Filipino American musicians, playing Jessa Zaragoza's hit "Bakit Pa?" over and over while looking up the translated lyrics online. I listened to One Vo1ce, a girl band from Vallejo. I also remember trying to make new friends by joining a student club geared toward Latinx students, but I didn't speak Spanish or know much about Mexico. At that age, I realized I lacked a set of assumed attributes and cultural traditions that others believed made someone legitimately Mexican American or Filipino American. Mexican American peers tended to accept that I was Mexican, but knew I couldn't speak Spanish. Filipino American peers didn't recognize I was Filipino upon seeing me frequently commented on my appearance after learning our shared heritage. I now looked white to many of my peers in the Bay Area ... but I wasn't ... *white.* How could I be "white" if my family came from the same islands, ate the same food, heard the same language spoken at family

[2] ABC7News. 2015. Union City school to be first named after Filipino-Americans in US. December 14. https://abc7news.com/bay-area-school-alvarado-middle-in-union-city-named-for-filipino-americans-larry-itliong-and-phillip-vera-cruz/1122779/.

[3] I use the term "ethnoracial" to describe the different groups of politicians I analyze (Garcia Bedolla 2014, 5). In the social sciences, race and ethnicity are commonly used interchangeably (e.g., Sen and Wasow 2016, 500). American courts have treated ethnic categories as racial categories (Bridges 2013, also see page 70). Using these terms interchangeably conflates the very real differences within racial groups and within ethnic groups. For example, consider the vast diversity of those considered "Latinx." Latinx people can appear Black, white, brown or something else. Using these terms interchangeably also muddles the distinction between the mixed ethnoracial ancestry between peoples generations ago, as is conceived by the notion of *mestizaje,* and mixed ethnoracial ancestry in the United States that derives from contemporary inter-ethnoracial couples having kids (Turner 2014).

Yet, ethnic groups are still *racialized* (Garcia Bedolla 2014, 5). For example, people often talk about "Latinx" people as if they constitute a racial group. Mixed people, when talking about their background, may say "I'm Blaxican" (Romo 2011) to note non-Black Latinx and African American ancestry. To resolve these conflations, I use the term "ethnoracial" to recognize how ethnic groups become racialized (Garcia-Bedolla 2014, 5). When I say ethnoracial groups, I'm talking about the social and political meaning of those ethnoracial group memberships (strmic-pawl 2014). For a more in-depth analysis that reconciles the tensions between "race" and "ethnicity," see Ifatunji (2024).

gatherings, worshipped in the same place, and lived in the same heavily Asian American community as my peers? As is common in studies of mixed people, I know now that how I saw myself was not always aligned with how people saw me.

Fast forward to present-day Danielle. As I developed what would become this book, I dove into the decades of sociological research on mixed identities. I learned about the Multiracial Category Movement of the 1990s, chronicled and analyzed by Kim Williams (2006) in *Mark One or More: Civil Rights in Multiracial America.* I read scholars such as Kerry Ann Rockquemore, David Brunsma, Kristen Renn, Jennifer Lee, Frank Bean, and more who helped me understand that the experiences of mixed people were context-dependent. I saw similarities between my experiences and what mixed persons shared with researchers.

I also became interested in the challenges that mixed identity posed for descriptive representation. Conceptually, a descriptive representative is a politician who shares experiences or characteristics, like ethnorace, with their constituents (Pitkin 1967, chapter 4; Mansbridge 1999, 628)—like how Vice President Kamala Harris may represent both Black Americans and Asian Americans. Hannah Pitkin (1967) was skeptical about the concept of descriptive representation, arguing that just because a representative "looks like" their constituents does not mean they will "act for" their constituents. By contrast, Jane Mansbridge (1999, 628) suggested that for ethnoracial representation in particular, having representatives in office who look like members of marginalized groups yields substantive representation when those groups have a reason to distrust the government or do not have clear policy preferences. Mansbridge (1999, 628) also argued that the experience of being a member of that group may then inform how they legislate and that their presence may legitimize our political institutions. Empirically, American politics research shows that legislators of color harness their experiences to advocate for their communities (e.g., Swain 1993, 211; Tate 1997; Canon 1999, 153; Haynie 2001; Casellas 2010; Grose 2011; Hero and Preuhs 2013; Minta and Sinclair-Chapman 2013; Rouse 2013; Broockman 2013; Brown 2014a; Minta and Brown 2014; Tyson 2016; Dancey and Masand 2019; Minta 2020).

But when I put the research on mixed identity and representation in American politics in conversation with my own experiences, I had more questions about descriptive representation, its empirical effect, and the approaches political scientists use to define and measure it. If in predominantly Asian American spaces, I am presumed to be white, if I ran for office, would I be considered a descriptive representative of Filipino Americans? If in predominantly Latinx spaces, I am accepted as Latina, would I lose votes from Asian

Americans if I ran as a Latina candidate? If I joined the Congressional Asian Pacific American Caucus and the Congressional Hispanic Caucus, would my bills be more successful? Would I even count as a legitimate descriptive representative for both groups? On the one hand, traditional definitions of descriptive representatives based on "visible" characteristics indicating some "shared experience," like skin tone or facial features we use to classify people ethnoracially, would mean I don't qualify to represent Filipino Americans, but I could possibly qualify to represent Latinx Americans (Mansbridge 1999, 629, 647). On the other hand, actual practices in political science would mean scholars would code me as both Latina and Asian American, and probably be unsure of what to do with me in a statistical analysis. How could I reconcile what I saw in the real world with what political scientists were doing?

Americans saw mixed candidates on four presidential tickets between 2008 and 2024.[4] At the same time, according to the US Census Bureau, the two-or-more races population grew by 276 percent from 2010 to 2020 (US Census Bureau 2021).[5] The rise of Barack Obama and Kamala Harris, two of the most powerful national leaders, most powerful Black leaders, and what we now call "mixed" leaders, is set against the backdrop of a historical legacy of the enslavement of Africans, settler colonialism, racist immigration laws, bans on inter-ethnoracial[6] marriages between whites and non-whites, and a mixed population that the census now recognizes as the "two-or-more races" population. Yet, the current scholarship on representation in political science cannot adequately speak to what these developments mean for the future of American representative democracy. This book fills that gap.

[4] Scholars use various terms, including multiracial, biracial, and mixed-race, to describe mixed people, while typically referring to those who are not mixed as "monoracial." All of these terms falsely imply that ethnorace is biologically inherited, that pure ethnoraces exist at all, and that mixed people are created through the biological mixing of the ethnoraces (Spencer 1999). In reality, ethnorace is made through social and political interactions (Omi and Winant 1994; Moya and Markus 2010). Even so, when we talk about our ethnoracial identities, biological lineage is a part of those conversations—our parents pass their ethnoracial memberships down to us through appearances, names, and culture (Chandra 2006). Rather than use terms that imply biology, I instead refer to people as mixed and non-mixed to emphasize their ancestry. By mixed, I refer to those who have parentage and/or grandparentage from different ethnoracial groups. By non-mixed, I refer to those who have parentage and/or grandparentage from the same ethnoracial groups. Everyday individuals who have mixed grandparentage may have social experiences that are distinct from those who who have mixed parentage (e.g., Pilgrim 2020; also see Morning and Saperstein 2018), but I include politicians who have mixed grandparentage because their grandparentage gives them the option to strategically deploy a specific identity, like US Representative Bobby Scott, who has Black and Filipino ancestry, and former US Senator John Ensign, who has white and Filipino ancestry (also see Ensign 2009).

[5] Notably, this estimate has come under scrutiny as being driven by statistical procedures rather than actual population growth (Starr and Pao 2024).

[6] Because I use "ethnorace" rather than "race," I also use "inter-ethnoracial" rather than "interracial" to describe mixed couples.

Identity Labor

How might politicians use their ethnoracial identities strategically when engaging with different political stakeholders? What does it mean to be a descriptive representative of American communities of color in an increasingly diverse democracy? What does the growth of the mixed population mean for how we think about and study representation? To answer these big questions, I theorize the concept of *identity labor* to understand and explain how politicians use their identities strategically.[7] Identity labor is the public, transactional, politically consequential work that politicians must perform to manage the public's perceptions of their identity in our "reality" of ethnorace.

By using the term identity labor, I assert that politicians attempt to manage others' perceptions of all of their identities, ethnorace being one, as part of a transaction. Politicians are powerful individuals who cultivate relationships with constituents (Fenno 1978). Managing others' perceptions is strategic and calculated, with various time horizons. Politicians must be mindful of how the media covers them, how voters form opinions about them and reward or punish them at the ballot box, and who becomes an ally or an obstacle within the legislature. Their actions have strategic purposes. They market aspects of themselves to various stakeholders with the hope that the labor will pay off with votes, a passed policy, favorable media coverage, favorable public opinion ratings, or genuinely better relationships with their constituents. The transactional nature of this labor does not imply ingenuity. For example, consider how in 2019, former New York City Mayor Bill de Blasio referenced having a Black son as part of his political narrative.[8] When de Blasio did this, it was an attempt to signal to voters, and perhaps Black voters specifically, that he cares about issues he may believe are of interest to Black parents, Black men, and younger Black people. When Jeb Bush speaks Spanish or talks about his Mexican wife, he attempts to signal to Latinx voters that he is a politician who will serve their interests (Alamillo and Collingwood 2017).

[7] In this book, I do not dive deep into the intersectionality of ethnoracial categories and other categories like class, gender, or sexuality because I am interested in multiple ethnoracial categories as the core analysis. I recognize how the way one experiences ethnorace depends on how they experience gender, or sexuality, or class (Crenshaw 1991; Hancock 2007; Davenport 2016b; Waring 2013; Sims and Njaka 2019, 93–101). I view multiple ethnoracial group membership as a layer of variation, or a type of intersection, within ethnoracial groups (Monk 2022). Moreover, I am conscious about deeply discussing the identities of representatives who participated in my research, beyond ethnorace, to protect their confidentiality. Future research should explicitly study how other identities affect descriptive representatives.

[8] Mays, J.C. 2019. Why "raising a Black son" is a de Blasio campaign theme. *Philadelphia Tribune*. July 5.

Politicians act strategically, and identity labor captures the general strategic public relations management that politicians attempt to perform.[9]

I argue that when a politician is classified into multiple ethnoracial categories, the classification raises questions about how well the politician adheres to the group identity—resulting in both favorable and unfavorable evaluations from different actors. For everyday mixed people, this is why "What are you?" is a common question (e.g., Bernstein and la Cruz 2009; Pew Research Center 2015, 55), and why some mixed people may experience challenges to their identities from others. The classification to more than one category disrupts the ability to make sense of ethnorace in a traditional sense (Moya and Markus 2010)—people cannot easily apply dominant stereotypes to someone to make quick inferences about them after learning they are mixed. In response to learning someone is mixed, people may classify that person according to the context and their own identities (Hogg et al. 1995; Sims 2025). How stakeholders classify a politician is an important aspect of the relationship building between politicians and their stakeholders. Mixed classification of a politician causes a disruption to stakeholders' ability to quickly make inferences about a politician's group loyalties and creates opportunities for a politician to use identity labor to manage perceptions of their identity.

I base my argument primarily on the social identity theory of leadership, a social psychological theory about how people come to occupy leadership positions of groups (Abrams and Hogg 1990; Hogg 2001; Hogg et al. 2012; also see Hogg et al. 1995). People nested in group identities "cognitively represent social categories as prototypes," or exemplars of what it means to be a social group member (Hogg and Reid 2006, 10). More prototypical people tend to rise to leadership partly because they "embody" the group (Hogg 2001, 189–190). Mixed politicians, by definition, don't fit into dominant ideas of what constitutes single ethnoracial categories—they're not prototypical.

Of course, mixed politicians are not the only individuals who perform identity labor. Politicians, mixed or not, commonly appeal to cultural authenticity (or to representing a supposed essential component of a culture), to demonstrate that they truly reflect the "typical" voter from that ethnoracial or ethnic group (McIlwain and Caliendo 2011, 39). Politicians of color may encounter accusations that they aren't "Black enough" if they have a particular social network (e.g., Dovi 2002, 737) or are not authentically Latinx if they do not speak Spanish (e.g., Lavariega Monforti et al. 2013). Politicians of any ethnoracial

[9] See Nancy Leong's (2013) *Identity Capitalists: The Powerful Insiders Who Exploit Diversity to Maintain Inequality* for an analysis of how institutions may capitalize on identity.

background may feel compelled to prove to voters that they are not some watered-down version of the group.

However, I contend that identity labor is acute for mixed politicians because they belong to more than one category. Because of their mixed classification, mixed politicians must strengthen their claims to group membership above and beyond cultural authenticity. Paula McClain and co-authors define "group membership" as the "assignment of an individual into a particular group based on characteristics that are specific to that group, in accordance with widely held intersubjective norms" (McClain et al. 2009, 473). In this book, I treat claims to cultural authenticity as related to, but distinct from, claims to ethnoracial group membership. The identity labor that one performs to claim group membership is motivated by a need to prove to others that you are, in fact, a member of an ethnoracial group *because* you lack "the characteristics that are specific to that group" (McClain et al. 2009, 473), including non-mixed parentage. Politicians who aren't mixed may feel pressure to show authenticity or group loyalty, but politicians who are mixed may more often feel compelled show that they are telling the truth about their group membership in ways non-mixed politicians are not.

I also argue that identity labor is complicated by questions about physical appearance. People may not always know a politician's ethnoracial identity just by looking at their faces, either because they present as ethnoracially ambiguous or do not appear to be a member of one of their ethnoracial groups. Again, this is not unique to mixed people. For instance, sociological research has shown that Filipino Americans are commonly confused with Latinx Americans (Ocampo 2014). Indeed, one study found that 6 percent of Asian, Black, Latinx, and white Americans surveyed (combined) reported they believed that others perceived them differently from their ethnoracial identity (Vargas and Stainback 2016, 450; also see Herman 2010). Additionally, others' perceptions of us are context-dependent. Jennifer Sims (2025) argues that in good or neutral contexts, people may sort individuals based on their appearances into higher status categories, and in negative contexts, into lower status categories. As Sims's own experiences show, you don't have to be mixed to have people misclassify you and ask, "What are you?" Although the experiences I describe in this book may apply to non-mixed politicians, I use the case of mixed politicians to argue that scholars of descriptive representation overlook this phenomenon. My focus is on the confusion that arises—and the identity labor that ensues—when politicians are classified into multiple categories and have appearances that do not obviously convey their ethnoracial backgrounds. As the following chapters will show, mixed politicians may encounter questions about their ethnoracial identity and their claims to group membership because of their multiple ethnoracial group memberships and how they look—a function of the constructed "reality" of ethnorace. I offer identity labor as a challenge to traditional descriptive presentation theory.

The work of identity

Identity labor, as I develop it here, is an interdisciplinary concept. I derive identity labor from the work of sociologists, primarily David Snow and Leon Anderson (1987) and Nikki Khanna and Cathryn Johnson (2010). Snow and Anderson (1987) use the term *identity work* to describe various tactics unhoused people use to construct their identities. Two of those tactics are relevant for studying politicians' behavior: embracement, which is the affirmation of assignment to a given category, and distancing, which is the disassociation from assignment to a given category (Snow and Anderson 1987, 1348, 1354). Khanna and Johnson (2010) expanded identity work into the concept of *racial identity work*, which refers to the various strategic interpersonal actions that mixed Black and white individuals take to manage how others, and sometimes bureaucracies, perceive their identities. For example, mixed persons may strategically develop "racial elevator speeches" that quickly provide information about their backgrounds to satisfy those curious (Heilman 2022).

Building on these concepts, I use *identity labor* to emphasize the strategic and transactional nature of this work and its application to how identities, in this case, ethnorace, function *for politicians*. The difference between everyday people managing their identities and politicians navigating society's expectations is that politicians' abilities to form authentic relationships with people, often based on shared ethnoracial identity, directly affect the welfare of their constituents. This distinguishes the work of politicians from that of everyday people. Doing identity labor is an integral part of becoming a descriptive representative in the first place.

As the title of the book, *Doing Identity Labor*, emphasizes, identity labor consists of actions. I build on Paula Moya and Hazel Rose Markus's (2010) *doing race* framework (which I refer to as doing ethnorace from here on), to conceptualize how individuals perform ethnorace. Simply put, "ethnorace" is created in our daily lives through actions tied to beliefs about ethnorace, racism, diversity, pride in one's group, and the so-called biological basis of ethnorace, to name a few (Moya and Markus 2010, 6). Ethnorace, as Moya and Markus (2010, 21) conceive of it, consists of actions that take place between people across time and space that impose ethnoracial categories onto people and assign them power based on those categories. For instance, consider the historical one-drop rule for African Americans in the United States. Historically, the one-drop rule was a social norm and legal practice that assigned anyone with a "drop" of Black blood to be classified as absolutely Black (Hollinger 2005). This meant that a person with one Black grandparent or great-grandparent could be classified as Black regardless of whether they appeared white and had more immediate white ancestors than Black ancestors. They would be counted as such on the US Census and subject to Jim Crow laws. In another time or geography, this person might be considered white because of how they looked and because most of their immediate ancestry was white, but in the 1900s, this person was Black. The people who wrote and enforced Jim Crow laws and championed false ethnorace science at the Census Bureau were doing ethnorace (e.g., McRae 2020; Nobles 2000). When the media, pundits, and opponents dismiss the value of descriptive representation as "just identity politics," they are doing ethnorace (Moya and Markus 2010, 6). When descriptive representatives publicly express pride in their ethnorace or the diversity of the United States, they are doing ethnorace (Moya and Markus 2010, 6). Ethnorace becomes contextually meaningful in our everyday lives because people, situated in relationships and structures of power, make it meaningful through action (Moya and Markus 2010, 19).

As I explore identity labor in the book, I show that mixed politicians' performances of identity labor hinge on how their families taught them to think about their identities, the power that society bestows to their ethnoracial groups, and how society maps their biological characteristics, like skin tone, to ethnoracial categories.

The performance of identity

At its core, identity labor is an interaction between a descriptive representative and society at large. Identity labor is a way that politicians "perform" their ethnoracial identities to meet others' expectations (West and Fenstermaker 1995, 23). Those expectations may involve meeting some criteria for what makes someone "legitimately" Asian American, like speaking an Asian language, or "acceptable," like being sufficiently "Americanized," to hold a political office.[10] Descriptive representatives may also perform identity labor to navigate negative generalizations people make about their ethnoracial group based on their individual actions (West and Fenstermaker 1995, 23). Black women politicians, for instance, may strive to genuinely be themselves while also remaining aware of how others will perceive them when they straighten or wear natural hairstyles on the campaign trail (Sims et al.

[10] See Kim (1999).

2020; Brown and Lemi 2021). To meet these expectations of their ethnoracial identity, descriptive representatives perform identity through identity labor.

Identity labor in the "reality" of ethnorace

Politicians do not perform identity labor in a vacuum. Although they exercise agency in their public performances, their performances are necessarily a response to the "reality" of ethnorace in American politics. Karen Fields and Barbara Fields (2014, 17) use the term *racecraft* to describe the literal construction, often through language and interpersonal interactions, of ethnoracial meaning in everyday life. The notion of ethnorace as a biological characteristic—that we can see it, inherit it, measure it in fractions, and use it to predict medical research and outcomes, is racecraft (Fields and Fields 2014, chapter 1; also see Spencer 1999). Ethnoracial categories are so ingrained in our lives that they constitute "common sense" (Omi and Winant 1994, 59): everyone belongs to one, and we can sort people into these categories based on facial features, names, language, and stereotypical behaviors. The notion that ethnoraces are "real" pervades contemporary social science research on racism, reinforcing the idea that ethnoracial categories, and not racism, lead to differences in social outcomes (Torres and Clemons 2022). I argue that ethnorace as biology also pervades current theorizing of descriptive representation when politicians are thought to "look like" a community defined by an ethnoracial category (also see Torres 2023). Politicians who perform identity labor may even inadvertently affirm the legitimacy of ethnoracial classifications and the social expectations that underlie those classifications (e.g., Heilman 2022, 2–3). When politicians perform identity labor, they respond to a broader ecosystem that dictates their ethnoracial classification and proper modes of behavior in American politics. Identity labor is not a disruption to the status quo. It's a dance with it.

Analyzing identity labor

Although all politicians perform identity labor, the degree to which they do so and how depends on their position within the ethnoracial hierarchy. Because of the way others respond to their multiple classification and their appearances, mixed politicians are especially likely to perform identity labor. I adopt Natalie Masuoka and Jane Junn's (2013) conceptualization of the "ethnoracial hierarchy" to refer to the general social and political organization of ethnoracial groups, specifically Black, Asian American, white, and Latinx Americans, in the United States. Historical processes created a hierarchy that consists of white people at the top, Black people at the bottom, and Latinx and Asian American between white and Black people, and a distinct relationship between Native Americans and the United States (Masuoka and Junn 2013, Figure 1.2, 22).[11] I view the position of mixed politicians in the hierarchy as the interaction of their ethnoracial backgrounds. For instance, the experiences of being mixed Black and Asian American and mixed white and Asian American are different because the ethnoracial categories interact differently (Hancock 2007). This context is critical to understanding why the experiences of mixed politicians differ by their specific ethnoracial backgrounds.

Finally, I use intersectionality and Critical Mixed Race Studies (CMRS) as analytical tools to understand the interactive relationships between multiple ethnoracial categories as individual politicians experience those categories (Hancock 2007; Daniel et al. 2014, 8; Monk 2022). My thinking is particularly influenced by Tanya Katerí Hernández (2018, chapter 2). Hernández shows that mixed people do not necessarily experience ethnorace-based discrimination because they are mixed; instead, they experience discrimination based on their specific backgrounds, mainly Black. Throughout the book, I harness CMRS's treatment of ethnoracial classification as "unstable" (Daniel et al. 2014, 8). I am not telling a story about how the future is mixed or how mixed politicians represent the consciousness of mixed people. Instead, I'm interested in how mixed politicians disrupt our fundamental thinking about ethnorace and descriptive representation. I show that the experiences of mixed politicians present challenges for how we theorize descriptive representation.

The Tensions of Traditional Descriptive Representation

The analyses of how mixed representatives perform identity labor in this book will reveal slippage in who qualifies as a descriptive representative, and more broadly, the tensions inherent in current descriptive representation theory. Traditionally, to descriptively represent a given ethnoracial group is to have "visible" characteristics that conform to an ethnoracial category in our head—we know "what" you are when we see you (Omi and Winant 1994; Mansbridge 1999, 647). However, studying mixed representatives helps us draw out three tensions in conceptualizing descriptive representation this way.

The first tension is that descriptive representation, as a concept applied to the United States of America and meant to benefit marginalized people

[11] Other scholars have discussed similar structural organizations of ethnorace, such as Bonilla-Silva (2004).

of color, reifies the supremacy of whiteness. For Mansbridge (1999, 641), one of the necessary conditions for the benefits of descriptive representation to outweigh its costs is a "context of distrust" as a result of "historical circumstances [that] interfere with adequate communication between members of" a dominant group and a subordinate group. Although unintentional, this specification does not name the specificity of the "historical circumstances" that impede communication—enslavement and settler colonialism on the part of white enslavers and colonizers (see Feagin 2013; Fields and Fields 2014).

While Mansbridge is writing from the immediate context of American white violence and anti-Blackness, this theorizing of descriptive representation obfuscates the institutionalized problem of white supremacy in American politics. Descriptive representatives effectively only exist for visible people of color, who are by default and to varying degrees, disempowered relative to whites (Kim 1999; Masuoka and Junn 2013). Descriptive representatives are defined by the extent to which they deviate from whiteness—and whiteness is held as the normative, "default category" for "normal" representatives (Masuoka and Junn 2013).[12]

The second tension is that current theory operationalizes ethnorace as a biological trait, invoking white logics that associate ethnorace with biology (Zuberi and Bonilla-Silva 2008). Hannah Pitkin (1967, 80) defined descriptive representation as the extent to "which a person or thing stands for others 'by being sufficiently like them.'" Importantly, Pitkin (1967, 81) did not specify that a descriptive representative is one who looks like anything, but instead that they "are" or "are like" something within their constituents. Pitkin (1967, 89) recognized that descriptive representation did not guarantee substantive representation—just because someone is like you does not mean they will represent you. Mansbridge (1999, 647) suggested that the power of descriptive representation, particularly of marginalized groups, stems from the "visible characteristics [that are] the outward signs of the shared experience" between the representative and the group. These "visible characteristics" are the "outward manifestations of belonging to the group" (Mansbridge 1999, 628), in this case, visual markers of ethnorace. Descriptive representation is thus defined by the presence of biological characteristics associated with ethnoracial categories. In this definition, Mansbridge (1999) leans on "race as common sense," or the scripts we have in our heads about what a Black, white, Asian, or Latinx representative "looks like" (Omi and Winant 1994, 59). Yet, as Fields and Fields (2014, 27) say: "Everyone has skin color, but not

[12] Location 177. The Kindle version of this book does not have page numbers.

everyone's skin color counts as race." Visual markers of "ethnorace," at least in the context of the United States, are markers that indicate someone is not white (Ahmed 2007, Song 2020). To be sure, Mansbridge (1999, 637–639) carefully noted the problems of "essentialism" and associating biological characteristics with key characteristics that define a group. For Mansbridge (1999, 637–639), however, the "benefits of descriptive representation" override these concerns. Suzanne Dovi (2002, 732) addressed how essentialism may have prevented scholars from defining preferable descriptive representatives, and contrary to Mansbridge, focused on a representative's social relationships with marginalized subgroups to define preferable descriptive representatives. Still, the working definition of a descriptive representative remains characterized by shared racialized biological characteristics (Dovi 2002, 736). Descriptive representation as conventionally theorized affirms white supremacy.

The third tension is the conflation of ethnoracial ascription with ethnoracial identity. Ascription refers to how others racially assign someone, and identity refers to how one personally thinks of oneself (Brunsma 2006; McClain et al. 2009; Hardy-Fanta et al. 2013). Both Pitkin and Mansbridge suggest, but do not explicitly explore, that a representative may have characteristics that do not align with their identity. In her discussion of descriptive representation, Pitkin (1967, 79) cited earlier arguments that centered on the idea that "the similarity in kind may be based in the voters 'identification' of himself with ... the office holder," highlighting the importance of shared identity, not solely shared descriptive characteristics. Pitkin's emphasis on a representative's similarity to their constituents suggests that something beyond appearances should inform desecriptive representation. For instance, Manbsridge (1999, 645) cites an example from Richard Fenno's (1978) interviews with members of Congress and adds that a Black "legislator's stance of introspective representation derived from far more than the color of his skin." Here, Mansbridge focuses on the representative's shared identity, not just his outward, visible characteristics that would define him as a descriptive representative of Black constituents. In the absence of a descriptive representative, Mansbridge (1999, 645) also argues that voters may use "pseudo description," or find affinity with representatives who "[mimic] descriptive behavior" or otherwise try to present themselves as "like" a particular community. When a representative does not "look like" a targeted constituent then, they may make explicit appeals to demonstrate affinity with that group. Both Pitkin and Mansbridge thus suggest that *identity*, independently of one's appearance, may be what both defines and drives a descriptive representative—but they don't dig in.

In effect, traditional theory on descriptive representation uses whiteness as an analytical anchor to theorize about the power of representatives of color in American democracy (Feagin 2013, 17). This foundation derives from the idea of "[ethno]racial difference" (Blatt 2018). How do you know a descriptive representative when you see one if whiteness often goes unseen? Mixed representatives whose appearances don't reflect dominant prototypes challenge this theoretical foundation—whether they appear Black, non-Black, non-white, or white. Politicians who must perform identity labor to explain their ethnoracial identities challenge traditional descriptive representation.

Like the sociologists who missed the rise of the Multiracial Category Movement because of a commitment to hypodescent (Daniel 2021), or the idea that mixed people inherit the lower status of their ethnoracial background, where someone who is white and non-white is considered solely non-white (Iverson et al. 2022), political scientists have neglected mixed representatives due the racist foundation of our discipline (Blatt 2018; McClain et al. 2016). This is why many political scientists have not considered what happens when a descriptive representative belongs to two or more ethnoracial categories or when constituents "cannot tell" that a representative stands for them descriptively. When we let go of biological essentialism, there is no descriptive representation.

Political scientists currently lack the theoretical tools to understand mixed representatives who vary in appearance and ethnoracial identity. If a mixed legislator appears white but self-identifies as non-white, how do we count them? If a mixed legislator appears Black and self-identifies as non-Black, how do we count them? And if a mixed legislator identifies with multiple non-white communities and appears ethnoracially ambiguous, how do we count them? Are any of these hypothetical cases even descriptive representatives?

Defining descriptive representatives by ethnoracial appearance is a relic of false ethnoracial science. Ethnoracial science historically undergirded census categories based on blood quantum (Nobles 2000). To identify a descriptive representative when we see one, according to conventional theory, we have to use biological characteristics assigned to ethnoracial categories—skin tone, nose shape, eye shape, hair texture, etc. At the same time, heritage passed down from parentage is also considered. Whether we classify a descriptive representative to one or more categories based on visible characteristics requires us to treat ethnorace as an immutable characteristic (Sen and Wasow 2016). Again, how do you know a descriptive representative when you see one?

We should use the experiences of mixed representatives to think more deeply about how we study and think about descriptive representation. By focusing on "visible" characteristics, Mansbridge neglects that some mixed representatives might slip in and out of their descriptive representative status depending on the context. Descriptive representation requires accepting that a set of necessary biological attributes makes one a member of an ethnoracial group and helps yield the benefits of descriptive representation. Mixed politicians are examples of representatives who defy this.

To be clear, I'm not saying we should ignore ethnoracial appearance and its relationship to substantive representation. A person whose appearance is read as non-white might carry experiences related to racism and colorism that matter for how they approach policymaking (Hunter 2005; Brown and Lemi 2021). However, political scientists must confront the refusal to acknowledge that one can hold multiple ethnoracial group memberships that are consequential for a representative's relationships with constituents and that ethnoracial identity does not always map cleanly to appearances. And political scientists should grapple with the fact that refusing to do so is rooted in white supremacy. By the end of this book, I will give political scientists the theoretical tools to understand and later account for mixed representatives who vary in appearance and ethnoracial identity.

Where We've Come From

To understand how contemporary mixed and non-mixed politicians use their ethnoracial identities strategically when engaging with different political stakeholders, we must first remember where the United States has come from. Throughout what became the United States of America, different laws and customs dictated the classification and treatment of different combinations of mixed persons (Nagai 2016). Colonization, enslavement, labor demands, immigration, and war facilitated opportunities for the "ethnoraces" to mix (e.g., Curington 2016; Newman 2021).

In many ways, how we study mixed people reflects their standing in the United States. In the 1990s, the Multiracial Category Movement consisted of self-identified mixed adults, student organizations, and mothers of mixed children—mostly "white women married to black men" (Williams 2005, 56; Williams 2006)—who advocated for changes to how the decennial census recorded ethnorace (Williams 2006). Some activists saw their efforts as an extension of the Civil Rights Movement (Davis 1991, 194; DaCosta 2007, 80–81). The movement put forth at least three reasons for wanting mixed recognition: to support children's self-esteem by not forcing children to choose between their parents on demographic forms, to improve data collection for medical purposes, and to improve data collection to track discrimination against mixed people specifically (Spencer 1999, Chapter 3, 134, 153–159). Activists disagreed on the appropriate way to recognize mixed identity. Some preferred a distinct "multiracial" category, while others preferred a multiracial category with the addition of a check-all-that-apply format (Williams 2006, 43). Ultimately, the Census Bureau opted for the current "mark one or more" option (Williams 2006).[13]

Today's public and scholarly discourse on inter-ethnoracial intimacy and ethnoracial classification (e.g., Spencer 1999; Dalmage 2000; Williams 2006; DaCosta 2007; Lee and Bean 2010; Masuoka 2017; Davenport 2018) is a response to and product of the social, political, and economic hierarchies that white colonizers and enslavers engineered (e.g., Davis 1991; Pascoe 2009; McRae 2018). The contemporary presence of "mixed" politicians is contextualized by white supremacy (King and Smith 2005), settler colonialism (Wolfe 2006), and the enslavement of Africans (Fields 1990; Wolfe 2006) as the fundamental building blocks for the American empire (King 2019; also see Harris 1993, 1714).

Biological treatments of ethnorace were critical to building the contemporary ethnoracial order. Laws regulating who was "white," "Black," and "American Indian" informed who counted as a citizen, the quality of that citizenship, and relationships with state and federal governments (Nobles 2000; Davis 1991; López 1994; Green 2006; Cuison Villazor 2008; Schmidt 2011; TallBear 2013, 31–66; Law 2015). For example, ethnorace was treated as a biological concept and weaponized to expand the number of people eligible for subjugation by anti-Black laws and to reduce the number of Indigenous people eligible to control land (Wolfe 2006, 338; Fields 1990, 107). Cheryl Harris (1993, 1734) argues that tying whiteness, or its absence, to eligibility to *be* property—as an enslaved person—and eligibility to *own* property—as an enslaver—resulted in the notion of "whiteness as property," whereby whiteness itself "is something that can both be experienced and deployed as

[13] The Multiracial Category Movement also had implications for policy issues (Williams 2006). For example, another purported goal of the Multiracial Category Movement was to use a "multiracial" category to broadly end the relevance of ethnoracial categories for American life (Hernández 1998, 109). However, critics have argued that in problematizing ethnoracial categories rather than white supremacy and institutional racism, the movement reinforced notions of "colorblind" racism (Hernández 1998, 110). The Multiracial Category Movement also had implications for reparations movements and efforts to recognize and compensate African Americans for the harm of enslavement because it raised questions about how Black persons who identified as mixed or had mixed ancestry could be counted (Davis 2006, 180–185). Williams (2017, 99–102) points to the role of the Multiracial Category Movement in shaping public conversations about ethnoracial identity.

a resource." One's ethnoracial classification thus determined the life one could live (e.g., Sharfstein 2007).

These categories were defined by blood and made meaningful through laws. For example, TallBear (2013, 56) discusses how the 1887 General Allotment Act, or the Dawes Act, extended full land ownership and citizenship to Native Americans who were "half-blood or less," and placed land in long-term trusts for those who had "more than half-blood." About a decade later, in 1896, the Supreme Court ruled in *Plessy v. Ferguson* that Homer Plessy could not sit in trains designated for whites because he was one-eighth Black (Davis 1991, 8–9, 193–194). From the late nineteenth century through the mid-twentieth century, the courts debated who counted as a white person (López 2004, Appendix A). With the 1965 Immigration Act, ethnoracial restrictions on immigration ended (Ngai 2014).

The one-drop rule in the United States is critical to understanding mixed politicians' positions in American politics. The historical origin of the one-drop rule is distinct for African Americans (Jordan 2014). From the mid-nineteenth century until the early twentieth century, individuals with Black and white ancestry were counted as "mulattoes" on the US Census,[14] and at times, held a political "buffer status" between Black and white Americans (Davis 1991, 11–12, 41). By the late nineteenth century, white workers had to compete with emancipated Black workers (Lung 2019). This resulted in a series of laws targeting Black workers that broadened the scope of who was counted legally Black—including anyone with up to an eighth of "Black blood" (Davis 1991, 44–45). By the 1900s, states codified the one-drop rule (Sharfstein 2007, 604), which determined whether one would be subjected to Jim Crow discrimination. Although the one-drop rule is no longer institutionalized and its use may only be used informally (Iverson et al. 2022), the idea that one inherits the status of one's non-white parent is an important contextual factor that helps us make sense of the experiences of mixed politicians who are not "fully white." In short, historically, flawed ethnoracial science and the law helped construct the ethnoracial categories we know today.

Mixed People Today

Mixed people develop their identities and their politics against the backdrop of the American ethnoracial hierarchy. Their identities vary with gender identification, religious identification, socioeconomic status (Davenport 2016a), and how they look (Sims 2016). They tend to be Democrats (Davenport et al.

[14] US Census Bureau. 2025. Infographic: "Measuring Race and Ethnicity Across the Decades, 1790-2010." https://www.census.gov/data-tools/demo/race/MREAD_1790_2010.html

2022). Mixed persons' appearances also garner extra attention. There is a stereotype that mixed people are "attractive" or "exotic" (Sims 2012; Curington 2020; Curington et al. 2015; Waring 2013; Feliciano and Kizer 2021; Newman 2019). Mixed persons' racialization also depends on their gender expression (Davenport 2016b; Sims and Joseph-Salisbury 2019; Waring 2013). The experiences of mixed people also vary according to their ethnoracial combinations. Mixed persons who are Black have fundamentally different experiences from mixed persons who are not Black. They may experience anti-Blackness, which creates constraints on expressing their ethnoracial identities and having those identities accepted by others (Lee and Bean 2010; Khanna 2010; Sims 2016; Feliciano 2016; strmic-pawl 2016).

People interpret mixed people in various ways. For example, Americans tend to classify mixed Black persons as singularly Black (Khanna 2010; Lee and Bean 2010; Feliciano 2016). Consider this experiment by Arnold Ho and colleagues: scientists presented participants with vignettes describing the family trees of mixed Black and white and mixed Asian and white persons (Ho et al. 2011). In scenarios where mixed people had equally white and non-white ancestry, participants tended to consider mixed people more non-white than white. However, when comparing participants' assessments of mixed Black and white and mixed Asian and white persons, participants tended to consider mixed Black persons "more Black" than the extent to which they considered mixed Asian persons "more Asian." These findings led them to conclude that while participants applied hypodescent to both cases, they more readily applied it to mixed Black persons. As the following chapters will show, the cultural and legal aspects of the one-drop rule and the socialization of mixed everyday people have ramifications for how we understand the identity labor of mixed political representatives.

What We Don't Know

The study of mixed identity is relatively new in political science—work on mixed representatives is nearly non-existent. Historically, the idea of candidates running on their mixed ancestry might have been inconceivable. Owing to the historical one-drop rule for Black Americans (Davis 1991), the idea of a "mixed" candidate arguably would not have applied to Black candidates prior to the Civil Rights Movement and the Multiracial Category Movement (DaCosta 2007). Yet, representatives with mixed ancestry are not new, specifically Black politicians with non-Black ancestry (e.g., Powell, Jr. 1971; Davis 1991, 6–8; Swain 1993, 26; Hochschild and Weaver 2007, 650).

Political scientists have only recently begun to talk about how ethnoracial identity changes over time (e.g., Davenport 2020), but the fluidity of ethnorace has historically been true for Black leaders. Take for example, the Democratic Congressman Adam Clayton Powell, Jr. who represented New York from 1945–1971,[15] who, on the one hand, described how a college friend terminated their friendship after suspecting that Powell was Black and how, on the other, a Congressional colleague indicated that Powell's appearance was not viewed as Black (Powell 1971, 32, 73). This meant that until white people knew Powell was Black, whites may have assumed he was white. Walter White, a leader of the National Association for the Advancement of Colored People (NAACP), is another example of a prominent Black leader who appeared white, so much so that he could visit the site of a lynching and interview white people about it (White 1995, 3, chapter 5). In a classic study of descriptive representation, one white member of Congress told Carol Swain (1993, 155) how they mistakenly attended a Congressional Black Caucus meeting because they believed a Black Congressmember in attendance was also white. One study found that from 1865–2007, most Black statewide or national representatives were lighter-skinned (Hochschild and Weaver 2007, 650). There has been a historical presence of public figures who present as white but were not white, specifically Black public figures.

Today, nearly 23 percent of elected officials, perhaps even more, may describe their backgrounds as non-singular in some way (Hardy-Fanta et al. 2013, 11). That is almost one in four elected officials who may be mixed—a stark contrast to the general population estimate of around 10 percent (US Census Bureau 2021).[16] In the 116th US Congress, three of the four women of color in the US Senate were mixed (Kamala Harris, Catherine Cortez Masto, and Tammy Duckworth). Two mixed members of Congress sought the 2020 Democratic presidential nominations (Harris and Tulsi Gabbard). Using our current definitions and tools in the study of descriptive representation (e.g., Shah and Davis 2017, 129), some of these mixed politicians would not even qualify as descriptive representatives because of how they look. Contemporary mixed politicians hold a national stage, yet we know surprisingly little about the ramifications of their presence for the politics of descriptive representation.

Current theory does not account for these representatives. To date, there are various typologies of mixed identity (e.g., Renn 2012), as well as studies about its determinants (e.g., Davenport 2016a; Rockquemore and Brunsma

[15] United States House of Representatives History, Art & Archives. Powell, Adam Clayton, Jr. n.d. https://history.house.gov/People/Listing/P/POWELL,-Adam-Clayton,-Jr--(P000477)/

[16] Again, see the debate regarding this estimate (Starr and Pao 2024).

2002; Harris and Sim 2002; Herman 2004; Masuoka 2011; Norman and Chen 2020), its consequences for social life (e.g., Doyle and Kao 2007; Shih and Sanchez 2005), and its implications for political life (e.g., Davenport 2018; Masuoka 2008; Masuoka 2017; Davenport et al. 2022; Leslie and Sears 2022). At present, we know little about how being mixed complicates campaign strategies, voter preferences, and experiences as legislators in American politics.

Separately, scholarship in political science, sociology, and social psychology suggests a few takeaways—and more questions—about mixed politicians in American politics. When people of color hold office, their communities tend to be represented in policy. Every day, people learn their ethnoracial identities and politics in a broader environment that now allows people to choose their identities (Masuoka 2017), contingent upon who they are and what they look like. Past research illustrates how mixed people differ from non-mixed people in political beliefs. Nearly all the research on mixed people in politics has focused on differences between mixed and non-mixed everyday people.[17] What about mixed representatives?

So What?

Skeptics may wonder why studying mixed representatives is necessary, given the relatively small size of the self-reported two-or-more ethnoraces population within the general population and the lack of clear policy interests for this group. Indeed, much like estimates of the general mixed population (e.g., Harris and Sim 2002; Pew Research Center 2015), estimates of mixed politicians are subject to inconsistency. Unlike countries such as Brazil (e.g., Janusz 2023), the United States does not collect the ethnoracial backgrounds of candidates for office. To study ethnorace and representation, scholars must frequently classify candidates based on public information or conduct surveys of politicians (e.g., Fraga et al. 2019; Klarner 2018; Shah and Davis 2017; National Conference of State Legislatures 2015a; NALEO 2019). Both classification methods are imperfect: categorization and self-identification are highly contextual (Davenport 2020; McClain et al. 2009).

Despite their small size, the inclusion of mixed representatives helps us address numerous issues. First, they are a part of the future of American politics. As of 2023, the median age of the two-or-more ethnoraces population

[17] But see research about Barack Obama and Charles Rangel (e.g., Price 2016; Adida et al. 2016; Gillespie 2020).

is about thirty years,[18] and these individuals are future city council members, state legislators, and members of Congress.

Second, voter responses to these politicians may be used to gauge our progress. Given the history of violence against Black men thought to have relationships with white women (e.g., Wells-Barnett 2005), it is significant that Barack Obama could become president and showcase his white mother to white voters. How voters receive these politicians offers one way to broadly surmise where the public stands on ethnoracial integration.

Third, these politicians help us envision the prospects and limitations for them as bridges for cross-ethnoracial coalitions, as they descriptively represent multiple ethnoracial groups simultaneously. As the country approaches majority-minority status, these candidates may be attractive to voters and party leaders seeking to maximize their reach to different voters—even as mere symbols of diversity (e.g., Williams 2006; Philpot 2007).

Beyond these issues, studying mixed candidates and elected officials helps us address normative, conceptual, theoretical, and methodological issues. Normatively, how voters respond to mixed candidates has implications for our efforts to recruit "preferable" descriptive representatives (Dovi 2002). Scholars have not seriously interrogated what a growing mixed population means for normative criteria for representatives (Dovi 2002, 732). Purposefully analyzing individuals who belong to multiple ethnoracial groups forces scholars and practitioners to think carefully about whether representatives who "stand for" multiple ethnoracial groups may legitimately "stand as" descriptive representatives (Pitkin 1967, chapter 4). Suppose voters deem mixed candidates more preferable than their non-mixed counterparts. In that case, we must consider whether increasing mixed identification indicates ethnoracial inequality and further marginalizes non-white, non-mixed, and darker-skinned people (Bonilla-Silva 2004; Davenport 2016a; also see Yancey 2003). Suppose voters deem mixed candidates less preferable than their non-mixed counterparts. In that case, we must consider what the presence of this newly recognized population means for our electoral institutions truly reflecting the United States. Practically, the increasing size of this population raises questions about party leaders' strategies for recruiting these candidates to advance party platforms—even platforms that are regressive on civil rights (e.g., Williams 2006; Philpot 2007).

Current conceptions of descriptive representatives do not reflect ethnorace as a social construction (Sen and Wasow 2016). Traditional research

[18] U.S. Census Bureau, U.S. Department of Commerce. "Selected Population Profile in the United States." *American Community Survey, ACS 1-Year Estimates Selected Population Profiles, Table S0201*, https://data.census.gov/table/ACSSPP1Y2023.S0201?q=Two+or+More+Races&y=2023&d=ACS+1-Year+Estimates+Selected+Population+Profiles. Accessed on 25 Aug 2025.

on minority representation typically conceives of descriptive representatives as mono-ethnoracial (e.g., Swain 1993; McConnaughy et al. 2010; Casellas 2010; Barreto 2010; Grose 2011; Rouse 2013; Tyson 2016; Fraga 2016; but see Bejarano 2013; Brown 2014a; Masuoka 2015; Adida et al. 2016). Representation scholars typically omit mixed candidates (e.g., Silva and Skulley 2019) or they do not conceive of mixed politicians as descriptive representatives of multiple ethnoracial groups (e.g., Barreto 2010, chapter 7; Grose 2011, 47). Explicitly engaging with mixed candidates moves this scholarship toward ethnorace as a social construction and challenges political scientists to be more precise with measurement.

Theoretically, mixed representatives offer challenging cases to test the strength of shared identity between voters and candidates. Mixed representatives are simultaneously insiders and outsiders. By belonging to multiple ethnoracial categories, these candidates raise questions about the limitations of current theory to explain voter preferences for descriptive representatives (Tajfel and Turner 1986; Adida et al. 2016; Manzano and Sanchez 2010). The absence of mixed representatives has likely led to studies and research designs that under-theorize and overestimate the effects of any descriptive representative on substantive outcomes.

Methodologically, mixed representatives introduce another layer of variation in research designs that correlate ethnorace with substantive representation. For example, few in-depth studies of descriptive representatives allow the explanatory variable—ascribed ethnorace—to vary by sampling multiple ethnoracial groups and incorporating mixed representatives. Using mixed cases, we may observe a social intermediate between an Asian American representative and a white representative (e.g., Harris 2019)—one who may identify as Asian American, white, or something else. By allowing the choice of identity to vary between representatives, we can better observe the mechanism that underlies the relationship between descriptive representatives and their constituents: their identification with the sociopolitical content of ethnoracial categories (e.g., strmic-pawl 2014, 64) or their own experiences with racialization (Mansbridge 1999, 628). For these reasons, examining the case of mixed representatives offers a vital opportunity to push scholarly theories forward and gain a glimpse into the future of American democracy.

Methodological Approach

Although this book began as a positivist project in which I sought to develop insights about ethnorace and representation that would generalize to the "real world" beyond the politicians I studied, readers may find that there are elements of interpretivism in the subsequent chapters (especially Chapter 4) (Schwartz-Shea and Yanow 2011). When I began this project, I didn't know that interpretivism as an epistemological framework was available, and perhaps more suitable, for the questions I was interested in exploring. That said, this project was born out of the disconnect between theory and my lived experience, identity labor was conceptualized *after* engaging with a variety of mixed politicians live or through texts, and what I learned in Chapter 4 was only made possible by the politicians who gave me *access* to their offices and shared whatever they were comfortable sharing on state time (Schwartz-Shea and Yanow 2011; Chapter 1, 113).[19]

I use qualitative and quantitative approaches to explore the constraints and opportunities for identity labor with the media, voters, and other legislators (see Appendix for detailed descriptions of the data and methods in each chapter). I take a multi-method approach to exploring identity labor because I am interested in both theorizing the phenomenon and testing its implications for elections (Creswell and Plano Clark 2018, chapter 1). While I had long thought that I was doing mixed methods work to "triangulate" across sources to reach some consistent truth or accurate finding, I also sought to maximize "exposure," or the range of perspectives regarding mixed politicians—their own perspectives told to me, their written perspectives shared with the world, their interactions with the media as depicted in news articles, and voters' perceptions of them to analyze the full contours of the experiences of mixed politicians (Schwartz-Shea and Yanow 2011, chapter 1; 84–89). Ultimately, what resulted was a blend of approaches, interpretivist and positivist, within a book that examines different questions about how mixed politicians use identity strategically (Schwartz-Shea and Yanow 2011, 134).

Positionality In The Field

Before I dive into the path forward for the rest of this book, I want to discuss my positionality in the data generation and interpretation process of this book. This discussion warrants more than a footnote. Some scholars of legislative politics grapple with the implications of their own ethnorace for soliciting personal interviews with legislators about ethnorace (e.g., Swain 1993,

[19] Politicians and their state staff cannot talk about campaign politics on state time. What constituted talking about "the campaign" during our conversation was up to them, and that's why I do not directly engage with how the conditions of the campaign might shape identity labor, such as whether a politician is an incumbent or a challenger. Future research should explore this.

229; Grose 2011, 196; Brown 2014a, 190–193). Ethnoracial categorization constrains who may even enter research sites (Harbin 2020). Our ethnoracial identities open or close opportunities for access to legislators, the nature of the conversations, and the quality of the data we obtain (Brown 2012). There is both insider and outsider privilege in gaining access to legislators.

As I conducted interviews, I realized my ethnoracial appearance might have conditioned the access and nature of conversations I was getting. Depending on who's asking and the various ethnoracial markers I choose to wear—the way I style my hair, wear my makeup, or the jewelry I wear, people classify me differently. My last name may be mistaken for French. The access and quality of conversations I had likely would have been different had "Danielle Martinez" sent the initial recruitment emails rather than "Danielle Lemi." These things influence how our research participants classify us.

My ethnoracial classification affected how legislators interacted with me. In one interview, a mixed legislator spoke to me as if they knew my ethnoracial background: "You may know, as well, within the [Asian American/Pacific Islander] community, being mixed is not necessarily smiled upon." This legislator must have been able to identify other mixed people. One legislator used my skin tone to reference another person's skin tone: "[they are] actually whiter than you are." Another legislator could not tell whether I was white on the phone, and another asked for my "nationality" while we were talking. My voice and appearance mattered in how legislators decided to interact with me. As a loved one has told me, "You don't look white, but you look somethin." Erica Mohan and Terah Venzant Chambers (2010, 276–278) argue that mixed researchers do not necessarily have insider status with mixed persons, nor is there necessarily a shared cultural mixed community. I agree with them. I do not feel a sense of kinship toward mixed legislators based on our mixed backgrounds, nor do I believe my experiences with racialization are the same as a mixed person with different ancestry.

Even so, many things mixed legislators said resonated with me. Brant Downey (2015) discusses how the flow of conversation in qualitative research is subject to each participant's ideas of appropriate conversation when the interview is live. Maybe I didn't follow up on specific responses because I felt I sufficiently understood them. Perhaps I didn't dig into particular answers because I thought that would be inappropriate. Maybe I neglected to detect comments I should have followed up on because they didn't register to me as relevant to the research. As Nadia Brown (2012) discusses, these interactions are part of the research. White legislators may have felt comfortable speaking candidly because I am not an "obvious" non-white person, and some non-white legislators may have felt comfortable because I was some non-white "other." Perhaps some were even less candid with me because I was not obviously a member of any one group. At other times, my interpersonal chemistry with interviewees shaped the conversation. Some legislators mainly spoke uninterrupted for the interview, while others responded to my questions with brevity. Others likely would have kept talking if their schedule permitted a longer meeting. My relaying of their stories is my current interpretation of their stories. We are a part of the data generation process, and the data we collect looks the way it does because we collected it.

Positionality is also relevant for the quantitative research shared in this book too. Our sociopolitical positions shape the questions we ask, the theories we're drawn to, and how we make sense of designing experiments and interpreting their outputs.

In Chapter 5, for example, had I possessed a strong "mixed" identity, perhaps I would've pursued questions that examined the extent to which mixed legislators represent the interests of mixed people. As my developmental editor reminded me in the final stages of writing, this book looks the way it does because *I* wrote it.

The Path Forward

Over four chapters, I analyze cases of mixed politicians to theorize the contours of identity labor. The book is organized into two parts. The first part focuses on this question: How do politicians use their ethnoracial identities strategically when engaging with different political stakeholders? Part I draws on qualitative case studies to theorize identity labor and its influences, and to show how politicians do identity labor. The nature of identity labor has much to do with familial processes, ethnoracial appearance, and mixed politicians' positions in the ethnoracial hierarchy.

Chapter 2 takes a deep dive into the case of Vice President Kamala Harris and explores how her upbringing and ethnoracial background as a Black person specifically shaped how she sees her identity. To capture how she performs identity labor to reporters and how the media in turn portrays her, I draw on articles from news venues that serve different ethnoracial communities, beginning just before she was San Francisco District Attorney General through her run for president in the Democratic primary in 2019. To capture an in-depth look at how she presents herself, I analyze her memoir, *The Truths We Hold: An American Journey*, newspaper articles that mention her, and archives of her website biography. Drawing on these sources, I show how the material politicians draw on to perform identity labor stems from familial socialization.

Chapter 3 examines how mixed politicians do identity labor. In interviews from thirty-seven state legislative offices around the country collected in 2018 and 2019, I show that mixed politicians draw on familial processes to contextualize their ethnoracial identities, and their experiences within the ethnoracial hierarchy parallel those of their non-mixed counterparts. Identity labor to show group membership is elevated for mixed politicians because of how people perceive their appearances. They use various tactics to let their stakeholders know that they share ethnoracial group membership. They perform identity labor with constituents, caucuses and colleagues, and the media.

Part II draws on qualitative case studies and quantitative surveys to examine the public's view of identity labor. Public depictions of mixed politicians and voters' reactions to them are rooted in the historical one-drop rule for Black Americans and contemporary intergroup relationships. In Chapter 4, I show that mixed politicians perform identity labor by capitalizing on their mixed backgrounds or navigating the questions the media raises about their ethnoracial identities. The media narrates mixed politicians depending on their constitutive parts' position in the ethnoracial hierarchy, with distinct treatment of mixed Black and mixed non-Black politicians.

In Chapter 5, I test the implication that emerges from Chapters 3 and 4: that there's an electoral support gap between mixed and non-mixed politicians. Using a survey experiment and a split-sample test embedded in a survey, I show that the benefit of a mixed politician's shared ethnoracial identity depends on the ethnorace of their opponent. Voters also react to mixed and non-mixed politicians within the constraints of their positions in the hierarchy. This chapter also shows that comfort with the idea of a family member marrying a member of another group may inform some voters' perceptions of mixed and non-mixed candidates. Consequently, this chapter argues that this electoral gap may be closed by identity labor.

In the last chapter, I return to my second and third broad questions: What does it mean to be a descriptive representative of communities of color in an increasingly diverse democracy? What do these changes mean for how we think about and study representation? I argue that we must revise how we theorize descriptive representatives. I introduce an alternative that engages with Black feminist thought and intersectionality (Crenshaw 1991; Hill Collins 2014; Taylor 2017; Hill Collins and Bilge 2020): *identity representatives*. The findings from this book ultimately encourage us to more forcefully confront the non-sense of ethnoracial categories in American life. In an increasingly diverse democracy, the benefit of politicians using their ethnoracial identities for political gain is not so clear-cut.

PART I

DOING IDENTITY LABOR

2

Family is the Foundation for Identity Labor

The Case of Kamala Harris

In November 2019, I was scrolling through Twitter when a video of Kamala Harris cooking with the Indian American comedian Mindy Kaling caught my eye.[1] At this point, Harris had not yet suspended her participation in the Democratic primary to select the Democratic presidential nominee. In this video, Harris enters Kaling's kitchen. Harris marvels that Kaling stores spices in Taster's Choice jars—just like Harris's mother did. As they cook, the discussion turns to Harris's heritage. Kaling explains they're cooking masala dosa "because [Harris is] Indian ... and I don't know that everybody knows that" (1:18). Kaling then draws out their common Indian heritage. At one point, Harris remarks, "You look like the entire one-half of my family" (1:36). Kaling's father joins the conversation, and Harris shares with him where her grandparents lived in India. The video was fun, albeit staged, and conveyed how Harris culturally connects to Indian Americans.

By referencing her mother's practice of storing spices in Taster's Choice jars and bonding with Kaling over shared cultural foods, Harris leverages her cultural capital as Indian American. Yet, Harris and Kaling also explicitly recognized that a gap existed between how Harris saw herself and how the public, and perhaps particularly Indian Americans, saw her—people don't always know she's Indian American. By noting that Kaling looks like her family members, Harris implicitly acknowledges the role of appearance in how people make ethnoracial classifications. By uploading this video to her YouTube channel during the primary campaign, Harris performed identity labor by highlighting her background as Indian American, demonstrating an ability to connect culturally with other high-profile Indian Americans.

In this chapter, I draw on the case of Kamala Harris to dive deeper into how mixed politicians perform identity labor. I explore how familial socialization

[1] Kamala Harris & Mindy Kaling Cook Masala Dosa. 2019. https://www.youtube.com/watch?v=xz7rNOAFkgE

Doing Identity Labor. Danielle Casarez Lemi, Oxford University Press. © Oxford University Press (2025).
DOI: 10.1093/9780197816851.003.0002

influenced her ethnoracial identity, how she is portrayed in the press, and how she has presented herself in her website biography over time. While identity labor is strategic, it begins with what family members, who have their own positions in the ethnoracial hierarchy, teach future politicians about their ethnorace, how to perform it, and, subsequently, how to do identity labor.

Why Kamala Harris?

Kamala Harris was born in 1964 in Alameda County to a Black, Jamaican father and a South Asian, Indian mother. Trained as a lawyer, her political career evolved from being the San Francisco District Attorney, the California Attorney General, and a US senator for California before being elected as the vice president of the United States in 2020 and running for president in 2024. In July 2024, Harris became the presumptive Democratic nominee for president after President Biden exited the presidential race. As a Black and Asian American woman, her election was historic at each level of office. As Harris rose from local office to the White House, the electorate shifted, and the media changed its focus on her candidacies.

In January 2019, Kamala Harris launched her 2020 presidential campaign for the Democratic primary from Oakland, California, about twenty minutes from my hometown of Union City. At the start of her presidential campaign, a reporter declared that "[Harris's] life story gives her not only entree to black voters who make up a significant share of the Democratic primary electorate but also Asian American voters whose ranks are growing" (Viser 2019). During the presidential primary campaign, Harris performed identity labor by using social media to assert her Black identity and Indian American identity.

Throughout the 2020 presidential cycle, news coverage of Harris raised questions about Harris's ethnoracial identities. Coverage ranged from comparisons of Harris's and Obama's Blackness (Peña-Vasquez and Kwakwa 2020), stories about Indian Americans' perceptions of Harris (Fuchs 2019; Sullivan 2019), and questions about how the public should talk about mixed people (e.g., Devarajan 2020; Ho 2020; Norwood 2020). Reuters even printed a story to "fact-check" how Harris has identified ethnoracially over time.[2] These themes broke into the news cycle again in 2024 when the 45th US President made comments about Harris's racial identity at the National Association for Black Journalists convention in Chicago, accusing Harris of

[2] Reauters. 2020. Fact check: Kamala Harris did not switch from identifying as Indian-American to Black. *Reuters*. August 24. https://www.reuters.com/article/uk-fact-check-harris-did-not-switch-raci-idUSKBN25H1RC

changing her identity, stating: "I didn't know she was Black until a number of years ago when she happened to turn Black and now she wants to be known as Black. So, I don't know, is she Indian or is she Black?"[3] Harris's story and the content she posted to her platform on YouTube illustrate how mixed candidates must manage how others see them (e.g., Citrin et al. 2014, 1126; Carter and Dowe 2015, 113; Masuoka 2017, 150).

Closely analyzing Kamala Harris's political career is valuable for two reasons. First, as a high-profile political figure with a career that spans multiple levels of office, Harris helps illuminate how family and the ethnoracial hierarchy influence the nature of the identity labor a politician performs as their star rises. Second, as a mixed politician from California, Harris presents the opportunity to observe identity labor from a specific context: a West Coast state with a diverse electorate, a high rate of inter-ethnoracial marriage, and a high concentration of mixed people. As a case study, Harris is ideal for exploring familial socialization as a contour of identity labor.

Dynamics of Inter-Ethnoracial Families

To understand the role of familial socialization in Kamala Harris's performance of identity labor, we must first understand the role of the family in identity socialization. Identity labor is strategic, and politicians exert agency in deploying family stories to discuss their ethnoracial identities. Still, the stories they have at all originate from their familial histories. The family is a site for the creation and meaning of ethnorace through different relationships (Pascoe 2010; Davenport 2018; Fielder 2020). We learn how to do ethnorace, in part, from our parents and caregivers who raise us.

In the United States, hegemonic notions of gender roles, family structures, and historical anti-miscegenation laws have worked together to uphold white heteropatriarchy (Pascoe 2010; Fielder 2020), or the social and political dominance of heterosexual white men (Strolovitch et al. 2017). White women having sex with and marrying non-white men, especially Black men, historically threatened notions of citizenship by whiteness and the social order enslavers institutionalized (Fields 1990, 107; Davis 1991, 48; Pascoe 2010, 27). Under the Cable Act of 1922, a white woman could lose her citizenship if she married an Asian man who was prohibited from becoming an American citizen (López 1996, 15; Cott 1998, 1465). The historical legal prohibition and

[3] Price, Michelle L. and Matt Brown. 2024. Donald Trump falsely suggests Kamala Harris misled voters about her race. *AP News*. July 31. https://apnews.com/article/trump-black-journalists-convention-nabj-1e96aa530e88013ed6f577feaf89ccb6

social stigma against marriage and sex between white women and non-white men, particularly Black men, reinforce the ethnoracial hierarchy.

Today, there is no prohibition on marriage between white women and non-white men, or any ethnoraces for that matter. Scholars often use inter-ethnoracial marriage to measure integration between ethnoracial groups (Song 2009). The dynamics within mixed families contextualize how mixed politicians develop their ethnoracial identities and politics.[4] These dynamics depend, in part, on the ethnoracial-gender composition of the couple. For example, non-Black inter-ethnoracial couples may not experience the same obstacles to their union that couples with a Black partner experience, and they may even perpetuate anti-Black stereotypes (Lee and Bean 2010, 91–97). White women who partner with Black men may be shunned by white men (Flores 2020, 273). Black women who partner with white men may be shunned by Black men (Dalmage 2000, 50–51). Black men may face questions about their masculinity from other Black men for partnering with white women (Dalmage 2000, 55–56). Within the relationship, white men might misunderstand their Black wives' identities (Osuji 2019, 90–91). Anti-Black stereotypes pervade some Latinas' perceptions of partnering with Black men too (Muro and Martinez 2018). When non-Black parents of mixed Black children hold negative stereotypes about Black people, their children may observe this and internalize or perpetuate those stereotypes (e.g., Rockquemore 2002). Contrary to popular belief, mixed marriages do not stop racism, not even within the family itself (Bratter and Campbell 2023; Nadal et al. 2013).

Parents play a role in teaching their mixed children their identities. Parents cultivate the environment in which children come to understand their identities (Csizmadia and Atkin 2022). Parents may do this by celebrating their children's multiple cultures or discussing racism (Robinson-Wood et al. 2021, 10–16). Parents may also expose mixed children to outdated biological language by calling them terms like "half-breed" (Chang 2016, 11). Parents decide how to classify their children on legal forms (e.g., Bratter and Heard 2009). Parents' physical presence may affect how a mixed child identifies in a given moment (e.g., Harris and Sim 2002). Although research on the politics of inter-ethnoracial families is scarce, existing work suggests that inter-ethnoracial couples may have relatively more liberal political orientations and, in turn, pass these orientations down to their children

[4] As Buggs (2020, 33:0) notes, this research on mixed families has tended to focus on heterosexual couples.

(Perry 2013, 255; Davenport 2016b). Having grown up with a mixed family, these dynamics are relevant for understanding Harris as a politician.

In Harris's Words: Family Stories and the Ethnoracial Hierarchy

In 2019, Harris published a memoir that reflected on experiences throughout her career and lessons learned. Analyzing Harris's memoir gives us deeper insights into how Harris understands her ethnoracial identity. Her ethnoracial identity was influenced by her family, the adults who raised her, and her specific status as a Black person in California. By presenting herself this way in her memoir, Harris performs identity labor by elaborating on her ethnoracial identity—as a Black woman.

Strategically Framing Family History

As Harris describes her life in the Bay Area and her career transition from local to state to federal politician, she discusses how relationships with close elders shaped her orientation of herself and her politics. Like contemporary mixed adults (e.g., Davenport 2018), Harris's political socialization began with her parents' politics. Again, identity labor is strategic, but the stories a politician can deploy stem from their familial socialization. At the time of her parents' marriage in 1963,[5] inter-ethnoracial marriage, specifically between whites and non-whites, was not federally protected in the United States (Pascoe 2009). Their marriage pre-dated *Loving v. Virginia* (1967), the US Supreme Court case that struck down prohibitions on inter-ethnoracial marriage. Her parents' marriage also occurred only fifteen years after *Perez v. Sharp* (1948), a California Supreme Court case that effectively ended California prohibitions against marriage between whites and non-whites (Lenhardt 2011). The 1960 census estimates that less than 1 percent of all married couples were in inter-ethnoracial unions (U.S. Bureau of the Census 1994). Some estimates indicate there were only 400 children with Black and "Asian Indian, Filipino, Korean, or Vietnamese" ancestry in the United States in 1960 (Liebler 2016, 554). While Harris's parents were not white, few families looked like hers.

[5] Bengali, Shashank and Melanie Mason. 2019. The progressive Indian grandfather who inspired Kamala Harris. *Los Angeles Times*. October 25. https://www.latimes.com/politics/story/2019-10-25/how-kamala-harris-indian-family-shaped-her-political-career

Contemporary scholarship on the mothers of mixed children suggests that they tend to perceive having less familial support than mothers of non-mixed children (Bratter and Whitehead 2018). Yet, Harris's account of her childhood shows how her Indian American mother was situated in a community that provided a network of care to Harris and her sister, particularly her mother's connections to Black women (Harris 2019, 15–17). For example, Harris describes how Mrs. Shelton, a neighbor in her mother's social network, was a "second mother" to her (Harris 2019, 19–20). With Mrs. Shelton, Harris attended a daycare program that featured "posters of leaders such as Frederick Douglass, Sojourner Truth, and Harriet Tubman" (Harris 2019, 20). Through Mrs. Shelton, Harris was exposed to major figures in African American history.

Harris must be discussed within the context of her parents' immigrant backgrounds (Newman 2021), as Harris is both a second-generation Jamaican American and Indian American. Sometimes, people don't recognize Jamaican Americans as "Black" because of their Caribbean heritage (Waring and Purkayastha 2017). However, Harris's narrative indicates that because she grew up in the Bay Area within an African American community, the identity to which she was socialized was African American. Although Harris says comparatively less about her Indian American background than her identity as Black in her memoir, she notes that her maternal family "[instilled Harris and her sister] with pride in [their] South Asian roots" (Harris 2019, 18).

Harris's mother may have practiced what Arpana Inman and colleagues (2007, 98) term "imparting cultural knowledge" on her daughters. She named her first daughter Kamala, which holds cultural meaning, and spoke to Harris and her sister Maya "in her mother tongue" alongside English (Harris 2019, 6, 18). Harris's mother also adopted what Atsuko Seto and colleagues (2021) call "fostering a child's multiple heritages" and "race-conscious parenting." As a child, Harris's mother regularly took her to Rainbow Sign, a community space that Harris described as "a pioneering black cultural center" that hosted Black political and cultural figures like former Congresswoman Shirley Chisholm (Harris 2019, 24–25). In an oft-quoted passage from her memoir, Harris says (Harris 2019, 18): "My mother understood very well that she was raising two black daughters. She knew that her adopted homeland would see Maya and me as black girls, and she was determined to make sure we would grow into confident, proud, black women."

In sharing these specific stories about her family and the people who raised her, the impression emerges that her mother and her mother's close friends were critical in cultivating a primarily Black, African American identity in

Harris. This reading should be considered alongside comments Harris made to the press in 2019, when she described the pressure to classify herself ethnoracially for others' sake—in that setting, she identified as "an American."[6] Harris could have told us a series of family stories that led us to believe she simply does not identify with ethnoracial categories. Yet, in her memoir, she strategically chose to share these specific family stories that paint a picture of a politician who identifies as Black.

Living in the Ethnoracial Hierarchy as a Black Person

Harris was born decades before the Multiracial Category Movement in the 1990s, and the idea of being "mixed," as it is understood today, may not have been a dominant societal idea in the 1960s. In her book, Harris shares formative experiences of her ethnoracial identity. For instance, as an elementary school student, she participated in busing during desegregation and was bused from her neighborhood, the flatlands, to Thousand Oaks Elementary School to go to school with white children from the Berkeley Hills (Harris 2019, 19). This story sets the backdrop of Harris's broader image as a Black woman politician and is important for how she experienced racialization as a child.

Sociologists have found that for mixed Black people, the ethnoracial composition of one's social network is associated with different categories of self-identification (Rockquemore and Brunsma 2002, 346). When reflecting on her Black identity as an adult, Harris uses examples that, for the reader, construct her Black identity in terms of her relationships with other Black people within her professional and socioeconomic strata.

In 1982, Harris enrolled at Howard University, one of the most prestigious Historically Black Colleges/Universities (HBCU), to prepare for a career in law.[7] While there, she joined Alpha Kappa Alpha Sorority, Inc., a Black Greek Letter Organization (Harris 2019, 31). In reflecting on her time at Howard, Harris (2019, 20–21, 31) references a song by singer Nina Simone, *To Be Young, Gifted, and Black*, "an anthem of Black pride," which she listened to often (as Aretha Franklin's cover) as a child at Mrs. Shelton's house: "That was

[6] Sullivan, Kevin. 2019. 'I am who I am': Kamala Harris, daughter of Indian and Jamaican immigrants, defines herself simply as 'American.' *The Washington Post*. February 2. https://www.washingtonpost.com/politics/i-am-who-i-am-kamala-harris-daughter-of-indian-and-jamaican-immigrants-defines-herself-simply-as-american/2019/02/02/0b278536-24b7-11e9-ad53-824486280311_story.html

[7] Valerie Strauss. 2020. Why Kamala Harris chose Howard University. *The Washington Post*. August 11. https://www.washingtonpost.com/education/2020/08/11/why-kamala-harris-chose-howard-university-what-she-did-weekends-there/

the beauty of Howard. Every signal told students that we could be anything—that we were young, gifted, and black, and we shouldn't let anything get in the way of our success."

She also led the Black Law Students Association at the University of California, Hastings (Harris 2019, 32). Black Greek Letter Organizations facilitate political socialization and access to resources to become a politician (Gillespie 2012, 50; Dowe 2020; Brown and Lemi 2021, chapter 5). Black law student organizations, like other organizations focused on specific ethnoracial groups, provide a network of support that can be drawn on professionally in the future (Deo 2013). By sharing this piece of her story in her memoir, Harris illustrates to readers that she has long been part of critical Black social and political networks (Gillespie 2012, 48; Clayton 2020).

Strategic Advantages of Mixed Parentage and Questioning Group Membership

While analyzing Harris's memoir allows us to observe the identity labor *she* wishes to portray to the public, analyzing newspaper coverage allows us to capture interactions between Harris, the public, and the media. Throughout Harris's career, reporters have drawn attention to Harris's mixed ethnoracial background or mixed parentage, creating the need for Harris to perform identity labor. The newspapers have made her mixed ethnoracial background salient to readers. For example, a 2010 article in *USA Today* characterized Harris as "the daughter of an Indian mother and a black father."[8] Some articles noted her connections to Obama and even explicitly compared her to him because of her mixed ancestry. One 2010 article in the *Sacramento Bee* about the California Attorney General election noted, "Harris, who in 2003 became the first African American district attorney elected in state history, was a California campaign co-chair for Barack Obama."[9] Another article elaborated on Harris's mixed background and directly likened her to Barack Obama: "Some have called the 46-year old Harris, whose father is Jamaican and whose mother is from India 'the female Barack Obama.' But to see Harris as that would be to misjudge her badly."[10] In 2010, the *Precinct Reporter* called Harris "the first African/Asian woman" San Francisco District Attorney and wrote: "She has been, called the female Barack Obama for her ability to open closed

[8] Schouten, Fredreka. 2010. Candidates of Indian ancestry on the increase; Spring from one of the USA's most affluent, educated immigrant groups. *USA Today, Final Edition.* September 13.
[9] Hecht, Peter. 2009. Contenders line up for attorney general. *Sacramento Bee (California).* March 16.
[10] Wichkam, DeWayne. 2010. Ever heard of Kamala Harris? You will. *USA Today.* December 21.

doors and obtain victories where they have never existed before [*sic*]."[11] Nearly ten years later, in 2019, an article in the *Sacramento Observer* described Harris in terms of her ethnoracial identity as well: "Her biracial background makes her the state's first Black and nation's first Indian American district attorney."[12] By drawing attention to her mixed parentage, the media raises the salience of Harris's mixed background to readers who will evaluate her. By mentioning Obama, who has arguably become a "mold" for all other mixed politicians, media sources cultivate the need for Harris to perform identity labor and elaborate on her identity to the public. In doing so, the media also implies that mixed politicians run in the same circles *because* they are mixed. This contrasts with the way she portrays herself: Harris's memoir does not portray her as a politician with a distinct "mixed" consciousness or who professes a desire to be "The Next Obama."[13]

Some commentators suggested that Harris's mixed background gave her an electoral advantage. For example, in 2004, *India West* printed that Harris's "mixed Indian and African American heritage has helped her connect to a diverse cross-section of voters."[14] When she won her election for California Attorney General, one of Harris's supporters, then-California Assemblymember Mike Davis, was quoted in *Chicago Citizen* stating, "the uniqueness of what Kamala Harris brings to the table is to give to California the opportunity to have ... minorities such as African Americans and Indian Americans to demonstrate their ability to be included in the criminal justice system of California in a significant way."[15] In other words, because she is Black and South Asian, she offers descriptive representation of African Americans and Indian Americans in California's criminal justice system and contributes to their sense of participation in governance.

By 2016, Harris was running for the US Senate. *India Abroad* printed, "The fact that both Indian Americans and African Americans lay claim to US Senate candidate Kamala Devi Harris ... is a representation of the true nature of America."[16] In 2019, pundit Nate Silver visited the University of Chicago and its campus paper, the *Chicago Maroon: University of Chicago*, quoted him stating that Harris "appeals to the various different parts of the party pretty well ... To be a woman who is Black and Asian and pretty darn smart on her

[11] Dowdy, E. 2010. NAACP hosts town hall. *Precinct Reporter.* September 30.

[12] Sacramento Observer. 2008. Harris vies for attorney general. *Sacramento Observer.* November 20–26, 2008.

[13] See Henderson (2015).

[14] Tsering, L. 2004. TiE forum empowers women. *India-West.* April 9.

[15] Simmonds, Y. 2010. Madame Attorney General Kamala Harris. *Chicago Citizen.* December 8.

[16] Haniffa, A. 2016. It shows what we are as Americans. *India Abroad.* March 25.

feet, she has a lot going for her."[17] Stories like this represent tension between how Harris has strategically presented her ethnoracial identity and how news sources discuss her. Harris's identity labor involves asserting her identity as a Black woman in her memoir and selecting venues to share her Indian heritage, but media sources and other politicians construct the image that her mixed background bestows a political advantage. Taken together, these stories create a public narrative that Harris's mixed ethnoracial background may be a resource to exploit for votes.

Although commentators suggest Harris's dual background offers strategic advantages, Harris has faced questions about the legitimacy of her claims to ethnoracial group membership. In terms of her Indian American group membership, *The Bakersfield Californian* printed an article in 2016 about a visit from then-US Senate candidate Harris to Bakersfield, California, and conveyed that "Resident Resham Singh said afterward Harris ... could have addressed issues near and dear to Bakersfield's Sikh community."[18] This story does not explicitly question the legitimacy of her claim to being Indian American. But this story implicitly constructs a supposed gap between Harris's Indian American heritage and her interest in speaking about issues of interest to Sikh Americans, many of whom are Indian American.

Some people refuted claims that she wasn't "Black enough." During her presidential campaign in 2019, the *Sacramento Observer* published a piece that pushed back against commentators who were skeptical of her ethnoracial identity, in part because she is a Black woman married to a white man:[19] "Some questioned her race suggesting she wasn't really Black because of her biracial and global heritage ... Who would think Black folk would accuse Harris of being 'suspicious' for being biracial and married to a white man with all of the influential Black men—some biracial—married to white women and non-Black women getting to keep their Black cards?"

Another article in *The Reveille: Louisiana State University* pushed back against criticism of Harris's mixed background: "Kamala's father is Jamaican, she went to Howard University and she is a member of the Alpha Kappa Alpha sorority. I'm not sure how much more black she can get."[20] *Philly.com* also printed an article that contained a quote from "Yvette Carnell, a cofounder

[17] Yee, William Yuen. 2019. In Return to Campus, Nate Silver defends 2016 forecast, bets "even money" on Donald Trump in 2020. *Chicago Maroon: University of Chicago*. February 12.

[18] Douglas, Theor. 2016. Senate hopeful Harris talks education, economy, bullet train. *The Bakersfield Californian*. February 20.

[19] Burton, N. K. 2019. Blacks need to give Harris A chance. *Sacramento Observer*. February 7–13, 2019.

[20] James, Olivia. 2019. Opinion: Policing political candidates' Blackness counterproductive. *The Reveille: Louisiana State University*. February 6.

of the #ADOS [American Descendants of Slavery] movement," who specified that the focus was on Harris's stance on policies for African Americans specifically, not whether she was considered Black: "'This whole argument that we're saying she's not black is really ridiculous.'"[21]

Overall, news coverage throughout Harris's career has created a tension between how she identifies herself and how newspapers portray her. In her memoir, she discusses her identity primarily as a Black woman. Newspapers highlight her mixed background as a resource and even print questions of her Blackness. This tension creates the opportunity for Harris to perform identity labor to explain her ethnorace.

Performing Identity Labor

When politicians engage in identity labor, they draw on familial history to publicly manage their ethnoracial identity. Harris's memoir shows that her family and childhood experiences influenced her ethnoracial identity as Black. Yet, reporters have homed in on her mixed background and discussed it as a strategic advantage by suggesting that her mixed background could collect favor from voters from different demographic groups. At the same time, her mixed background could be a liability when appealing to voters who question her identity. How has Harris performed identity labor over time? Two venues in which Harris has strategically and publicly managed her ethnoracial identity are her website biography and public statements to the press.

Table 2.1 analyzes terms denoting ethnoracial group membership on her website biography from 2003 to 2019. As the table shows, "African" (N = 197) occurs the most frequently. In all 197 instances of the word "African," Harris identifies as African American. She uses the words "India" and "Tamilian" in three individually archived biographies to describe her mother as Tamilian and from India in her 2010 biography during her campaign for California Attorney General. The rarity of her use of Asian and Indian in this collection of her website biographies indicates that she has generally publicly self-presented her ethnoracial identity as African American.

Over the years, Harris has referenced her ethnoracial background strategically for news venues when talking to different audiences. The *Sun Reporter* quoted Harris during her campaign for a California US Senate seat in 2015

[21] Russ, Valerie. 2019. It's not whether Kamala Harris is "Black enough," critics say, but whether her policies will support native Black Americans. *Philly.com*. February 11.

Table 2.1 Kamala Harris.org Biographies (2003–2019), *N* = 132 biographies*

Term	Word count, Biography count	% of Biographies
Biracial	0	0
Multiracial	0	0
Mixed	0	0
Jamaican	0	0
Jamaica	0	0
Black	**61, 49**	**37.12**
African	**197, 108**	**81.82**
Tamilian	3, 3	2.27
India	3, 3	2.27
Indian	0	0
Asian	16, 16	12.12

Kamala Harris has used Black/African the most on her website biographies.
*Values indicate the total word count in the biographies and the count of archived biographies with the term. For instance, the word "Tamilian" occurred three times in three archived biographies, or in 2.27 percent of 132 archived biographies. Ninety-five archived versions of the website are duplicates.

as saying: "There are obviously no African American women in the Senate. I will bring a perspective informed by that."[22] Four years later, in 2019, when discussing Harris's stance on legalizing cannabis, *New York Amsterdam* described Harris as "jokingly saying 'half [her] family's from Jamaica.'"[23] Harris's mixed ethnoracial background serves as a resource to establish credibility (and perhaps to draw on stereotypes) to connect to the representation of Black women and policy issues like the legalization of cannabis.

Harris has also performed identity labor by elaborating on her relationships with her ethnoracial constituents. In 2010, after winning her election for California Attorney General, *India-West* reported Harris stating that "the Indian American community has been very supportive of my campaign, which is a great source of pride for me."[24] In 2019, *Philadelphia Tribune* noted Harris's relationship with Howard University "and sorority Alpha Kappa Alpha Inc., whose members she Constantly singles out for selfies and makes time for conversation at various campaign events [*sic*]."[25] In doing so, Harris draws on her cultural capital in both communities to cultivate relationships with Black and Indian American constituents.

[22] Berkley-Armstrong, G. 2015. Harris running hard for Boxer's Senate seat. *Sun Reporter.* April 23.
[23] Boyd, H. 2019. The halves of Kamala Harris. *New York Amsterdam News.* February.
[24] Sohrabji, S. 2010. Historic Harris victory. *India-West.* December 3.
[25] Wright, J. 2019. Kamala Harris nabs high-profile endorsement in S.C. *Philadelphia Tribune.* June 14.

At the same time, Harris is aware that people question her Blackness. In 2019, the *Philadelphia Tribune* cited an interview between Harris and the radio show *The Breakfast Club* that discussed how others have questioned Harris's claims to Blackness in part due to her mixed immigrant parentage, to which she responded by comparing the questions as similar to those lodged at Obama. In this interview, she stated, "'I'm not going to spend my time trying to educate people about who Black people are.'"[26] In this instance, Harris performs identity labor by refusing to engage in debates about her claims to Blackness.

Discussion

Society's fascination with politicians' parentage and identity creates the need—and opportunity—to perform identity labor. Identity labor, an interaction between politicians and society, consists of the strategic actions that politicians take to manage public perceptions of their identity. Exploring the case of Kamala Harris offers the opportunity to observe the role of the family and the ethnoracial hierarchy in her performance of identity labor.

Parental influence informs the content of politicians' identity labor. Harris performs identity labor by expressing pride in who she is, primarily as a Black woman, in her memoir (Moya and Markus 2010, 14). Harris's mother made a conscious choice to raise her children as Black women, which perhaps played a role in Harris deciding to attend an HBCU and publicly declare her identity as African American early in her career. By exposing Harris to Indian culture as a child, her mother also gave her the option to strategically affirm cultural affinity with Indian Americans as a politician. Through cultural exposure and identity socialization, parents and families give mixed politicians material to draw from to craft their public story.

Parentage and the group membership it bestows become political resources to exploit, both for the politician and the media. Harris can reference her parentage in statements to the press or speeches. She can also reference parentage in her official biography—swapping out her mother's heritage on her website when doing so makes sense for her political image. For reporters, having mixed parentage may be a novelty that offers interesting news stories for their audiences. When news articles mention mixed parentage as an electoral advantage, they create the idea that being mixed is a strategic benefit and

[26] Reston, M. 2019. Kamala Harris takes on questions about her Blackness. *The Philadelphia Tribune*. February 12.

an opportunity for a politician like Harris to exploit. Covering Harris's mixed background as a political benefit suggests that mixed politicians, and perhaps mixed women politicians specifically, are more marketable than non-mixed politicians (see Streeter 2002; DaCosta 2007; Locke and Joseph 2021). More broadly, by noting Harris's ethnoracial parentage at all, news venues implicitly suggested that Harris inherited her ethnoraces—not just her membership to socially constructed ethnoracial groups—from her parents through biology (Moya and Markus 2010, 15). In short, her mixed ethnoracial background, in addition to the substance of her work as a politician, is an important aspect of describing her and her political opportunities.

Taken together, using Kamala Harris as an example, this chapter shows that identity labor is a dance between the politician and the public. Mixed politicians convey their personal stories in their written biographies and interactions with reporters. Reporters, in turn, categorize them. How do other mixed politicians across the United States perform identity labor, and what does it look like? In the Chapter 3, I report my interpretations of interviews I conducted with state legislators around the country and show how state legislators perform identity labor within the legislature, with constituents, and with the media.

3
How Legislators Perform Identity Labor

When my older sister was born in the 1970s, a Chinese American nurse carried her into a shared hospital room to return her to our mother, calling out her Chinese surname. We have different fathers. When my mother raised her arms to claim the baby, the nurse said, "This baby is Chinese," suggesting that my sister was not our mother's child. In the early days of my sister's life, she didn't share skin color, hair color, hair texture, eye shape, or surname with my mother—all markers that would indicate they "belonged" together.

In response, my mother pointed to their matching identification tags—administrative paperwork—that indicated they were mother and daughter—Mexican mother and Chinese daughter. My mother had to "prove" they were related by pointing to documentation that they indeed belonged together because "this baby is Chinese" and my mother is not. Claims of kinship were insufficient because biological essentialism pervades how everyday people interpret appearances and familial relationships (also see Moya and Markus 2010, 15–16).

As we grew, my sister and I interpreted our appearances as we received comments from people about how we looked and who we resembled. The way we interpret and think of our ethnoracial appearance has much to do with our connections to our family members.[1] I grew up interpreting my appearance nearly always in relation to my dad, who people read as Filipino and sometimes Hawaiian. At the same time, people interpreted my sister's appearance in relation to my mom, who people read as white or Mexican. When my sister was younger, they looked nothing alike. And we looked nothing alike. Today, my sister and I both look like my mom. But I don't look think we look anything alike.

Politicians in the public sphere navigate the predominance of biological essentialism as they do identity labor. The public assigns their group membership based on their appearance, and membership denotes one's place in the ethnoracial hierarchy. From there, politicians draw on their familial socialization to tell stories about themselves and their identities. The nature of their stories and the way people respond to them, depend in part on how they look.

[1] See Fielder (2020) and Waring and Bordoloi (2019).

Doing Identity Labor. Danielle Casarez Lemi, Oxford University Press. © Oxford University Press (2025).
DOI: 10.1093/9780197816851.003.0003

How do politicians perform identity labor when engaging with different political stakeholders? In this chapter, I share findings from interviews with thirty-seven state legislators' offices around the country. I explore how mixed politicians understand their identities and subsequently do identity labor. Familial socialization, the ethnoracial hierarchy, and ethnoracial appearances structure the opportunities to perform identity labor. Although mixed legislators have similar experiences, their experiences better parallel their non-mixed counterparts *because* of the ethnoracial hierarchy. Identity labor is most apparent when interacting with constituents and the ethnoracial caucuses. The degree to which one must perform identity labor hinges partially on how others interpret politicians' ethnoracial appearances, as perceived by politicians themselves. These interviews suggest that there's an identity labor gap between mixed and non-mixed representatives, in which mixed representatives must use identity labor to close the distance between themselves and their ethnoracial groups.

Group Membership and Identity in the Legislature

When I first began this research back in 2015 (Lemi 2018), I was a lot more interested in teasing apart the distinction between ethnoracial identity and ethnoracial classification and how we understand the role of identity in descriptive representation (Brunsma 2006). Previous interviews with legislators offered inconsistent evidence that legislators *themselves* believed their ethnoracial identities made them uniquely positioned to represent their ethnoracial groups (e.g., Swain 1993; Fraga et al. 2006; Casellas 2010; Rouse 2013). At the time, few studies dug deeply into personal ethnoracial identity and tended to assume that descriptive representatives identified with the groups to which they were assigned (but see Brown 2014a). I thought this was a weak assumption given what we know about mixed people in particular—people often misinterpret their appearances or can't read them at all (e.g., Khanna 2004; Rousseau Anderson 2015, 15–16; Vargas and Kingsbury 2016; Sims 2016). And, one study indicated that having an ambiguous appearance as a legislator may be politically advantageous (Brown 2014b). Past research also suggested that legislative institutions are microaggressive settings where legislators of color experience racism from their colleagues (Hedge et al. 1996, 90–91; Tyson 2016, 145). Legislators' appearances, and how they experience ethnorace and identity within the legislature, were an underexplored area.

When I set out to do field work, I sought to combine the insights of research on descriptive representation—that there's something about being a person of color that makes one legislate differently—with the insights of research on everyday mixed people—that their ethnoracial appearances complicate how others read them and how they understand their identities. How did mixed descriptive representatives understand their roles as legislators? Did other peoples' perceptions of their ethnorace drive their behavior, or did their own identities drive their behavior? How did they differ from their non-mixed counterparts and from legislators from other groups?

I found that some mixed legislators experienced questions about group membership, in part, because of their appearance. For example, one Black legislator who identified as "African American of [Latinx ethnic group] descent" experienced questions about his place in the Latino Caucus, likely because he appeared Black (Lemi 2018, 736). Yet, he didn't mention that his membership to the Black Caucus was questioned. And when it came to his memberships to multiple ethnoracial caucuses, he was careful "to avoid being perceived as a 'double agent'" (Lemi 2018, 736). Another legislator, with Black and white ancestry, was initially perceived as white when seeking the endorsement of the state legislature's Black Caucus, and was eventually asked, "So are you Black or are you white?" (Lemi 2018, 736). People also wondered if a mixed Asian American legislator, who was a member of the Asian Pacific Islander Caucus, was even Asian American (Lemi 2018, 734). And one mixed white and Latinx legislator explained that their mixed status was "irrelevant" for their standing as a Latinx legislator in the Capitol (Lemi 2018, 736). The reception of mixed legislators in this legislature depended on how people interpreted their appearances and their specific ethnoracial backgrounds.

That study inspired new questions. How common was this in other states? For other ethnoracial combinations? And how were mixed legislators around the country navigating their identities during the campaign, with constituents, with their colleagues, and with the media? How do politicians use their ethnoracial identities strategically when engaging with different political stakeholders? In 2018 and 2019, I interviewed thirty-seven state legislators' offices and their staff by phone and in person to tackle these questions (see Appendix for details on data and methods). What I learned was that much like everyday mixed people (e.g., Waring and Bordoloi 2019; strmic-pawl 2016; Rockquemore and Brunsma 2002), familial socialization, the ethnoracial hierarchy, and ethnoracial appearance all structure how mixed legislators talk about their backgrounds and identities, and ultimately, how they perform identity labor.

Findings

Methodological Choices

The specific data and methods discussion is in the Appendix. However, a few details are worth discussing before we turn to the findings. Table 3.1 summarizes the characteristics of the thirty-seven legislators' offices in this sample. I made some coding choices to create this table. One was no longer in office at the time of the interview. Most of the sample has Asian or white ancestry. This is a diverse purposive sample that captures different ethnoracial contexts nationwide. I make no claims about the veracity of my interviewees' backgrounds—their self-identification of their own ancestries is what constitutes their understandings of themselves. As I talked to legislators, I learned some had mixed grandparentage. One mixed white legislator described having Indigenous ancestry through a parent and shared that they could not trace their history much, so I tabulated this legislator as having mixed Indigenous heritage. Other non-white legislators seemed to reference distant heritage—or what they learned about themselves in a 23andMe test. I do not consider them members of those groups in this tabulation. Distant ancestry, especially that recovered from a DNA test, may not actually be meaningful for their identities or lived experiences (see Roth and Ivemark 2018, 152; Roth et al. 2020; Roth et al. 2024).

Reporting this qualitative research requires balancing ethical considerations while synthesizing their stories. In this book, I made some choices to protect the identities of the people willing to talk with me. I have omitted specific categories such as gender or sexuality that, if combined with ethnorace and region, may aid in identifying some legislators. In reporting these narratives, I also cloak specificities like cities, languages, specific ethnic groups, and in some cases, specific combinations of ethnoracial categories that may make the participant more easily identifiable. For example, it would be easy to find a legislator who is a Black and Asian American lesbian from the South. I also purposely omit partisanship—in regions controlled by Republicans, it is straightforward to identify a person of color, especially a mixed person, when identified by party. One legislator had a distinct ethnoracial background, so for this legislator, I did not consistently use a unique identifier to avoid linking their quotes. For these reasons, I use labels such as "Mixed Legislator #1" to refer to the participants. In the interviews, I asked legislators to tell me about their family histories, the circumstances under which ethnorace was salient, and where they thought our country was headed in terms of diversity (see Appendix for full questionnaire).

Table 3.1 Summary of sample from 2018 and 2019

Interviews with state legislators (thirty-seven offices) in 2018 and 2019	
Non-mixed or mixed	***N* Individual interviews**
Non-mixed	18
Mixed	20
Ethnoracial ancestry	
Asian alone	3
Asian mixed	10
Black alone	3
Black mixed	3
Indigenous alone	1
Indigenous mixed	7
Latinx alone	5
Latinx mixed	6
Middle Eastern or North African (MENA) alone	0
Middle Eastern or North African (MENA) mixed	3
Pacific Islander alone	0
Pacific Islander mixed	2
White alone	6
White mixed	15
Region	
West	26
East	4
South	2
Midwest	6

Note: The individual number of interviews sum to 38 because a legislator and a staff member from the same office participated, for a total of two individuals from that office.

Familial Socialization and Early Life Structures Identities of Mixed Legislators

Like Kamala Harris, the legislators I spoke to, mixed and non-mixed, shared how family members and moments from earlier life shaped how they thought about their ethnoracial identities.

In some cases, mixed legislators described how their parents took particular care to explain the implications of their backgrounds for how society would interact with them. For example, I spoke to Mixed Legislator #5, who was Black and MENA and steadfast in identifying with both of their heritages. As a child, they grew up in the Midwest and lived in an "affluent area" before moving to a "working-class suburb." They attended a predominantly white school after their parents' divorce. In their words, they are "medium to dark-skinned." They described how their parents anticipated that others would be confused about this legislator's background:

> My parents were great from the time I was three years old, I remember that was when the discussions about color and race started ... we started to have those as a family because they wanted me to be confident and prepared and they always told me, "People are going to try to put you in a box." And so when you're biracial you often get that question of, "Well what do you identify as?" Well I'm Black and [MENA]. "Well, what do you see yourself as?" Well I'm Black and [MENA]. "Yeah, but what do you feel more ... " You know, and they just don't get it. I am Black and [MENA]. I am equally Black as I am equally [MENA].

This legislator had minimal tolerance for the expectations people put on them to choose one category. Because of their parents' influence, this legislator responded to questions that boiled down to, "What are you?" by identifying with two categories, regardless of pressure from people to choose one. When people could not grasp that they could possibly belong to more than one ethnoracial group—and identify "equally" with two distinct groups of people—the legislator used repetition to get the point across.

Likewise, Mixed Legislator #18, a Black and white legislator, also grew up in a suburb in the Midwest. Despite being sometimes white-presenting as an adult, as a child, this legislator was aware of how teachers treated them differently from their white peers: "Growing up, I was often the only kid of color in my school or in my classes ... I can see some racial overtones. Like I had teachers who would say that I was disrespectful for asking questions or challenging them ... I do recall that students would look at me to speak on behalf of all Black people."

As a consequence, this legislator described how:

> when I was a kid I did a lot less rule breaking stuff than my friends did. We had that conversation when I was pretty young—your friends are going to be able to get away with stuff that you're not gonna be able to get away with ... so I didn't do some of the typical teenage—drinking, throwing parties, because I was never under the impression that I would be able to get away with it as some youthful indiscretion.

This legislator's parents explicitly communicated the double standard in the behaviors that white society will tolerate for white children and Black children. Whereas white children would be given the benefit of the doubt, this legislator knew they would not be given that courtesy.

In one case, Mixed Legislator #15 internalized the experiences of their parents and was socialized into their Indigenous culture by their father. When I asked how they identified, they didn't leave room for ambiguity: "Well, first of all, I'm [Indigenous], I've always identified that way." Their mother was Indigenous and white, and their mother gravitated toward her Indigenous heritage because people from her white side "were racist. They were mean to her." Mixed Legislator #15's father was Indigenous, and he was:

> raised in the culture, and he spoke the language. When I tried to get him to teach me the language, because he was in the boarding schools for a while, he would just say, "They beat it out of me." But when we'd come home to the reservation, he would speak fluent [Language], the [Indigenous] language here, quite fluently with the elders.

The combined experiences of this legislator's parents ultimately resulted in this legislator identifying as solely Indigenous on demographic forms—"if [Indigenous] wasn't on the form, then I wrote in [Indigenous]." I then asked how they identified their white heritage on forms. They noted they don't identify as such, "Cuz there's never a box for it to be checked and because of how my mother was treated." Knowing that their mother was treated poorly by racist family members created the opportunity for this legislator, like their mother, to gravitate closer toward their Indigenous identity and strongly affirm that aspect of their heritage.

In other cases, mixed legislators' relationships with their grandparents shaped their identities and expressions of those identities. For example, Mixed Legislator #3, from a Western state, had Indigenous ancestry and credited their mixed ethnoracial background to the military—frequent moves to report for duty create opportunities for inter-ethnoracial relationships and mixed kids. Because of the influence of their grandfather in particular, this legislator had a strong (though not exclusive) Indigenous identity. They described their grandfather, noting that he:

> very much cherished his [Indigenous] heritage and it was extremely important to him that all of his kids be enrolled into the tribe. And that's not a simple task. You don't get it at birth, right? You have to lay it all out, all kinds of stuff. So as a

> consequence, because of his strong hand on the family, that got imprinted pretty strongly on me.

I learned that the influence of this legislator's grandfather—at least from our conversation—did not extend to this legislator's sibling. As they put it:

LEGISLATOR: If you had asked my brother that same question by the way, he would probably say [Latinx ethnicity].

ME: Really? Why?

LEGISLATOR: I have no idea. It's something that happened when he was in high school. I think that—I don't know what your experience was in high school—you kind of start self-associating and joining clubs and whatever, and I think for me that was the place to go. I think maybe it was a safe place to be, it was maybe larger numbers ... but yeah, he—he would say that.

ME: Is he older or younger?

LEGISLATOR: Older. So that's also been a complexity of my upbringing—"Hold on your brother's over in [Latinx Organization] and you're starting the [Indigenous] club—what's that about?" You've gotta hold people's hand ... Okay, well, there's a little bit of everything going on here, and he's not being inauthentic, he's just choosing to emphasize a different part of our heritage. That was just a long way of saying my grandfather was just way into it, and you know that kind of influence.

Much like how children within the same family have different relationships with their parents and grandparents, this legislator expresses their ethnoracial identity differently from their sibling.

Of course, ethnoracial identity on its own wasn't explicitly important to every mixed legislator—not everyone shared stories about personally navigating others' curiosity, racism, or tracing one's genealogy. Mixed Legislator #10, a Latinx and Asian American Western state legislator, did not immediately identify with any ethnoracial category. They shared that people perceived their appearance to be ambiguous—"Mixed. I mean I get all kinds: [Indigenous to their state], Samoan, part Chinese."

As I asked about their experiences at different life stages they responded: "Well it doesn't concern—I'm not obsessed about my ethnic background." Moments later, they elaborated on how the experiences of their grandparents inform their political views:

> My grandmother was a custodian at a elementary school in [Local City] ... and she only caught the bus. That's how she went to the doctor, that's show she went to the store, that's how she went to work. So, because of that, I've always been a

> big supporter of public transportation, because I see the impact it has on people's lives—like my grandmother. My grandfather was a plantation worker with different ethnic groups and despite different ethnic groups being treated differently in the camp he worked at, he was never prejudiced … or resentful.

As the conversation went on, it was clear that the added layer of the local context shaped this legislator's perception that their ethnoracial background wasn't that consequential for them. At multiple points in our conversation, they highlighted the diversity of their state and their legislature. When I asked about the role their ethnoracial background plays during campaigns they replied:

> People may vote for you because you have some ethnic—they have some ethnic connection, but I—because [Western state] is more and more diverse and there's so much—through several generations there's a lot of mix—or I guess interracial or multiethnic marriages. I guess it's—it plays less of a role.

For this legislator, rather than point to their own negative experiences at the intersection of ethnorace and class, they internalized their grandparents' experiences. The expression of their ethnoracial identity did not carry the same weight as other legislators' identities did.

The Ethnoracial Hierarchy Structures Expressions of Identities

When I asked legislators how they identified and why, some of them laughed, answering with a version of: "because that's what I am." Their laughter offered a window to observe how they thought about ethnorace in the United States. Ethnorace in America is "common sense" and understood to be biologically inherited through parentage and discernible by physical features like skin color (Omi and Winant 1994, 59; Moya and Markus 2010, 15–16). My question was so absurd it was a joke.

For some, their laughter seemed to stem from their context. One mixed state legislator explained to me that their state "is very different from anywhere else because we're all minorities here." When I asked them to elaborate on their experience being the only member of one of their ethnoracial groups in their legislature, they replied, "Nobody cares—" they paused and laughed, "—nobody cares." This laughter suggested that perhaps I was looking for potential racism that they didn't perceive in their legislature.

This question also gave me insight into how the ethnoracial hierarchy manifested itself within the legislature. One non-mixed Black legislator, who did not laugh, answered, "I think it's kind of funny when you say, 'How do you identify?' because at one point in time we didn't have a choice, to have Black blood in your family in America at one point in time for many folks was looked upon as a stain." This legislator was referencing the historical one-drop rule in the United States, which classified anyone with a "drop" of "Black blood" as absolutely Black. To be asked "How do you identify?" was ironic.

Mixed and non-mixed Black Legislators

The ethnoracial hierarchy also showed up in the references mixed and non-mixed legislators made to the historical experiences of their ethnoracial group and their personal experiences (or lack thereof) with racialization. Legislators shared similar narratives with respect to anti-Blackness, anti-Indigeneity, xenophobia, within-group hierarchies, and understandings of white privilege. Multiple Black legislators pointed to institutional racism and prejudice endured by themselves or their families, including experience with violence from police.

For example, Non-mixed Legislator #17 is a Black legislator from a Southern state who grew up in the 1960s. When I asked about their experience in the legislature, they described how they use their personal experiences to take action:

> I'm bringing my experiences, my—my experiences to the table. You can't help but do that ... I wanted to have a conversation and we did this on the House floor. I asked [another legislator], "What does the term 'Black Lives Matter'—what does that mean to you?" These are the kind of conversations that I have on the House floor. And I have that because when somebody introduces a bill [that is hostile to Black Lives Matter] I'm trying to understand where's he coming from and what are his thoughts—what's his thought process? ... We say, "What type of different experience do you have?" Well, I'll go driving through my neighborhood—I don't have a criminal record—and I'll be stopped by the police, 'kay? And they'll pull me over and they'll say—they'll tell me I did something wrong even though it's not true and—and those are real experiences that I've had.

For this legislator, their personal experiences with anti-Black police violence contributed to them engaging with the other side to defend the interests of Black people—even if they're one of the few to do so.

Similarly, a staff member for Mixed Legislator #18, a Black and white legislator, pointed to their legislator's work on police shootings in their state.

Their staff member described how this legislator was concerned about police shootings of Black men because they "could see that as being [their] father or brother." This led to action in their state legislature:

> STAFF: [Mixed Legislator #18] organized [direct action] about gun control earlier this year, and as an African Amer—you know part African American [person] was a driving factor in that, is seeing some of the injustices around some of the police shootings that have been going on especially if you're in [State] . . . and it kind of came to a head with a number of protests.

Much like how Non-mixed Legislator #17 above drew on their experiences with getting pulled over in debates with colleagues, this legislator drew on the experiences of their ethnoracial group and immediate family members to exercise direct action in the state legislature. These legislators were not just advocating for their constituents, but for their families and themselves.

Black legislators also expressed feeling compelled to overcome, or being praised for (apparently) overcoming, negative generalizations of Black people (West and Fenstermaker 1995, 23). I spoke to Non-mixed Legislator #7, a Black legislator from a Western state. They were born to a relatively large family in the South. Their father taught them about the institutional racism they could encounter:

> I had a clear understanding that . . . that for me it would be difficult because I was African American, and I was going to have to fight for every opportunity I had. And my dad drilled that into us . . . I remember when I graduated from high school I didn't get a scholarship from my dad's company. Some white girl in [the Midwest]—somewhere—got the scholarship and my dad was angry. Okay? But, what he did was, every award I ever got while I was in college, he took it to his job and put it on the bulletin board to say, "And this is the [child] you didn't give a scholarship to" . . . He wanted me to understand, "You didn't get a scholarship not because you weren't good," but this country—company—that he worked for at the time was so racist. . . . I was raised with a real sense that you know that racism was real, that there was no fantasy about it . . . that I had to be twice as good in order to be considered good.

Like Mixed Legislator #18's experience as a child, the ethnoracial hierarchy dictated that white society would hold this legislator to a higher standard than their white counterparts.

By contrast, Mixed Legislator #5, who is Black and MENA, described being praised by their friends *because* they didn't fit stereotypes in their friends' heads:

> I really appreciate the term privilege now, because I think that was a term—it was something I always experienced in my life—being affected by white privilege but there wasn't a term for it. I knew that most of my friends and community weren't racist, but they would say things that—that still were very hurtful or insensitive ... they didn't realize that they were saying it. When you get ... "You're smart for a [Black person]," you know you get that compliment that ends with, "for a [Black person]," and you're kind of like, "Well—well, what does that mean? Are you saying that generally [Black people] are not these things?"

Likely because they were mixed, this legislator's friends treated them as an exceptional Black person (see Joseph 2013)—a perverse way of granting this legislator "white privilege." Receiving backhanded compliments like this, from friends, didn't feel good.

Mixed and non-mixed Indigenous legislators

Indigenous legislators commonly referenced land and group persistence. In our introduction, Mixed Legislator #7, who had white, Indigenous, and Asian American ancestry, explicitly named their connection to the land as part of their identity:

> I'm [an Indigenous person] in [State]. So, this is my home, this is the homeland, this is the fatherland, this is the motherland. And everything we do associated with politics is aimed towards equality of life for the Native and all of the rest of the peoples of [State].

Their status as an Indigenous person drove their policy work as a legislator.

Mixed Legislator #4, who also had white, Indigenous, and Asian American ancestry, told me: "the majority of the community would perceive me as ... child of the land" because of their family's longstanding ties to the state. I asked this legislator if their background contributed to their political views. They indicted the United States government:

> I guess, being [Indigenous] from [State], it does give a little bit extra connection to the land, which is where we're from and ... I mean [Indigenous people in this state] are very opinionated ... America taking over [our land] is not—is not a very ... nice thought for a lot of [Indigenous people in this state], because of the force that was used ... if anything, that push to try to ... well not so much reparations, but you know, try to keep—keep our society, you know, our culture, still alive as much as possible.

This legislator's relationship to the land at least partially motivated them to participate in the fight for cultural preservation in their state.

When I asked Indigenous legislators if there was something unique about having their backgrounds in America today, multiple legislators brought up survival. As Non-mixed Legislator #5, who is Indigenous, from the West, put it: "We're survivors, you know. We are survivors and we're not gonna go away ... we are the Indigenous people of this country, and we—and the rest of the people need to ... respect us."

In the Midwest, Mixed Legislator #14, who is white and Indigenous, also pointed to survival and historical attempts to erase their group:

> Indigenous folks are starting to speak up and say, "We were screwed so many times over, and we have been made invisible, and there have been so many intentional acts done in order to terminate us." But we survived. And we're still, we're still here, and we're still prideful, we're still proud of our heritage. There's all this language rejuvenation. I mean our legislature has funding for [Indigenous] arts, for the rejuvenation of the languages, of community events and recognizing the contribution of the [Indigenous people] in our state.

Seeing members of their community thrive through language and art brought this legislator pride in the persistence of their Indigenous culture and their group.

Mixed and non-mixed Latinx legislators

Some mixed and non-mixed Latinx legislators connected their backgrounds to immigration as an issue. Mixed Legislator #6 is white, Latinx, and MENA from a Western state. Growing up, they experienced racism directed at them for being Latinx and for being MENA. When I asked if there was anything unique about being someone with their specific ethnoracial backgrounds, Mixed Legislator #6 connected their heritages to how they view immigration policy:

> I am able to see connections and similarities across racial groups that other people don't have the fortune or the knowledge to make those connections. One example is my [grandparent] grew up with the Berlin Wall ... Then you have us trying to stand up against the border wall that [the 45th US President] is trying to construct ... I see walls as a very oppressive divisive tool that's not really about gaining more security, it's about aiding and trying to divide these from one another.

Mixed Legislator #2, who is white and Latinx from a Southern state, expressed a similar sentiment regarding the climate toward immigration. They grew up along the border between the United States and Mexico, and they thought of themselves as "Caucasian" racially and "Hispanic" ethnically. Whereas Mixed Legislator #6 saw walls, they saw bridges:

> The [border between Mexico and the United States] is not something to be feared, it's something that's a way of life ... I have a different understanding about immigration because ... the bridges between [Mexico and the United States] were numerous, and heavily used, and were a way to do commerce and tourism and visiting family ... the bridges were just another bridge ... it wasn't something that, in today's political atmosphere, has become something that's ... been more divisive than unifying.

Two Latinx legislators pointed to the hostility of the 45th US President's Administration to Latinx immigrants in particular. Non-mixed Legislator #2, a Latinx immigrant in an Eastern state, told me, "I think I also represent the resistance ... under this current administration because we constantly see our president portraying people who look like me, or anyone who doesn't fit the profile of a white American, that we don't belong here." As we wrapped up our conversation, I asked Non-mixed Legislator #1, a Latinx immigrant from an Eastern state who has been in the United States since the 1980s, where they thought the United States was headed in terms of increasing diversity. They felt a "backwards" shift comparing "discrimination" in the United States back then to present day: "People feel more entitled now to say what they feel about immigration, about Latinos. And we feel them target the Latino community more than any other community." Similar to Non-mixed Legislator #1, this legislator felt that Latinx Americans were being singled out. All four legislators, mixed and non-mixed, were concerned that the discourse on immigration policy was fueled by racism, security theater, and divisiveness.

Mixed and non-mixed Asian American legislators

In my conversations with mixed and non-mixed Asian American legislators, I found similarities in how they named the often-overlapping hierarchies of ethnicity, color, and class that exist among Asian Americans. For instance, one mixed Asian American legislator believed that the Asian and Pacific Islander Caucus in their state tended to treat representatives who are not Northern or East Asian as lesser members of the caucus. When I asked Non-mixed Legislator #11, a Western state legislator, about their experiences as a member of their group, they pointed out the colorism among Asian Americans:

> That's a complicated question ... if you're a lighter-skinned Asian person, namely a Chinese, Korean, or Japanese person in [State], you're kinda at the top of the food

> chain, because you have all of the advantages of being Asian, and ... none of the disadvantages of being, like a—receiving discrimination.

Non-Mixed Legislator #3, an Asian American legislator from the Midwest, discussed how data disaggregation among Asian Americans reveals class differences among Asian American ethnic groups:

> There's the model minority perception where Asian Americans do well in the [State] or across the country, and the data shows that. But when you break it down by race and ethnicities, we see that the community members that struggle most in the state in regards to the Asian American ... communities come most from Southeast Asia or those who have ... that refugee experience compared to East Asian and South Asian who are here in the US ... I would generalize mostly because of education and higher paying jobs and what not.

Taken together, these legislators recognized the ramifications of the hierarchies among Asian Americans for caucus membership, discrimination, and economic well-being.

Mixed and non-mixed white legislators

For some mixed and non-mixed legislators who were white, the ethnoracial hierarchy showed up in references to privilege or expressions of feeling solidarity, specifically in relation to Black people. For example, Mixed Legislator #1, who is white and Indigenous from an Eastern state (but was unable to trace their Indigenous heritage), shared that they were:

> very much cognizant of white privilege ... growing up in the city of [City] ... under the regime of a very tyrannical mayor at the time, who had a brutal police force, and talking with my Black friends that they lived a very terrifying life at that time under that mayor ... so I'm much more aware of [how] privileged I am.

In response to my question about the advantages and disadvantages of being "Caucasian," Non-mixed Legislator #8, from a Western state, shared that:

> There's been various times when I've gotten in a little trouble and I think ... I probably was treated much better because I was white ... in an age of "check your privilege," and Black Lives Matter stuff ... I think if I had been Black, it would have been much worse.

Like Non-mixed Legislator #8, Mixed Legislator #17 also located their whiteness, or lack thereof, in relation to Black Lives Matter. When I asked Mixed

Legislator #17, who is white and Asian American from a Western state, if their background has contributed to their political views, they shared that:

> I have gravitated towards prejudices and injustices and trying to fix those things ... I think maybe I notice them more ... because I'm not white, I gravitate more towards causes like Black Lives Matter and other kind of causes that are related to minorities.

Although this legislator had white ancestry, they understood that because they were Asian American, *they weren't really white*. Like these three legislators, Mixed Legislator #18, who is Black and white from the Midwest, also located their "privilege" in the ability to sometimes "pass as white," comparing their skin tone to a darker-skinned cousin who is also "biracial." These legislators had very different experiences with racialization in their contexts, and each understood their whiteness in terms of their relationship to Black people—their awareness of white privilege, their support for Black Lives Matter, and their recognition of the benefits of colorism. Overall, the ethnoracial hierarchy structured how some legislators talked about their identities and experiences.

Ethnoracial Appearance Creates the Need for Identity Labor

Multiple mixed legislators described how others' classifications of them were ambiguous and context-dependent. When I asked Mixed Legislator #13, an Asian American and MENA legislator, if their background ever came up when they work in states beyond theirs, they replied:

> Not so much now, because looking at me people don't know what—what I am, my ethnic background. If I'm in Arizona, people think I'm Mexican, if I'm in Europe—if I'm in Spain, they think I'm Spanish ... when I was in Peru, they thought I was Peruvian. When I'm in [Asia] they think I'm [Asian], so I have one of those faces that people don't quite—is able to pin the ethnicity without knowing.

The composition of the local population also shaped how legislators believed others saw them. Mixed Legislator #3, from a Western state, pointed to how others interpret their appearance as a result of the local demographics: "When I'm in my district they think I'm [Latinx]. I have gotten everything from Euro white [person] with a nice tan ... from some people I get [Asian ethnicity], some get Native. But by and large, just because of demographics, geography, I think they would probably classify me as Latino." Mixed Legislator #8, a white and Asian American legislator from a Western state, suggested a regional difference in how others saw them based on the size of the local Asian American population: "When I'm in [State] people will say, 'You don't look very Asian.' But when I'm on the East Coast people will say, 'You look very Asian.'" Both legislators received different comments from people that reflected the local demographics.

Mixed legislators' perceptions of how others interpreted their appearances also depended on the social setting or who's asking. Mixed Legislator #6, who is white, Latinx, and MENA in a Western state, noted that others' perceptions of them depend on who's around. In their words, "If I'm on the street, and it's just someone white or Latino looking at me, they think I'm [Latinx]. If I'm in a [MENA] space, they think I'm [MENA]." Mixed Legislator #5, who is Black and MENA, also pointed to the importance of the eye of the beholder—people from numerous ethnoracial groups have thought this legislator belonged to their group:

> I've had both [Black and white people] think that I was all Black and I've had both of them think I wasn't Black at all ... I've had East Indian people claim me as East Indian ... when I was a kid I worked at a Filipino and Hawaiian restaurant and the Filipino people who would come in would speak to me in Tagalog and ask me if I was born here or back home ... I've had ... Latino people thinking I'm Latino, Italian people thinking I'm Italian ... I've had, you know, Middle Eastern people–they see the Middle Eastern.

Appearances, coupled with surnames, also shaped how legislators believed people saw them. One former mixed legislator I spoke to, Mixed Legislator #16, is white and Latinx. They described themselves as "not as dark complected as [their] other two sisters can get when they're in the sun." Earlier in life, they had naturally dark hair. People have mistaken this legislator for French, Greek, or Italian. This legislator shared that as a college student, someone with anti-Mexican beliefs did not realize that this legislator was Latinx:

> I had an experience in college where somebody thought that I was [French, Greek, or Italian] because that person was very anti-Mexican, and we had only been introduced by first name. So, I had to share, or felt the need to [say], "Hey, well, we weren't formally introduced, here's my name, and I'm sorry that you feel that way ... please don't judge people as a whole group, get to know people individually because we're all different."

According to this legislator, people thought they were Greek or Italian because "[people] were just grasping at straws not wanting to come to the realization that [their] last name was" a common Latinx name. This legislator felt offended that people would feel comfortable expressing anti-Mexican prejudice to them.

Mixed Legislator #17, who is white and Asian American, pointed to the role of their name and observers' perspectives in how people classified them. They explained that, "If they're Asian, they'll consider me half white. People who are white, they'll consider me Asian." As a child, they grew up in an area with a large Asian American population and other mixed people around. They recalled, "I didn't look exactly like all the other Asians, I had like freckles and curlier hair than everybody else." Yet as an adult, because of their appearance, this legislator believed that people commonly mistake them for "Hispanic," and because of their name, identify them as Asian:

LEGISLATOR: People don't know what I am, people will generally speak to me in Spanish instead of English depending on where I am in the United States ... people are not sure how to categorize me. And that probably happens the most often and next would be Asian. People go straight for Asian now rather than any kind of white.

ME: Mm-hm. Why do you think that is?

LEGISLATOR: Part of it is because of my last name. People will naturally gravitate toward what's different. So the more that I gain sort of national attention, the more that I found that people will assume that I'm just full Asian, because they gravitate toward what they know, and so they will—sort of latch on to whatever's different about you, being Asian is what makes me different.

People from their own ethnoracial groups do not think of this legislator as a member of those groups. Yet, people are more inclined to identify this legislator as Asian American, perhaps because there are relatively few nationally recognizable Asian American politicians.

Styling choices also shaped how legislators believed others perceived them. Wearing a beard, straight hair, or having a certain hair color may be used by others as clues for classification (see Sims et al. 2020). For instance, a mixed legislator explained that outside of their local context, "I mostly come off as either a white person or if I haven't shaved for a few days, probably Hispanic." Another mixed legislator mentioned that others' classification of them shifts with their hairstyle: "I've gotten anything from Jewish to Polynesian to ... Native ... Puerto Rican or Latinx." A third mixed legislator suggested that the color of their hair might introduce uncertainty for people recognizing them as "Hispanic": "I'm fair skinned and dark hair. So, it's not fitting into anyone's stereotype of what a [Latinx] is."

Taken together, these mixed legislators navigate others' questions about their identities within the contexts of their names, geographies, local demographics, and styling choices. Again, while these individuals are politicians, their experiences with racialization are similar to everyday mixed people. And while the experience of being mistaken for something else is of course not unique to mixed legislators, it is nonetheless a common experience among the mixed legislators I spoke to. As I show below, their responses to others' interpretations of their appearances and multiple group memberships have shape how they perform identity labor with constituents, caucuses, colleagues, and the media.

Performing Identity Labor: Campaigns and Constituents, Caucuses and Colleagues, and the Media

When mixed politicians manage perceptions of their identities in public life, they do so both proactively and reactively. They may use their identities to speak on issues relevant to their communities and establish credibility. At the same time, they must react to how others respond to their identities or to others' confusion resulting from their appearance. In various interactions with constituents, legislative caucuses, other legislators, as well as the media, they perform identity labor.

Campaigns and constituents

During the campaign and in interactions with constituents, mixed legislators have the advantage of appealing to multiple communities because of their ancestry. For example, Mixed Legislator #4, who is white, Asian American, and Indigenous, shared that when they won their election, someone explained to them, "You didn't get elected because you're the smartest one. It's because you're the most relatable to your district." This legislator explained that having ancestors who were Indigenous, as well as ancestors who came to the state as laborers, equipped them with the ability to understand multiple perspectives. When I asked what role their background plays during the campaign, they shared that they purposely highlight certain heritages when they visit ethnoracial enclaves:

> I'm also [Asian ethnic group] and I represent [Asian ethnic group neighborhood]. When I go to [Asian ethnic group neighborhood], I make sure I hark that a little bit

> extra ... You know people—they might see me and might think I'm [Asian ethnic group] but if I let them know, you know, it just opens up doors. I don't know if it's a direct advantage, but at least they might be a little more friendly to me knowing I'm [Asian ethnic group].

For this legislator, purposely playing up their Asian American heritage may strengthen their effort to cultivate support among this particular set of voters in their district. Whether highlighting that particular background, as a form of identity labor, pays off electorally is unclear. To this legislator, it certainly can't hurt.

Mixed legislators also have opportunities to leverage their family histories to bolster their credibility. I spoke to a staff member for Mixed Legislator #12 from a Western state with Indigenous, Asian American, and Pacific Islander ancestry. According to their staff, this legislator was in the minority of legislators "here at the Capitol that actually speaks [the Indigenous] language." Because of this legislator's seniority, they had become a fixture of "institutional knowledge" on Indigenous issues in the state. Their staff member described how this legislator's relationship to the land was an integral part of their advocacy for Indigenous constituents:

> STAFF: In [their] district [they've]—[they've] seen a lot of people come in, a lot of transplants come in and try to, you know, pull the, "I lived here for ten years, I know what it's like to really like to live here," you know but [this legislator pulls] the card of, "Hey sure, you—you've lived here for ten years. Hey my family's been living here for the past 600 years. (Mm-hm). You know, so yes, you do have a connection, but my connection is deep. It's—you know it's rooted in this land." So there are instances where—not just [them] but the other [Indigenous] legislators, they'll pull the [Indigenous to state] card, because they need to be a voice for the people.

For some mixed legislators, the public's perceptions of their appearance necessitate them proactively explaining their identities. When Mixed Legislator #18, who is Black and white, was running for office, the public was curious about their parentage. Because this legislator is lighter-skinned and, in some contexts, can present as white or some ambiguous non-white person, people do not always grasp that this legislator is Black. They shared with me that people would search for information about their parents online "because people wanted to see what my parents looked like." Mixed Legislator #18's staff member explained that in town halls, people would look to this legislator's parents to try to understand why this legislator advocated for issues relevant to Black constituents in their state:

STAFF: [People] don't realize [Mixed Legislator #18 is] part African American til [Mixed Legislator #18] vocally identifies it and [Mixed Legislator #18 does] it often ... it's like a jarring moment when [people]—like in a town hall when [the legislator will] point to [their] parents and [people] see that one's Black and one's white ... you see the wheels turning up there and [people] go, "Oh well that's why [they're] so [out] spoken on this issue, that's why [they're] so outspoken on that issue, that's why." You know, it starts to make sense ... it's a brief moment of disconnect and then people understand.

People could not reconcile Mixed Legislator #18's appearance with their commitment to protecting Black people—it violated common sense (Omi and Winant 1994, 59)—why would an apparently non-Black person, or even a white person, advocate for Black people? Once their confusion was settled by the sight of the legislator's parents, suddenly things made sense.

Mixed Legislator #18 became aware of how others perceived their appearance earlier in their political career. When they were a staff member for a member of Congress, they were responsible for building relationships with Black constituents:

LEGISLATOR: When I was doing outreach in the Black community I would kind of have to like drop hints to let them know that like I'm Black. Not just a [person] of color who happens to be doing outreach in the Black community.

ME: Mm-hm. And when you say when you were staffer you would have to drop these hints, how would you do that? What does that look like?

LEGISLATOR: It would be things like meeting at a place like a Black-owned coffee shop where they already know me and know that I'm Black. And so like having that external validator, or talking about things with my family that we do, or you know like my dad is from [city with a relatively large Black population], so oftentimes that's code for Black. Or oftentimes talking about Thanksgiving and collard greens ... So, these little things that clue people into: I am related to Black people and this is something that is part of my life and we share this.

At one point in our conversation, they explained the pressure of meeting the expectations of group membership for both Black and white people: "You're not Black enough for Black people sometimes and you're never white enough for white people, and it can feel very isolating to not have a home in either place." For Mixed Legislator #18, their appearance necessitated them making their Blackness explicit and even treating Black institutions, like businesses, as validators of their identities. These actions constitute identity labor.

Some mixed legislators reported receiving discouraging feedback about their candidacies because of their heritage or appearance, while others' group membership was dismissed entirely. In one case, a legislator was advised that their name could be a political liability. Mixed Legislator #13, who is Asian American and MENA, shared that, "When I was first running, people would say, 'A [person] named [Name]—nobody's gonna vote for [them].' And I just—I told 'em, 'Well if a guy named Barack Obama can get elected as president, I can—a [person with my name] can easily get elected into the State House." Similar to how the media associated Kamala Harris with Barack Obama, this mixed politician also understood their electoral prospects in relation to Obama.

By contrast, Mixed Legislator #3 shared that their name was a double-edged sword:

> I remember when I was first running for office, I was told to hide my ethnic differences or, combination—whatever, in part because people do rely upon that and people can perceive—they cannot readily figure out what I am and that makes them uncomfortable. At the same time, my last name was seen as something that was positive because it was something that was pronounceable. It was ethnic without being scary. "Ethnic" was the way it was phrased to me.

Because people "cannot readily figure out" this legislator's ethnorace, they've realized that the confusion "can create distance between individuals, and the success in this business is by connecting with people and connecting with them on a really authentic level." To cultivate that connection, this legislator uses speeches and social media to proactively explain who they are. They described how they "frontload" their heritage by naming their ethnoracial backgrounds in introductions to constituents:

> And again, that's part of why I frontload often. I mean ... it's in my biography, you sort of frontload it. Most of my speeches, it's [the] kind of thing I'll put out at the beginning, again, to help people navigate, "What the heck is this [person]?"

For these legislators, their names could either be political liabilities or political novelties. As Obama has become the mixed politician that many mixed politicians will be compared to, Mixed Legislator #13's self-comparison to Obama was apt. For Mixed Legislator #3, the risk was that their name would amplify their ambiguous appearance by triggering others to ask, "What are you?" and create confusion that could be counterproductive to building relationships. Their experiences represent the calculations that legislators with "ethnic" names have to consider when performing identity labor.

Mixed Legislator #5, who is Black and MENA, had a campaign experience that was directly tied to anti-Blackness. During Mixed Legislator #5's campaign, they were advised not to print their face on their campaign materials:

> Someone made the comment to me, that I might not want to put my face on—on my signs. On my road signs and stuff like that, because well, you know—"because you're Black." And, you know, I just was like, "First of all, I am who I am and if they don't want to vote for me because of my color, well there's nothing I can do about that." But I'm also not gonna hide who I am, cause I'm proud of who I am. And again, to even be deceitful—I'm gonna show up at their door. They're gonna eventually know, so why would I hide who I am? That's just not an option for me.

While this same legislator had an appearance that they believed was highly ambiguous, they were still advised to hide that they were Black when they ran for office. Although they refused that advice, their experience underscores that regardless of their appearance, some people believed that voters would lodge anti-Blackness at this legislator upon seeing their photo because they classified this legislator as Black. This legislator had to decide how they would perform identity labor—by ignoring that advice.

Some mixed legislators have to defend their identities from those who dismiss or question their group membership, either because of their appearance or because their non-white ancestry makes them unmistakably not white. Mixed Legislator #17, who is white and Asian American, had an experience where an opponent exploited this legislator's ancestry:

> LEGISLATOR: One of the things that came up during the election that was fascinating to me is one of my opponents, when [they] jumped into the race, [they] jumped in and people said [they were] going to have an automatic—[they were] going to pick up the white vote. And because there was nobody who was white in the race, [they were] going to pick up the white vote, and I had to make the argument—I had to say "Wait a second, you're missing half my identity," and saying that [they are] the only person who's white in the race, you know. [They] might be the most white, you know, [but] that you can't discount half of who I am. That—that came out during the campaign. But I think identity politics has always played a role in any campaign I've been in.
>
> ME: Mm-hm. So, when all of that was happening, and you're like, "You can't dismiss my other half," how did you process that, like, with your team, like—how did you handle that?

LEGISLATOR: I've been in this long enough to know that if you're any amount of something other than white, you're not white. That's the way people view you. I don't think it matters. It didn't bother me.

Although they expressed that the experience "didn't bother" them, ultimately, they "ended up [issuing communication] ... about the experience of being part white" and experiencing racism from white people as a child "because I wasn't white. Or white enough." They viewed the experience as "a good opportunity to highlight a problem." This legislator was cognizant of the norm of hypodescent, whereby people in the United States inherit the "lower" status ethnoracial category for their background. For African Americans, this was historically known as the one-drop rule, where any "drop" of "Black blood" made an individual absolutely Black. For this legislator, because they were also Asian American, their opponent did not view them as a legitimate white person or a viable white competitor. This white competitor prompted Mixed Legislator #17 to perform identity labor by asserting their identity and calling out how they have experienced white people enforcing the boundaries of whiteness. The campaign experience *did* affect them, even if it didn't bother them.

One mixed legislator described how their appearance complicates how people receive their work on Indigenous issues in their state. Mixed Legislator #14, who is white and Indigenous, explained that sometimes people dismiss their Indigenous identity:

> Sometimes you have to—I have to—prove that I'm [Indigenous] because I don't have [those] stereotypical, physical characteristics of being [Indigenous]. I mean I have brown eyes, I have darker hair, but my hair is curly, my skin is, is lighter, I didn't grow up on a reservation or in direct proximity, I don't speak the language, you know there's all these things that, that people look for and think [an Indigenous person] should be, and I don't always present that way. And so there have been times especially since I've been elected where people will sort of discount me, or say, "Oh [they're] not really [Indigenous]" you know, blah blah blah.

In contrast to Mixed Legislator #17, people dismiss this legislator's identity not because they aren't white enough, but because they are apparently *too* white to be Indigenous. And yet, they were Indigenous enough to work with other Indigenous legislators in their state legislature to create an Indigenous caucus. Notably, this legislator is an Indigenous descendant, and because they do not qualify for tribal enrollment via blood quantum, they are not enrolled in a tribe. As this legislator worked on a bill of interest to Indigenous communities, an Indigenous woman—who this legislator did not know intimately—called them to relay gossip:

> She said, "You know I just want you to know that there are people that are making disparaging remarks, that you're not really [Indigenous], that you don't really carry credibility, and you know, they're just saying you know, maybe some negative things about you" ... I said, "Well, you know, those people probably don't know me, they don't know my story, they don't know my history, they don't know a lot of the things about me and if anybody has any questions, I'm more than happy to give them my historic background, my genetic background when it comes to the [Indigenous] side of me."

People were accusing this legislator of lying about their stated Indigeneity. In response, this legislator asserted their Indigenous identity and performed identity labor by appealing to their history and their genetics. Their family history provided the "proof" that they were not lying about being Indigenous.

While these legislators explicitly leaned into their ethnoracial backgrounds during the campaign or in interactions with constituents, either by explaining their identities or asserting their identities, in one case, a mixed legislator intentionally aimed to downplay their ethnorace. Mixed Legislator #8, who is white and Asian American, described how they avoid highlighting their background during the campaign:

> I wouldn't want to play [my backgrounds] up too much, because it appears like a crutch or you're just saying that, "Because this is my ethnic background, you should support me." I—I just tried to present it and leave it at that. So, I feel that presenting one's ethnic background, it's one of several indicators on a person's personality.

Unlike other mixed legislators who may leverage their heritages for political gain, either by campaigning extra hard to a particular ethnic group or appealing to shared culture, this legislator hoped to simply state their ethnorace as fact. In doing so, they performed identity labor by choosing to engage with ethnorace only minimally.

Caucuses and colleagues

Mixed legislators may have a complicated status within the legislative ethnoracial caucuses. Some may experience racism from people within the legislature and carry the burden of fighting for their communities when there are only a few of them (see Kanter 1977; Dahlerup 1988). Two mixed white and Indigenous legislators reported similar experiences in their legislatures.

Mixed Legislator #14 described encountering ignorance about Indigenous law, which was coupled with "prejudice":

> There are plenty of my fellow legislators that . . . don't understand what sovereignty, especially sovereignty between the tribes and the state really means. They don't understand treaties or treaty rights, have a prejudiced attitude toward our [Indigenous people] here in [State].

Mixed Legislator #15 spoke with candor:

> LEGISLATOR: The problem is—is that my [non-Indigenous] legislators, the majority of them have white privilege so ingrained in them, they don't realize that they're behaving inappropriately . . . . it's a constant education process, explaining what something is.
>
> ME: Mhm. Now when you say that you have sometimes like colleagues behaving inappropriately, do you have any examples of when that's happened?
>
> LEGISLATOR: Out and outright racism. When I first came to the legislature, it was blatant, it was openly talked about on the legislative floor, in their floor debates. Well, most of that has gone away now, or at least I've driven it underground where legislators are being careful about how they address some of these things.

At one point, Mixed Legislator #15 even "tried to invite people to come out to the reservation . . . and they wouldn't come. In fact, they won't go visit any reservation, so even if it's in their district." For both of these legislators, there's a sense of exasperation. While these legislators advocate for Indigenous communities because of their identities, they are also strongly positioned to do so because of their knowledge of Indigenous law. In having to do the work of teaching Indigenous law to their colleagues, as Indigenous people—in the face of racism—they perform identity labor. And it's exhausting.

Others may experience racism and invalidation of their identities. For example, Mixed Legislator #18 recalled how early in their career, a white colleague casually used a racist and antiquated term to refer to people who are Black and white in conversation with them. In the course of fulfilling their legislative duties, this legislator also experienced blatant disrespect from white colleagues, such as being ignored while giving speeches. Despite experiencing anti-Blackness within their legislature, Mixed Legislator #18 described how they were also dismissed as a person of color while participating in an event with other legislators:

> So like today there was [an event] with myself and [a Black legislator] and [another legislator] whose name is [Name], and then [Name] who's my colleague but [they

> are white and Indigenous], and so there's a picture of this [group] ... and someone had commented like, "Oh we only have one person of color," and all of us were [people of color], but we didn't look it. So having to consistently continually assert yourself as a person of color ... and also having to speak on behalf of [people of color] can be kind of tough.

As a consequence, this legislator had to balance both their advocacy work with their identity labor—to simultaneously manage anti-Black colleagues and people who do not interpret them as Black. They were tired.

The ethnoracial caucuses are a site of complication for legislators who have multiple non-white heritages. For instance, a mixed legislator with Latinx and Asian American ancestry belonged to the Latino and the Asian American and Pacific Islander caucuses in their state, which at times presented policy conflicts on issues such as affirmative action. This legislator astutely recognized the fine line they walked:

> Suddenly just because I am who I am and have the relationships I have, I have a running start to get my bills passed, and that's good. When there are points of departure, or when one caucus has one particular opinion, and the other one maybe has a different, that becomes awkward and strange. I think certainly within the two ethnic caucuses, I may not necessarily be perceived as a full member. I don't know if anyone would ever say that, but I also don't think I'm projecting on this. So, it's often, pointed out that I'm a member of multiple caucuses in conversations. And I don't know if that's a way of disclosing that maybe this won't be kept confidential—what we're saying in this caucus about the other one, or if they really see a natural tension between the two. But either way you still end up being an outsider even in these groups where you self-affiliate and you know, have a pretty good claim to [be in the caucuses], right?

This legislator enjoyed having the political advantage of multiple caucus memberships that function as "running starts" to their bills. Yet at the same time, they felt a nagging suspicion that members of their ethnoracial caucuses did not trust them because they belonged to two ethnoracial caucuses simultaneously. That feeling extended to what they inferred their colleagues thought about the *legitimacy* of their membership to the ethnoracial caucuses. Tenuous acceptance of their group membership was salient to them. They compared themselves to another mixed Asian American legislator in their legislature and remarked, "At some point, a full-blooded will come along, and I understand and will expect that they will be embraced more strongly than either of us, right?" They told me about an experience from earlier in their career that illustrated this feeling of exclusion:

LEGISLATOR: I had this experience when I was on the city council, where we elected someone who is full-blooded [Asian Pacific Islander] and the difference between the two of us in terms of how we were treated by the community was night and day.

ME: Really? What happened?

LEGISLATOR: Just, "[They are] one of us," where you know I'm sometimes forgotten about or an afterthought. And again, I acknowledge that. Again, I'm not 100%, culturally, that was a part of my family that didn't really come along. That kind of got left back in [Asian Country]. So I get it. I totally understand it. But what does that do? When you're out talking to people and saying, "As the [Historically Notable Asian Ethnicity] American elected to the [State legislature]," but you know that doesn't always resonate or connect with members of that actual community. Again, it's situational. If I have a deeper personal relationship with the folks involved, they're absolutely lovely and you're really fully embraced. But if you don't present, like my face may not completely tip you off right away that my family—a portion of my family—came from there, then you don't get quite the same reception, if that makes sense.

To connect with Asian Americans, they have to build deeper relationships that their "full-blooded" counterparts may not have to build at the start.

Again, mixed legislators' experiences are not monolithic. For example, Mixed Legislator #8, who is white and Asian American, does not participate in any ethnoracial caucuses in their state. And not all mixed legislators reported questions about their loyalty within the legislature. However, the narratives of these legislators suggest that some mixed legislators experience racism and tokenism because of their specific ancestries. At the same time, because of others' skepticism, they also face challenges to completely politically leveraging all of their ancestries through the ethnoracial caucuses.

The media

Interactions with the media offer opportunities for mixed legislators to market their identities. For instance, some legislators may speak a specific language when engaging with particular news venues. Two mixed Latinx legislators mentioned speaking to Spanish news media, and one mixed Indigenous legislator has been interviewed in their Indigenous language. Mixed Legislator #14 explained how they use media engagement to let the public know they are Indigenous, in part because doing so offers their caucus "a unique sort of leverage or identity and folks will pay more attention to [the press release or article]." Their Indigenous ancestry legitimizes their work as a legislator.

However, media access may be conditional. For instance, Mixed Legislator #17, who is white and Asian American, explained that at times, they are contacted to offer "an Asian American voice." Yet, they anticipated losing their stature as more Asian Americans enter office:

> I often wonder what it would be like if there were more Asian voices, but I may not be Asian enough. Do I get coverage because I'm one of the few Asian voices, but if someone comes along who looks more Asian and is more Asian, does that become the better voice to have, right. If you're looking specifically for Asian voices, and that's part of the problem with doing diversity the way we've been doing it. What if they find someone Asian—enough? I think that's sort of a next—next problem.

This legislator worried about future access to the media and the potential loss of the current benefit of being one of the few Asian American politicians. Right now, being mixed is a resource. But in the future, being mixed could undermine their visibility to the public as other people who are "more Asian" assume office.

Of course, sometimes mixed legislators' ethnoracial backgrounds aren't salient in their media engagement. Mixed Legislator #8 noted that their ethnoracial background "doesn't really come up unless the issue is about race, or there's some component of the interview that has to do with culture," like holidays. Likewise, Mixed Legislator #6 stated, "Nobody's done a feature on my ethnic background."

Discussion

How do politicians use their ethnoracial identities strategically when engaging with different political stakeholders? Over the course of my conversations with these thirty-seven legislators' offices, I learned how mixed legislators do identity labor. The legislators I interviewed were diverse in terms of their ancestry, region, and how they expressed their ethnoracial identities. For some, ethnoracial identity simply wasn't that salient in their lives as legislators. For others, ethnoracial identity, often as a non-white person, structured how they thought about certain issues and how they related to the rest of their ethnoracial group. In contrast to the trope of mixed persons "struggling" with their identities (e.g., Gardner and Hughey 2019), these representatives are not struggling. They are managing other people's expectations. They manage with identity labor.

Their stories echo much of what social scientists outside of political science have found regarding how everyday mixed people navigate their identities—their families play a role in socializing their identities, they deal with questions about their appearances, and while they often share the experience of others' confusion about their appearances, the ethnoracial hierarchy structures their experiences and how others perceive them (e.g., Waring 2013; strmic-pawl 2016; Csizmadia and Atkin 2022;). These legislators perform identity labor through tactics such as proactively referencing shared culture, making their identities explicit to the public, balancing competing ethnoracial interests in the legislature, and reactively claiming their identities when they are dismissed. They do this during campaigns and with constituents, within their legislatures, and in media engagement. Like everyday mixed people (Pew 2015), they deal with peoples' questions about their identities and respond accordingly (e.g., Heilman 2022). However, unlike everyday people, as politicians, performing identity labor has ramifications for cultivating relationships with constituents and colleagues and ultimately serving as descriptive representatives. As these narratives show, some legislators believe that people don't always recognize them as descriptive representatives.

These findings indicate that legislators work within a political system that does ethnorace to them—and they do it back through identity labor. While mixed representatives complicate dominant understandings of ethnorace, their identity labor does not disrupt ethnorace as a whole. From the perspective of intersectionality, their experiences with identity labor depend on their constitutive parts (Hancock 2007). Although mixed representatives have common experiences, being white and Asian American is not the same as being Black and white. Mixed legislators may assert or encounter challenges to their identities depending on their ethnoracial combination and their appearance. Their experiences lie under the broader sociopolitical position of their groups (e.g., Hill Collins 2014).

As Part I of this book has shown, there are three contours of identity labor from politicians' perspectives: familial socialization, the ethnoracial hierarchy, and ethnoracial appearances. Politicians have agency over when and what parts of their identities they perform publicly, but they do so within the structures set up by their families, the ethnoracial hierarchy, and how others interpret their appearances. In the next half of the book, I focus on another perspective: the public's view of identity labor.

PART II

PUBLIC VIEWS OF IDENTITY LABOR

4
Depictions of Identity Labor Are Rooted in Historical White Supremacy

In 2023, Justin Jones, a mixed Black and Filipino American politician originally from Oakland, California, was expelled from the Tennessee House, where he serves as a Democratic state legislator.[1,2] The House Republicans charged that Jones, along with his colleagues, Black Democratic state legislator Justin Pearson, and white Democratic state legislator Gloria Johnson, violated House decorum rules by chanting with protestors calling for gun control after a mass shooting at an elementary school.[3] After a vote, Jones and Pearson were expelled from the legislature. Johnson was not. When asked for her perspective on why, Johnson stated, sarcastically: "It might have to do with the color of our skin."[4] When asked if race, age, and ideology had anything to do with his expulsion, Jones told *NPR*, "That's absolutely correct. We're the two youngest Black lawmakers ... we represent the voices of our generation. And race, most definitely."[5]

During the coverage of Jones's expulsion, there was also discussion of Jones's ethnoracial background. Emil Guillermo, a blogger for the American Legal Defense and Education Fund, remarked that mainstream news sources such as the Associated Press and NBC Nightly News were incorrectly classifying Jones as solely Black: "Justin Jones isn't just Black ... He's a mixed race Asian American."[6] To this blogger, acknowledging Jones's Filipino American

[1] Jones, Justin. n.d. Meet Justin. https://www.votejustinjones.com/about/

[2] Chappell, Bill and Vanessa Romo. Tennessee House votes to expel 2 of 3 Democratic members over gun protest. 2023. April 6. https://www.npr.org/2023/04/06/1168363992/tennessee-expel-3-democrats-house-vote

[3] Breen, Kerry. 2023. What to know about the "Tennessee Three": Why were two of the Democratic lawmakers expelled, and what happens now? https://www.cbsnews.com/news/tennessee-expulsion-house-democrats-expelled-what-happens-now/

[4] Chappell, Bill and Vanessa Romo. Tennessee House votes to expel 2 of 3 Democratic members over gun protest. 2023. April 6. https://www.npr.org/2023/04/06/1168363992/tennessee-expel-3-democrats-house-vote

[5] Chappell, Bill and Vanessa Romo. Tennessee House votes to expel 2 of 3 Democratic members over gun protest. 2023. April 6. https://www.npr.org/2023/04/06/1168363992/tennessee-expel-3-democrats-house-vote

[6] Guillermo, Emil. 2023. Emil Guillermo: Justin Jones is still black...and Asian American Filipino. Asian American Legal Defense and Education Fund. April 23. https://www.aaldef.org/blog/emil-guillermo-justin-jones-is-still-blackand-asian-american-filipino/

Doing Identity Labor. Danielle Casarez Lemi, Oxford University Press. © Oxford University Press (2025).
DOI: 10.1093/9780197816851.003.0004

side was a more accurate presentation of his ancestries.[7] According to this blogger, because of Jones's appearance, "Jones can't just be Black. Not when his physical presence (his hair, skin, size) clue us in that he's also representing another ethnic minority as well, Asian American Filipinos."[8] Jones wears his long curly black hair pulled back in a low bun. If you saw Jones on the street (López et al. 2017), depending on who you are and where you are, you might assume he's Black, Latinx, Filipino, or South Asian. When I first saw the photos of Justin Jones online, I immediately recognized him as Filipino American.

What was striking about the coverage of Jones was the connection between his reported experiences, appearance, and how others saw him—fellow politicians and commentators were doing ethnorace to Jones (Moya and Markus 2010). In the Tennessee House, Jones believed his predominantly white colleagues saw him as Black and expelled him because he was Black. And on his website, although he names the influence of his Black and Filipino grandmothers on his beliefs,[9] back in 2019, Jones told Professor Emerita Lenny Mendoza Strobel that "the Black and brown communities in the East Bay made him aware that he is always perceived as a Black person."[10] Yet this blogger, Guillermo, interpreted Jones's physical characteristics as Asian American and wanted the media to acknowledge that Jones was also Filipino American. While Jones *is* Filipino American, he is *also* Black, and his expulsion was because his colleagues were racist toward Black people in particular, not mixed Asian Americans (see Hernández 2018). In the case of Jones, we see how the ethnoracial hierarchy constructs how mixed representatives must publicly manage their identities and navigate others—sometimes from their own communities—trying to manage their identities for them. Much of that dance depends on how mixed representatives look.

In this chapter, I consider how mixed politicians perform identity labor in the press. Media depictions of mixed politicians align with historical tropes of mixed people and the ethnoracial hierarchy. Politicians undertake various forms of identity labor to manage their personas in the press, and the media plays a role in shaping their narratives. A mixed politician may leverage

[7] Guillermo, Emil. 2023. Emil Guillermo: Justin Jones is still black...and Asian American Filipino. Asian American Legal Defense and Education Fund. April 23. https://www.aaldef.org/blog/emil-guillermo-justin-jones-is-still-blackand-asian-american-filipino

[8] Guillermo, Emil. 2023. Emil Guillermo: Justin Jones is still black...and Asian American Filipino. Asian American Legal Defense and Education Fund. April 23. https://www.aaldef.org/blog/emil-guillermo-justin-jones-is-still-blackand-asian-american-filipino

[9] Strobel, Leny Mendoza. 2023. Justin Jones: Black, Filipino, Civil Rights Activist. CoverStory. April 8. https://coverstory.ph/justin-jones-black-filipino-civil-rights-activist/

[10] Strobel, Leny Mendoza. 2023. Justin Jones: Black, Filipino, Civil Rights Activist. CoverStory. April 8. https://coverstory.ph/justin-jones-black-filipino-civil-rights-activist/

their ethnoracial identity when interacting with different ethnoracial audiences. However, media depictions of mixed politicians constrain the range of strategic options a mixed politician has to use their ethnoracial identity. My analysis of media depictions of mixed politicians shows they may carefully highlight their identities when it is politically opportunistic—but within the constraints of their position in the ethnoracial hierarchy. I call this form of identity labor *constrained shifting*. A mixed politician's options, and how the press reacts, are both a function of the mixed politician's position in the ethnoracial hierarchy and the position of the community that the press serves.

When Candidates of Color Manage the Media

Identity labor is strategic. How it looks depends on a politician's contextual goals—often, on whose votes they must win. On the one hand, identity labor is proactive image management that a politician can control. The media is a platform for politicians to strategically manage their public personas (see Canon 1999, 222). A candidate might dial down their ethnoracial identity and stances on issues related to racism (Perry 1991; McCormick and Jones 1993, 76–77; Stout 2015, 8–13; Price 2016, chapter 2; Stephens-Dougan 2020, 6; also see Orey 2006), depict oneself as antithetical to ethnoracial stereotypes (McIlwain and Caliendo 2011, 26), or speak as though ethnorace no longer matters in American life (Wamble and Laird 2020, 517). Identity labor might also involve purposefully highlighting one's ethnoracial identity when speaking to specific audiences (Collet 2008, 711–714; McIlwain and Caliendo 2011, 39).

Although politicians control the messaging coming out of their campaigns, they cannot fully control how the media depicts them. Politicians' public personas are shaped partly by what the media chooses to run about them. In this sense, identity labor is also reactive.[11] For example, Black politicians who opt for a campaign strategy that dials down ethnoracial identity and discussions of racism might still need to perform identity labor to strategically manage the newspapers quoting them talking about racism (Barber and Gandy 1990, 221). Asian American politicians might need to combat newspapers covering their candidacies with anti-Asian stereotypes (Wu and Lee 2005). Sometimes politicians wish to downplay their heritage. The media has depicted Republican Bobby Jindal, former governor of Louisiana, as someone who strategically disassociates himself from Indian Americans at times (see Sriram

[11] Also see McIlwain and Caliendo (2011, 41).

and Grindlife 2017).[12] Yet, newspapers highlight his heritage anyway (Major and Coleman 2008, 324). Newspapers also serve different ethnoracial communities (Canon 1999, 229–230; Grose 2006; Sui et al. 2018). So, identity labor might involve a candidate needing to manage how multiple communities depict them. The media plays a role in shaping their narrative. In short, politicians undertake various forms of identity labor to manage their personas in the press.

Mixed politicians, because of their classification into more than one ethnoracial category, might be seen as distinct from their counterparts. They do not represent group prototypes (Hogg and Reid 2006), and they are commonly stereotyped as "beautiful" or "exotic" (Sims 2012; Waring 2013). As a result, their mixed ancestries become novelties they can capitalize on, as Barack Obama often did (McIlwain 2013, 137; Price 2016). For instance, shortly after his election in 2008, when discussing the Obama family's search for a dog for the White House, he joked to the press that "shelter dogs are mutts like [him]."[13] For some mixed politicians, their mixed ancestries serve as a resource to connect to a broad set of American voters.

Mixed politicians' ancestries become novelties the media capitalizes on too. Mixed politicians operate against the backdrop of historical tropes of mixed people—tropes rooted in white supremacy, the ethnoracial hierarchy, and social norms around interethnoracial sex in the United States (Pascoe 2010). For example, a dominant trope of mixed Black and white persons in particular is the *tragic mulatto* trope (Joseph 2013), hereafter referred to as the *tragic mixed person*. The trope has its origins in the early colonial period in the United States, where marriage between whites and Black and Native American people was prohibited, and the rape of Black women by white men was a key feature of maintaining the order of slavery (Joseph 2013, 11–12). Films and books in the 1900s characterized mixed Black and white persons as sexual objects, as highly "intelligent," and as having "mental instability" (Joseph 2013, 14–17). In nineteenth-century American literature, the trope was often applied to women who were "always doomed by [their] racial liminality" (Clark 2016, 260). Ralina Joseph (2013, 17–19) points to the 1959 film, *The Imitation of Life*, as an example that depicts the trope of the tragic mixed person. In the film, one of the main characters, Sarah Jane, has a Black mother. Due to Sarah's appearance, she can pass as white (see Hobbs 2016

[12] Venkatraman, Sakshi. 2020. Nikki Haley, Bobby Jindal and on-and-off relationships with Indian American identity. *NBC News*. August 28. https://www.nbcnews.com/news/asian-america/nikki-haley-bobby-jindal-relationships-indian-american-identity-n1238266

[13] Fram, Alan. 2008. 'Mutts like me' shows Obama's racial comfort. *NBC News*. November 8. https://www.nbcnews.com/id/wbna27606637

on passing). A key conflict in the film revolves around Sarah Jane wanting to be white. In her storyline, she dates a white boy and eventually experiences violence from him when he finds out she's Black.[14] Sarah Jane appears white, but is also not white because of the one-drop rule. If a politician is depicted as "doomed" or "unstable" because of their mixed background, this trope is at play.

Another common depiction of mixed Black people is what Joseph (2013) calls the *exceptional multiracial*, hereafter referred to as the *exceptional mixed person*. The origin of this trope lies in nineteenth-century abolitionists holding up mixed Black and white persons as people who would invite "sympathy" from whites for the abolition of slavery (Clark 2016, 264; Joseph 2013, 21). In this trope, mixed Black and white persons are characterized as attractive and representative of the post-racial future (Joseph 2013, 21–23). Joseph (2013, 23) points to the discourse around Barack Obama in 2008 as an example of the exceptional mixed person trope—he was "a racial [bridge] to a new United States." The tragic and exceptional mixed person tropes are common in depictions of mixed Black people (Harrison et al. 2017; Deeb and Love 2018, 104–105; Mills 2019; Gardner and Hughey 2019; Nunn 2021; Woldemikael and Woldemikael 2021). If a politician is depicted as worthy of celebration because of their mixed ancestry, this trope is at play.

Asian American politicians' identity labor takes on a global dimension because of American society's treatment of Asian Americans as foreigners (Kim 1999). One trope for mixed Asian Americans is the Eurasian, depicted similarly to the tragic mixed person (Ma 2007, 167, 170), and similarly to the exceptional mixed person as "cosmopolitan" (Poulsen 2012, 10). Likewise, the Amerasian, or the American and Asian, is typically white and Asian and depicted as the exceptional mixed person (Gage 2007, 97; Cheng 2014, 188; Graves 2019, 197). Mixed Black and Asian Americans, or Blasians, might be depicted as either tragic or exceptional (Washington 2017, chapter 2). To be exceptional, mixed Asian American politicians might be depicted as the future of America. To be tragic, they might be depicted as torn between two nations. These tropes about mixed people are situated in different political contexts of the American ethnoracial hierarchy and all have much to do with fears of mixing between whites and non-whites (Pascoe 2010). As I argue in my analysis of selected cases of mixed politicians, for some of them, the media draws on these tropes.

[14] Freya. 2013. Harrowing scene from Imitation of Life. *YouTube*. November 29. https://www.youtube.com/watch?v=0WgenwfYmwk

Cases of Mixed Representatives

To explore how the media depicts the identity labor of mixed representatives, I analyzed news coverage of five purposefully selected cases of mixed representatives (see Appendix for more details on data and method, which follows work by Squires 2007 and Thornton 2009). These politicians had careers long enough to collect coverage over time, yet they weren't so longstanding or well-known that coverage of them was idiosyncratic to them (e.g., Barack Obama was no longer *just* a mixed member of Congress, he was first Black president of the United States, so coverage of Barack Obama would necessarily be unique to him as Obama rather than a mixed politician). To collect news coverage, I relied on newspaper articles from LexisNexis and Ethnic NewsWatch, two repositories that store newspaper articles for a variety of audiences, including newspapers for specific ethnoracial group audiences (see Appendix for the list of newspapers contained in this analysis). In this analysis, I focus on coverage collected over the course of their careers through 2014. In what follows, I preview each case analyzed here and then show how the media uses tropes about mixed people in its coverage of these politicians. Interestingly, three of them have noted their connections to Obama in their biographies, as they were within Obama's professional and political network. With the exception of Tammy Duckworth, these politicians ran in geographies with local two-or-more races populations that tended to approach the national percentage of the two-or-more races population in 2010,[15] 2013,[16] and 2014.[17] With the exception of Tammy Duckworth and Anthony G. Brown, they also tended to run in geographies where non-Hispanic whites comprised less than half of the population.

Anthony G. Brown

Anthony G. Brown is an attorney, military veteran, and Democrat from Maryland.[18,19] His mother is white, and his father is Black. He is lighter-skinned with brown eyes. Earlier in his career, he had brown-black hair that has

[15] U.S. Census Bureau. "DETAILED RACE." American Community Survey, ACS 1-Year Estimates Detailed Tables, Table B02003, 2010, https://data.census.gov/table/ACSDT1Y2010.B02003?q=two or more races. Accessed on May 5, 2024.

[16] U.S. Census Bureau. "DETAILED RACE." American Community Survey, ACS 1-Year Estimates Detailed Tables, Table B02003, 2013, https://data.census.gov/table/ACSDT1Y2013.B02003?q=two or more races. Accessed on May 5, 2024.

[17] U.S. Census Bureau. "DETAILED RACE." American Community Survey, ACS 1-Year Estimates Detailed Tables, Table B02003, 2014, https://data.census.gov/table/ACSDT1Y2014.B02003?q=two or more races. Accessed on May 5, 2024.

[18] Biographical Directory of the United States Congress. Brown, Anthony Gregory. https://bioguide.congress.gov/search/bio/B001304.

[19] Ballotpedia. Anthony Brown (Maryland). https://ballotpedia.org/Anthony_Brown_(Maryland)

since grayed. Based on his photos, one might classify him as Black, Black and white, or possibly white. His career spans multiple levels of office. He began in 1999 as a member of the Maryland state legislature and eventually entered statewide office, where he served as Maryland's Lieutenant Governor between 2007–2015. In 2014, he lost against Republican Larry Hogan for Governor of Maryland. During his gubernatorial campaign, his website biography identified him as "the son of immigrants" and elaborated on his Jamaican father's immigration story to the United States.[20] He also mentioned his connection to Obama, as they overlapped as students at Harvard Law School.[21] From 2017–2023, he was a member of the US House of Representatives, where he represented Maryland's Fourth Congressional District. As of 2023, he is Maryland's Attorney General. For a summary of the demographics of Maryland during Brown's run for governor in 2014, see Table 4.1.[22]

Hansen Clarke

Hansen Clarke is an attorney and Democrat from Michigan.[23,24,25] His mother is Black, and his father is South Asian. He is brown-skinned with black hair and dark eyes, and passersby might assume he is South Asian or Latinx. Earlier in his career, he was a staff member for former Member of Congress John Conyers. His career in elected office began in 1991 in the Michigan state legislature, where he served two non-consecutive terms until 2010, punctuated by multiple unsuccessful campaigns for local office.[26] He ultimately served one term in Congress as the US House Representative for Michigan's Thirteenth Congressional District from 2011–2013. Heading into the general election in 2010, his website biography mentioned that "he is also a member of Alpha Phi Alpha Fraternity, Inc." a Black Greek Letter Organization.[27] In 2014, Clarke lost the Democratic Primary election for Michigan's

[20] Brown, Anthony G. 2014. Meet Anthony. https://web.archive.org/web/20141107100508/http://anthonybrown.com/meet-anthony/

[21] Brown, Anthony G. 2014. Meet Anthony. https://web.archive.org/web/20141107100508/http://anthonybrown.com/meet-anthony

[22] U.S. Census Bureau. "HISPANIC OR LATINO ORIGIN BY RACE." American Community Survey, ACS 1-Year Estimates Detailed Tables, Table B03002, 2014, https://data.census.gov/table/ACSDT1Y2014.B03002?q=maryland&t=Race and Ethnicity&y=2014. Accessed on April 29, 2024.

[23] Biographical Directory of the United States Congress. Clarke, Hansen. https://bioguide.congress.gov/search/bio/C001085

[24] Ballotpedia. Hansen Clarke. https://ballotpedia.org/Hansen_Clarke.

[25] History, Art & Archives United States House of Representatives. Clarke, Hansen. https://history.house.gov/People/Detail/11827.

[26] Michigan Votes. 2025. Sen. Hansen Clarke (D-1, 2010). https://www.michiganvotes.org/Legislator.aspx?ID=51

[27] Clarke, Hansen. 2010. About Hansen Clarke. https://web.archive.org/web/20101028215439/http://hansenclarkeforcongress.com/about-hansen-clarke

Fourteenth Congressional District to Brenda Lawrence. For a summary of Clarke's district demographics in 2014, see Table 4.1.[28]

Tammy Duckworth

Tammy Duckworth is a military veteran, Purple Heart recipient, and Democrat from Illinois.[29,30] Her mother is Asian, and her father is white. She is lighter-skinned with brown hair and brown eyes. At first glance at her photos, one might assume she is Asian American, Asian American and white, or white. Her career in elected office began in 2013 as the US House representative for Illinois's Eighth Congressional District. Like Anthony G. Brown, her website also referenced her connection to Obama, noting her service as the Assistant Secretary of Veterans Affairs under the Obama administration.[31] She also touted her family's military service: "a family member has served during every period of conflict since the Revolution."[32] She represented Illinois's Eighth Congressional District for four years between 2013–2017. Since 2017, she has served as a US Senator from Illinois. For a summary of Duckworth's district demographics in 2014, see Table 4.1.[33]

Laura Richardson

Laura Richardson is a businesswoman and Democrat from California.[34] Her mother is white, and her father is Black.[35,36] Prior to entering office, she was a staff member for former US House Representative Juanita Millender-McDonald. She is lighter-skinned with brown hair and brown eyes. Upon seeing Richardson, one might assume she's Black, Black and white, or possibly white. Before entering office, she was a staff member for former US House Representative Juanita Millender-McDonald. Her career in elected office began in 2000 as a Long Beach City Council member. She went on to serve in California's State Assembly representing the 55th Assembly District from 2006–2007. Her final post in elected office was from 2007–2013, when she

[28] U.S. Census Bureau. "HISPANIC OR LATINO ORIGIN BY RACE." American Community Survey, ACS 1-Year Estimates Detailed Tables, Table B03002, 2014, https://data.census.gov/table/ACSDT1Y2014.B03002?q=ACSDT1Y2014.B03002&g=040XX00US26_500XX00US2614. Accessed on May 5, 2024.

[29] Biographical Directory of the United States Congress. Duckworth, Tammy. https://bioguide.congress.gov/search/bio/D000622.

[30] Ballotpedia. Tammy Duckworth. https://ballotpedia.org/Tammy_Duckworth.

[31] Duckworth, Tammy. 2013. About Tammy. https://web.archive.org/web/20131009182600/http://www.tammyduckworth.com/about/

[32] Duckworth, Tammy. 2013. About Tammy. https://web.archive.org/web/20131009182600/http://www.tammyduckworth.com/about

[33] U.S. Census Bureau. "HISPANIC OR LATINO ORIGIN BY RACE." American Community Survey, ACS 1-Year Estimates Detailed Tables, Table B03002, 2014, https://data.census.gov/table/ACSDT1Y2014.B03002?t=Race and Ethnicity&g=040XX00US17_500XX00US1708&y=2014. Accessed on May 5, 2024.

[34] Biographical Directory of the United States Congress. https://bioguide.congress.gov/search/bio/R000581

[35] Kapochunas, Rachel. 2007. Early Brush With Racism Set Rep.–Elect Richardson on Political Path. *CQPolitics.com*. August 22. https://web.archive.org/web/20070926231437/http://www.cqpolitics.com/2007/08/early_brush_with_racism_set_re.html

[36] Ballotpedia. Laura Richardson. https://ballotpedia.org/Laura_Richardson.

represented California's Thirty-Seventh Congressional District. Like Brown and Duckworth, her website also noted her connection to Obama: he enacted her bill, the Diesel Emissions Reduction Act of 2010 (DERA).[37] For a summary of Richardson's district demographics in 2013, see Table 4.1.[38]

Alberto Torrico

Alberto Torrico is an attorney and Democrat from California.[39,40] His mother is Asian, and his father is Latinx. He is brown-skinned with black hair and dark eyes. Looking at him, one might assume he's Latinx. He began his career in elected office on the Newark City Council in 2001 and represented California's 20th State Assembly District from 2004–2010. During his campaign for California Attorney General in 2010, he noted the significance of his membership to the Latino Caucus and the Asian Pacific Islander Caucus in the California State Legislature, highlighting that he "made history as the first member of the California Assembly to sit in both the Latino Legislative Caucus and Asian Pacific Islander Legislative Caucus."[41] In 2010, he lost the Democratic Primary for California Attorney General to Kamala Harris. For a summary of the demographics of California during Torrico's run for California Attorney General, see Table 4.1.[42]

Findings

Identity Labor as Strategy: Exploiting Mixed Ancestry

In coverage of Alberto Torrico, both the media and Torrico constructed an image that being mixed is strategically advantageous. For example, reporters nodded toward the power Torrico's ethnoracial background gave him in the legislature. In one article about Torrico's career as a California state legislator in 2005, a reporter described how "Torrico talked proudly about belonging

[37] Richardson, Laura. 2012. Biography. https://web.archive.org/web/20121016230430/http://richardson.house.gov/index.php?option=com_content&view=article&id=2928&Itemid=500246

[38] U.S. Census Bureau. "HISPANIC OR LATINO ORIGIN BY RACE." American Community Survey, ACS 1-Year Estimates Detailed Tables, Table B03002, 2013, https://data.census.gov/table/ACSDT1Y2013.B03002?q=race and ethnicity&g=040XX00US06_500XX00US0637&y=2013&d=ACS 1-Year Estimates Detailed Tables. Accessed on May 5, 2024.

[39] VoteSmart Facts for All. 2021. Alberto Torrico's Biography. https://justfacts.votesmart.org/candidate/biography/29471/alberto-torrico.

[40] Ballotpedia. Alberto Torrico. https://ballotpedia.org/Alberto_Torrico.

[41] Torrico, Alberto. 2010. About Alberto. https://web.archive.org/web/20100325192453/http://www.albertotorrico.com/about

[42] U.S. Census Bureau. "HISPANIC OR LATINO ORIGIN BY RACE." American Community Survey, ACS 1-Year Estimates Detailed Tables, Table B03002, 2010, https://data.census.gov/table/ACSDT1Y2010.B03002?q=california&t=Race and Ethnicity&y=2010&d=ACS 1-Year Estimates Detailed Tables. Accessed on April 29, 2024.

Table 4.1 Summary of district demographics*

Case	Geography	Asian American	Black	American Indian and Alaska Native	Native Hawaiian and Other Pacific Islander	White	Latinx	Two or more races	Two or more races (National)
Anthony G. Brown	Maryland (2014)	6.16%	29.20%	0.18%	0.03%	52.43%	9.31%	2.44%	3.01%
Hansen Clarke	MI Congressional District 13 (2014)	4.72%	56.73%	0.18%	0.00%	31.07%	4.72%	2.68%	3.01%
Tammy Duckworth	IL Congressional District 8 (2014)	13.22%	3.98%	0.07%	0.07%	52.51%	28.61%	1.34%	3.01%
Laura Richardson	CA Congressional District 37 (2013)	9.26%	22.09%	0.06%	0.19%	26.31%	38.81%	2.65%	2.96%
Alberto Torrico	California (2010)	12.95%	5.77%	0.40%	0.36%	40.00%	37.72%	2.58%	2.71%

*Values are rounded to the nearest hundredth.

to the Latino and Asian legislative caucus."[43] In 2006, the *Contra Costa Times* covered Torrico's rise in the California legislative caucus system when he became the Chair of the California Asian and Pacific Islander Caucus:[44]

> Torrico's parents are immigrants from Bolivia, and his mother is of Japanese descent. He said he is proud to serve as the first biracial chairman of the caucus. "It is a reflection that members of the Legislature are beginning to look like the face of California today," said Torrico, who is also the first person to be a member of both the API and the Latino Legislative Caucus.

Torrico performs identity labor by strategically leaning into this and pointing to the cliche that "we're all going to be mixed eventually" by suggesting that he represents Californians because he is "biracial." Implicitly, in this article, the press draws on biological notions of ethnorace to link Torrico's parentage to his ethnoracial background by using the term "biracial," affirming the myth that there's some biological basis for ethnorace (e.g., Fields and Fields 2014). Moreover, by stating that he "looks like the face of California today," Torrico implies that the face of California today is mixed Latinx and Asian American.

By 2009, Torrico was running against Kamala Harris for California Attorney General. A reporter from the *Oakland Tribune* covered the launch of Torrico's campaign:[45]

> So Torrico has been the first California lawmaker to be a member of two ethnic caucuses, the Legislative Latino Caucus and the Asian Pacific Islander Caucus [*sic*]. That should stand him in good stead with crucial voting blocs, he said, as should his status as a Silicon Valley Democrat.

According to the article, membership to the Latinx and the Asian American communities and Torrico's position in the two ethnoracial caucuses should grant him access to Latinx and Asian American voters in a statewide election. In 2010, *La Prensa San Diego* profiled the roster of candidates running for California Attorney General and noted that Torrico "was heavily involved in both the Latino and Asian-Pacific Islander Caucus." In portraying Torrico this way, the *Oakland Tribune* and *La Prensa* both depicted caucus work as a tool

[43] Garcia, Edwin. 2005. Rising voice in Capitol; Democratic born-again Christian lawmaker embodies state's diversity. *San Jose Mercury News (California)*. July 10.

[44] Contra Costa Times. 2006. Capitol notebook: Times Sacramento Bureau. *Contra Costa Times (California)*. April 2.

[45] Richman, Josh. 2009. Torrico to announce 2010 run for state AG. *Contra Costa Times (California)*. February 20.

to appeal to Asian American and Latinx voters, perhaps because the caucuses legitimized his group membership.

In some articles from Asian American newspapers collected from Ethnic NewsWatch, Torrico's status as an Asian American politician is conveyed as matter-of-fact. For example, when Torrico was a state legislator, in one article from 2005 in *Asianweek*, a reporter included Torrico in a list of Asian American politicians with "influence" in the California State Legislature.[46] Indeed, a 2007 *Asianweek* article stated that: "the current chair [of the Asian/Pacific Islander Caucus] Assemblyman Alberto TorriCO … has helped make the API Legislative Caucus a force to be reckoned within the state Capitol [*sic*]."[47] Because half of his ancestry is Asian American, Torrico gains access to an Asian American legislative institution and has the opportunity to exert influence within it. By highlighting Torrico's caucus memberships, the media conveys Torrico's ethnoracial background as an institutional resource.

Identity labor is also about proactive public management, not just reacting to questions about ethnoracial identity. Some mixed politicians may perform identity labor by *not* attempting to capitalize on their mixed backgrounds. Newspaper coverage may create a public narrative about a politician that limits a politician's openings to perform identity labor. For instance, newspapers rarely discussed Laura Richardson's mixed background. In 2009, the *Press-Telegram (Long Beach, California)* covered Barack Obama's first presidential inauguration and described Richardson as someone "who, like Obama is biracial," while discussing how Richardson's mother and the Civil Rights Movement influenced her interest in legislative office.[48]

Another article from 2009 used "mixed race" to describe a group of parade marshals that included Richardson: "they are black, mixed race, and Asian," but the article did not specify whether "mixed race" referred to Richardson.[49] The article did not mark Richardson as a non-prototypical politician, closing off the opportunity for Richardson to need to answer questions about her identity.

Perhaps the media did not focus much on Richardson's mixed background due to a strategic decision from Richardson's team not to showcase it. In 2007, Richardson was running for Congress against a Latina opponent, Jenny Opreza, and one article about the implications of the election for the Black and Hispanic Congressional Caucuses labeled Richardson as

[46] Tom, M. 2005. Capitol watch; will a jury-rig prevent gerrymandering? *Asianweek*. November 2.

[47] Tom, M. 2007. Ted Lieu calls for order in the courts. *Asianweek*. August.

[48] Canalis, John and Pamela Hale Burns. 2009. Long Beach luminaries feel excitement as they head to D.C. *Press-Telegram (Long Beach, California), Distributed by McClatchy-Tribune Business News*. January 17.

[49] Mellen, Greg. 2009. MLK parade's marshals hail from all walks of life. *Press-Telegram (Long Beach, California), Distributed by McClatchy-Tribune Business News*. January 17.

"black."[50] In another article, *Roll Call* covered Richardson's contest, noting that "Richardson's top strategist, called [Richardson] the best cross-cultural candidate in the field," highlighting her previous success with Black, Latinx, Asian American, and white voters.[51]

In newspaper articles from Ethnic NewsWatch that serve African American audiences, Richardson barely elaborates on her parentage. In a *Los Angeles Sentinel* article about Richardson's involvement with a Cambodian arts academy, she notes that her "father was a musician and so I understand the benefits of being surrounded by various forms of art during adolescence."[52] Given that she was running for Congress in parallel to Obama's first presidential run and was even compared to Obama because she is mixed,[53] if Richardson's campaign wanted to include highlighting her mixed background as part of her outreach strategy, this would have been the time to do so. We can infer that Richardson's strategy did not include capitalizing on her mixed background. This might be why non-African American newspapers did not heavily focus on it in the middle of a closely-watched election. Moreover, because Richardson does not have or explicitly discuss immigrant parentage, perhaps non-African American newspapers did not view Richardson's background as novel or "foreign" to American voters (e.g., Kim 1999).

Constraints on Strategy: The Ethnoracial Hierarchy, Mixed Race Tropes, and Challenges to Group Membership

Perhaps because of his dual non-white background, the image that the non-Latinx/non-Asian American press constructed for Torrico was one of celebration, diversity, and power. In 2005, when the *San Jose Mercury* published an article detailing Torrico's biography, the newspaper printed:[54]

> And yet the thirty-six-year-old baby-faced legislator is a unique character in Sacramento: the embodiment of California's social, cultural, religious, and political diversity.

[50] Yachnin, Jennifer, and David M. Drucker. 2007. CHC Aims at California seat. *Roll Call.* May 22.
[51] Drucker, David M. 2007. Grass Roots Key to California's 37th District. *Roll Call.* June 14.
[52] Los Angeles Sentinel. 2009. Congresswoman Richardson announces $100,000 for the Arts. *Los Angeles Sentinel.* July.
[53] Canalis, John and Pamela Hale Burns. 2009. Long Beach luminaries feel excitement as they head to D.C. *Press-Telegram (Long Beach, California). Distributed by McClatchy-Tribune Business News.* January 17.
[54] Garcia, Edwin. 2005. Rising voice in Capitol; Democratic Born-Again Christian Lawmaker Embodies the State's Diversity. *San Jose Mercury News (California).* July 10.

Torrico was hardly "unique." In the 2000 Census, the two-or-more races population made up about 4.7 percent of the state of California.[55] However, the rarity of legislators like Torrico in the State Capitol was considered newsworthy enough to celebrate. This article also used biological language to describe Torrico as a symbol of California's ethnoracial diversity: Torrico *embodies* it. That a politician could embody diversity harkens back to the idea of blood quantum and the idea of ethnorace as biologically inherited from one's parents (e.g., Spencer 1999). With this description, Torrico is depicted as an exceptional mixed person.

Some coverage of Tammy Duckworth aligned with the idea of the cosmopolitan Eurasian who is "transnational" (Poulsen 2012, 10). For example, in 2013, *The New Zealand Herald* printed a story that discussed Duckworth's visit to a Bangkok university.[56] Although the article is primarily about American foreign policy in Syria, it printed two sentences about Duckworth's parentage and language ability: "Born in Thailand to a U.S. Marine Corps veteran and a Thai mother, Duckworth lived in the Southeast Asian country until she was in third grade. She can still speak Thai fluently, with only minor mispronunciations in tone." The brief mention of Duckworth's connection to the United States, Thailand, and the Thai language depicts Duckworth as a transnational figure.

When she began her term in Congress in 2013, Duckworth's claim to a Thai background was celebrated as a political resource. In one article about human trafficking from *The Bangkok Post (Thailand)*, Duckworth's ethnoracial background was characterized as a diplomatic resource: "She said she is proud of her Thai heritage and she would use it to seek a stronger relationship between the US and Thailand in many areas, including in anti-human trafficking and in economic cooperation [*sic*]."[57] Having Thai heritage seemingly grants her access to international influence.

Duckworth's Thai heritage was also a focal point in articles from newspapers that serve Asian American audiences. Two articles used "Thailand" to describe Duckworth as "the daughter of an ethnic Chinese woman from Thailand and a U.S. war veteran who can trace his family's military history

[55] U.S. Census Bureau. "Profile of General Demographic Characteristics: 2000." Decennial Census, DEC State Legislative District Demographic Profile (100-Percent), Table DP1, 2000, https://data.census.gov/table/DECENNIALDPSLDH2000.DP1?q=&g=040XX00US06&y=2000. Accessed on May 5, 2024.

[56] The New Zealand Herald. 2013. US Congresswoman Duckworth opposes Syria strike. *The New Zealand Herald*. August 29.

[57] The Bangkok Post (Thailand). 2013. Step up fight on trafficking, says Tammy. *The Bangkok Post (Thailand)*. September 4.

back to the Revolutionary War."[58,59] Like other articles, this description traces Duckworth's genealogy through different countries, depicting Duckworth as a cosmopolitan Eurasian.

In coverage of Clarke, there were elements of the tragic mixed person and the exceptional mixed person. Questions about his Blackness were particularly acute and highlighted in both Asian American and non-Asian American media. In 2007, *India West* covered comments Clarke made at an event called the Indian American Leadership Initiative Democratic Dialogue, noting that he "said he had a hard time convincing his black constituents that he was of African American descent."[60] Years later, comments he made in a speech to the Indian American Leadership Initiative were reprinted: "A drop of black blood makes you Black. But in my re-election campaign in 1992, my opponent said I was not black enough. No black looks like me."[61] In 2010, as Clarke ran for governor of Michigan, *India Abroad* printed a story indicating that Clarke did not feel supported by Indian Americans, quoting Clarke stating that "he was elected because of his African American roots. 'Being Indian has not helped much. Once an Indian said he is a brother and promised to collect money, which I never got.'"[62] After suspending his campaign for governor,[63] Clarke ran to represent Michigan in Congress and defeated former US Representative Carolyn Cheeks Kilpatrick, a Black woman politician, in the Democratic primary.[64] As he began his Congressional term in 2011, *News India-Times* noted that, "Clarke is going to ruffle some feathers as he plans to join the Congressional Black Caucus, the only South Asian ever to do so. He tells Newsweek he has probably upset some members of that caucus who were close to Kilpatrick."[65] Another article reported that "there were some reports that the Congressional Black Caucus gave Clarke a 'cool reception' in Washington, but Clarke downplayed any ruffled feelings, saying he has joined both the Asian Pacific American Caucus and the Black Caucus."[66] In these articles, his relationship with Black people was depicted as being fraught at worst, and

[58] Spring, R. 2012. Ricky Gill, Syed Taj turn in impressive vote totals in defeats. *India—West.* November 16.

[59] Springer, R. 2012. Krishnamoorthi losses to Duckworth in congress primary. *India West.* March 30.

[60] Anand, R.S. 2007. IALI dialogue: Promise of 2nd generation Indian Americans. *India-West.* August 31.

[61] Joseph, G. 2010. Hansen Clarke is the first Bangladeshi American elected to Congress. *India Abroad.* November 12.

[62] Joseph, G. 2010. Indian-origin Senator Hansen Clarke to run for Michigan governor. *India Abroad.* January 15.

[63] Associated Press. 2010. State Sen. Hansen Clarke drops out of govern's race, could run against Rep. Carolyn Cheeks Kilpatrick. *Mlive.* January 16.

[64] James, Frank. 2010. Rep. Kilpatrick Vanquisher, Hansen Clarke, Has Some Story. *NPR.* August 4.

[65] Dutt, E. 2011. Freshman Congressman Featured in Newsweek. *News India-Times.* January 7.

[66] Springer, R. 2011. Rep. Clarke in Exclusive Interview. *India-West.* February 18.

inconsistent at best, while his relationship with Indian Americans is depicted as distant.

At other times, non-Asian American and non-African American media printed stories about whether he was lying about being Black. In 2012, Clarke ran for Congress again. A political scandal emerged when "a robo call had gone out in the 14th District claiming that Clarke is not black."[67] Although it was unclear what the robocall specifically told voters, the article detailed how his mother's death certificate classified her as white, not Black. Opponents latched onto this controversy to suggest that Clarke used his ethnorace opportunistically. The *Detroit Free Press* reported that one opponent, Mary Waters, a former state representative and Black woman candidate, said "she feels she's the only black Detroiter in the race," noting that, "He used to say he was raised by a Black woman, now he's saying he's Asian ... I don't like that kind of shifting, saying one thing in front of one group, another thing in front of another."[68] To quell the rumors that he was not Black or that his mother was white, Clarke told the *Windsor Star (Ontario)*, "his voice husky with emotion," that his mother "was black. But she was light-skinned, and, yes, she wanted to pass for white."[69] Due to the controversy surrounding his Black identity, Clarke did not attend an event hosted by the Detroit chapter of the National Association of Black Journalists (NABJ) and was quoted stating, "he 'respects NABJ highly, but these forums are only set up to inflame racist rhetoric.'"[70] As a result, Clarke blocked opportunities for live debate of his ethnoracial identity in a public setting. As a Black and South Asian politician, Clarke's experience of being accused of "shifting" his identity is strikingly similar to accusations the 45th US President levied against Kamala Harris, also Black and South Asian, at the NABJ's convention over a decade later in 2024.

By contrast, newspaper articles collected from Ethnic NewsWatch that serve African American audiences did not portray Clarke as struggling to secure support from Black communities or institutions. For example, a 2002 *Michigan Citizen* article honoring Vincent Chin, an Asian American man who was brutally beaten to death by two white men in Michigan in 1982, discussed how some Asian Americans in Detroit, such as "the father of State Representative Hansen Clarke (an immigrant from India) found their

[67] Gray, Kathleen. 2012. US Rep. Hansen Clarke complains race baiting has entered congressional campaign. *Detroit Free Press*. June 30.

[68] Gray, Kathleen. 2012. US Rep. Hansen Clarke complains race baiting has entered congressional campaign. *Detroit Free Press*. June 30.

[69] Lessenberry, Jack. 2012. When politics get personal in Michigan. *Windsor Star (Ontario)*. July 12.

[70] Gray, Kathleen. 2012. Hansen Clarke, John Conyers, Shanelle Jackson to skip congressional candidates forum. *Detroit Free Press*. July 26.

homes in the African American community."[71] This is another striking similarity to Kamala Harris, as her mother found community with African Americans in Oakland, California. During his 2012 Congressional run, the *Michigan Chronicle* endorsed Clarke alongside Representative John Conyers and lamented the potential loss of African American representation due to redistricting: "the thought, in this day and age, of an African-American population as large and important as Detroit's sending no member of that community to Congress, is an ugly problem that should make everyone in the state of Michigan uncomfortable,"[72] indicating that Clarke was considered a Black representative that would represent Black voters from Detroit in Congress.

In multiple newspaper articles that Ethnic NewsWatch classified as serving African American audiences, reporters quoted or portrayed Clarke talking about policies with an explicit focus on Black men, such as literacy,[73] incarceration,[74] and high school graduation rates.[75] In 2003, the *Michigan Chronicle* included Clarke on a list of Detroit leaders who hold membership to Alpha Phi Alpha Fraternity Inc., a Black Greek Letter Organization and an institution that provides political credibility for latent Black politicians (Gillespie 2012, 49–50).[76]

Clarke was also depicted as an exceptional mixed person. During his campaign for Congress in 2011, the *Windsor Star (Ontario)* discussed the voting dynamics by ethnorace in Clarke's district, noting that Black voters "vote less frequently than whites."[77] The article compared Clarke and a primary opponent, a white candidate named Gary Peters: "Hansen Clarke spans the rainbow. He is multiracial (his father was from what is now Bangladesh), charismatic and appealing, and is married to an adopted Korean orphan who was raised by a Roman Catholic mother and a Jewish father."[78] This article does not specify that Clarke is also Black. Yet, while talking about how Black voters might respond to Clarke's opponent, the article suggests that Clarke's "rainbow" background, as well as his spouse's background, might give him

[71] Kurashige, S., and G. L. Boggs. 2002. Asian Detroit and the legacy of Vincent Chin. *Michigan Citizen*. July 13.

[72] Michigan Chronicle. 2012. We endorse John Conyers and Hansen Clarke for Congress. *Michigan Chronicle*. July.

[73] Keating, P. 2012. Hansen Clarke co-sponsoring bipartisan literacy program. *Michigan Chronicle*. July.

[74] Wright, M. 2012. Peters, Clarke run in the 14th. *Michigan Citizen*. July.

[75] Michigan Citizen. 2009. A proposal for Detroit schools. *Michigan Citizen*. April.

[76] Moore, M.D. 2003. Detroit faces you may know. *Michigan Chronicle*. July 30.

[77] Lessenberry, Jack. 2011. The topsy-turvy world of Michigan politics. *Windsor Star (Ontario)*. October 18.

[78] Lessenberry, Jack. 2011. The topsy-turvy world of Michigan politics. *Windsor Star (Ontario)*. October 18.

an electoral edge, depicting him as an exceptional mixed person, much like Alberto Torrico.

This collection of articles reveals how news reporters and the stories they run create opportunities for mixed politicians like Clarke to perform identity labor. Non-African American media sources create the image that on one hand, Clarke is as diverse as a "rainbow," yet struggles to secure support from Black and Indian American voters. At the same time, Clarke performed identity labor by making it clear to a non-Black audience that he identifies as Black. By referencing the one-drop rule, Clarke pushed back against his detractors. Clarke understood that part of why people could raise these questions as far back as 1992 was because of how he looked. When people saw him, they did not immediately assume he was Black. Others' interpretations of his appearance created the need for Clarke to perform identity labor by elaborating on his background. Questions about his Blackness became an issue for his campaign, as he was compelled to talk about his dead mother with the press to clarify his ancestry. Despite this, news articles from African American newspapers make it clear that Clarke is a Black politician. These depictions also show that mixed politicians may be construed as individuals who shift their ethnoracial loyalties, further reinforcing negative historical stereotypes of mixed persons as "unstable." Overall, Clarke can leverage both identities as a Blasian (Washington 2017, 23), but within the constraints people place on his Blackness.

The tragic and exceptional mixed person tropes were present in some depictions of Anthony G. Brown too. In 2004, *The Washington Post* ran a story about then-state legislator Brown's upcoming military deployment to Iraq and discussed his biography.[79] The article stated that "Brown is a Maryland version of Barack Obama, the U.S. Senate candidate from Illinois who electrified the Democratic National Convention with his speech last month," partly because of Brown's mixed parentage—a comparison strikingly similar to those that call Kamala Harris the "female Obama."[80] By connecting his mixed parentage as part of his "crossover potential," the article depicted Brown as an exceptional mixed person. It implies that non-mixed candidates do not have the same appeal as politicians like Brown and Obama. That same article also featured a discussion about how Brown answered questions about his ethnoracial identity as a college student:

[79] Barr, Cameron W. 2004. Md. Lawmaker trades politics for new fight; Delegate-reservist leaves for Iraq duty next month. *The Washington Post. Final Edition.* August 9.

[80] Barr, Cameron W. 2004. Md. Lawmaker trades politics for new fight; Delegate-reservist leaves for Iraq duty next month. *The Washington Post. Final Edition.* August 9.

> The child of a Jamaican father and a Swiss mother, Brown initially practiced what he calls a colorblind approach to race. He answered the inevitable question—"Are you black or white?"—by saying, "My father's black; my mother's white," and no more. At Harvard, a fellow student told him to get off the fence. He did and became more self-consciously African American. "I knew I couldn't get off the fence and identify myself as white."

In sharing this story from his college days, the article depicts him as someone who "struggles," much like the tragic mixed person trope, between whiteness and Blackness, and sets the tone for how he will have to navigate questions about his identity later in his career.

Ten years later, in 2014, Brown was the Lieutenant Governor of Maryland and was running for governor. Brown's mixed background warranted a discussion at the end of a 2014 *Washington Post* article primarily about his political career and the election.[81] The article invoked both the tragic and exceptional mixed person tropes and prompted Brown to perform identity labor. The exceptional mixed person trope was invoked in a discussion of white politicians who supported Brown earlier in his career. The article quoted Maryland Delegate Mike Busch, who was white, then Maryland's House Speaker, describing his impression of Brown early on: "I made him my first draft pick that year [for committee assignment] ... here was a versatile, attractive African American with unlimited potential." As Busch reflected on Brown, he "[recalled] another 'promising' black delegate had just left office." In making this statement and drawing a comparison between Brown and "another 'promising' black delegate," Busch invokes both tokenism and the exceptional mixed person trope. Busch's statement, as depicted in the article, tokenizes Brown and the other Black delegates by emphasizing that they are *Black* delegates, portraying them as "symbol[s]" and drawing comparisons between two politicians who may be nothing alike (Kanter 1977, 968). In the same vein, the statement also invoked the exceptional mixed person trope *because* Brown is mixed—Brown's mixedness is part of his status as a Black politician.

In a discussion of how Brown had lost support from Black politicians in Prince George's County, the article invoked the tragic mixed person trope and suggested that Brown, like Clarke, struggled with cultivating support from Black political actors. In the article, Eugene Grant, the then-Mayor of Seat Pleasant in Prince George's County, questioned Brown's legislative

[81] Fisher, Marc and John Wagner. 2014. A chain-of-command guy. *The Washington Post*. Suburban Edition. June 17.

record and his ability to serve "the everyday worker."[82] The article also featured Grant and Julius Henson, "a campaign operative,"[83] who each made comments about Brown's identity. According to Henson, "'Brown had the Ivy League thing going on and said he wasn't black,'" and Grant "heard Brown 'call himself 'multiracial,' and that's fine, but now, all of a sudden, he says he's black. I have a problem with that.'"[84] As in the case of Clarke, this article suggests that fellow Black political actors take issue with apparent identity shifts over time, much like Clarke's opponent Mary Waters did. Such questions brought up memories from high school, and "Brown's face [tightened as he heard] criticism about how he's defined his racial identity."[85] To address these comments, Brown performed identity labor by explaining his identity as Black and referencing his parents: "I am the child of an interracial relationship ... I'm African American."[86] In printing questions about Brown's ethnoracial identity as a topic of discussion during an election, particularly questions from Black political figures in Maryland, *The Washington Post* invoked the tragic mixed person trope and depicted Brown as someone who was "unstable" in his own identity. By quoting individual Black political figures commenting on his identity, the article constructs the image that Brown must alleviate concerns about his identity to secure political support from these figures—even though part of their criticisms focused on his record.

By contrast, some articles in African American newspapers from Ethnic NewsWatch depicted Brown's heritage as part of his biography—but not necessarily something to analyze. For example, after Brown won the Democratic gubernatorial primary in 2014, *The Washington Informer* reported: "The son of a Jamaican father and a Swiss mother, Brown, 52, stands to become the third elect- ed African-American governor in the U.S. should he go onto win the Nov. 4 general election [*sic*]."[87] In 2008, the *Chicago Defender* named Anthony G. Brown as a "biracial" politician and placed the history of "biracial 'Black' leaders" in context with enslavement, colorism, and historical Black

[82] Fisher, Marc and John Wagner. 2014. A chain-of-command guy. *The Washington Post*. Suburban Edition. June 17.

[83] Fisher, Marc and John Wagner. 2014. A chain-of-command guy. *The Washington Post*. Suburban Edition. June 17.

[84] Fisher, Marc and John Wagner. 2014. A chain-of-command guy. *The Washington Post*. Suburban Edition. June 17.

[85] Fisher, Marc and John Wagner. 2014. A chain-of-command guy. *The Washington Post*. Suburban Edition. June 17.

[86] Fisher, Marc and John Wagner. 2014. A chain-of-command guy. *The Washington Post*. Suburban Edition. June 17.

[87] Garner, J. 2014. Brown cruises to victory. *Washington Informer*. June.

political power.[88] Whereas *The Washington Post* highlighted criticisms of Brown's identity from Black leaders and invoked stereotypes of mixed Black people, these articles included Brown as part of a long history of Black leaders with mixed ancestry in the United States. This coverage was similar to how African American newspapers contextualized the 2000 Census change to recognize two-or-more races (Squires 2007, 161–162). In these news venues that serve African American audiences, Brown, like Clarke, is a Black politician whose "biracial" background is recognized within broader African American history.

Discussion

The media does ethnorace to mixed politicians by printing (or not printing) stories that highlight their mixed ancestries (Moya and Markus 2010). As a result, mixed politicians have opportunities (or carry burdens) to perform identity labor in public.

In many ways, the identity labor that mixed politicians must perform is not much different from how all politicians of color perform: mixed politicians still have to navigate a political system that marks them as non-white and imposes institutional racism upon them. Mixed candidates may appeal to a specific ethnoracial identity when it is politically opportune or helps them establish a more genuine connection with an audience. But they can only shift within the constraints of how others will ethnoracially classify them. I call this strategy *constrained shifting*.

The constraints under which mixed politicians shift may also differ by venue. For example, whereas non-African American newspapers focused on debates about Brown's and Clarke's Blackness, African American newspapers in this sample of newspaper articles did not. It is possible that in the contemporary period, with conversations about "increasing diversity" and "increasing intermarriage," the presence of mixed Black politicians presents more of an enigma or curiosity for non-African American newspapers than African American newspapers.

Press coverage of mixed politicians' identity choices may also be constrained by how reporters react to a mixed politician's gender. Although Richardson's campaign strategy might have contributed to non-African American newspapers not profiling her "biracial" background the way they

[88] Curry, G.E. 2008. Taking a second look at bi-racial "Black" leaders. *Chicago Defender*. August.

did Brown and Clarke, perhaps because Richardson is a woman, her "biracial" background is treated differently. Reporters in non-African American newspapers may grant mixed women more flexibility in their ethnoracial identities, an option that may not exist for mixed Black men specifically (Davenport 2016a, 72). By contrast, because Brown and Clarke are men, reporters may latch onto their mixed backgrounds with interest. These are public men figures trying to identify with multiple ethnoraces, and to the press, perhaps that's interesting and strange. These findings lie in contrast to sociological research on the experiences of everyday mixed Black men, which suggests that mixed Black men may experience fewer challenges to their Blackness than mixed Black women (Sims and Joseph-Salisbury 2019, 62–63). As these cases are politicians who may have to "prove" their identities more often than everyday people, it is possible that mixed Black men experience more scrutiny than mixed Black women upon becoming public figures.

The media may also narrate mixed politicians differently depending on their position in the ethnoracial hierarchy. Non-Black mixed politicians are celebrated for their diversity and transnationalism, akin to the exceptional mixed person and the cosmopolitan Eurasian. The media may draw on tropes of the tragic mixed person in coverage of mixed Black men politicians, but not necessarily mixed Black women politicians. The one-drop rule remains relevant for mixed Black elected officials, but its relevance may be more prominent in non-African American newspapers. To some extent, the media treats mixed politicians as both minority tokens and mixed tokens (Kanter 1977)—their ethnorace is relevant news. They may "embody" the future of ethnorace in America, as their mere presence is viewed as a measure of ethnoracial progress (e.g., Ahmed 2009).

Mixed Black politicians faced questions of ethnoracial authenticity and loyalty that mixed Asian American politicians did not. One implication is that the nature of constrained shifting differs in degree between mixed politicians. Only some will be permitted to shift their identities without answering to others or being forced into a single category. While mixed Asian American officials might enjoy more control over strategically using their ethnoracial identities (McCormick and Jones 1993; Collet 2008), mixed Black officials may face obstacles to acting strategically. In coverage of these politicians, reporters raised questions about ethnorace that candidates such as Brown and Clarke presumably sought to avoid. The campaign strategies for mixed Black candidates might revolve around credibly communicating one's Black identity while avoiding racist attacks (McIlwain and Caliendo 2011, 40). Still, instead of dealing with racist political attacks from opponents, mixed Black candidates may have to defend against the media's coverage of their claims to

Blackness. By contrast, non-Black mixed Asian American politicians might have more opportunities to capitalize on the novelty of their backgrounds (McIlwain and Caliendo 2011, 121), but they still operate within the confines of being "foreigners" (Kim 1999).

Whereas Torrico's status as "biracial" is celebrated, and Duckworth's Thai heritage is a diplomatic asset, non-African American newspapers depict both Clarke and Brown as unable to gain acceptance from African Americans. Clarke's Blackness is debated because of his appearance, and he's accused of lying to the public, but the media does not depict him as under "pressure to choose." By contrast, Brown's Blackness is not debatable, likely because of his appearance. And, the press depicts him as facing pressure to identify as Black.

Public preoccupations with mixed politicians' parentage, such as Duckworth's "American father" and "Thai Mother," whether Clarke's mother was "really Black," and if Brown identified as Black or white, suggest that contemporary mixed officials represent taboos that harken back to laws against inter-ethnoracial sex and marriage between whites and other ethnoraces. Press coverage of these politicians' identities suggests that newspapers serve as vehicles for the public to work through worries about mixing between Black and non-Black ethnoraces. Clarke's treatment in the media indicates that even in the twenty-first century, ethnorace is defined by how one looks—a relic of ethnoracial science (e.g., Sharfstein 2007). Throughout all of this, there is an implied acceptance of ethnorace as biologically inherited from one's parents and observable in appearance. As mixed politicians become more common, their campaign calculus will likely have to consider how they will perform their identity labor in the press based on how they look. By covering questions of ethnoracial identity, reporters essentially ask these mixed politicians, "What are you?"

Chapters 3 and 4 suggest that politicians are aware of the need to perform identity labor, and the press may amplify attention to mixed politicians' ethnoracial backgrounds. In both chapters, we see how mixed politicians can either capitalize on their mixed status or work to close the perceived gap between themselves and their ethnoracial group. Is there an electoral support gap for mixed politicians? In the next chapter, I test this.

5
Is There an Electoral Support Gap?

In 2021, Ritchie Torres, a Democratic congressmember from New York's fifteenth Congressional District, gave an interview to *The Washington Post* with reporter Eugene Scott in a video titled, *Race in America: The Power of Representation.*[1] Torres is from the Bronx, he identifies as Afro-Latino, and he presents as a Black man. In his own words, "my mother is Puerto Rican, and my father is Black and Puerto Rican." He explained to Scott that "identity is not binary. It's intersectional. I've had several people tell me, 'You do not look Latino.' To which I reply, what does it mean to not look Latino?"

The year before, in 2020, Torres, then a candidate, penned an op-ed in *The Washington Post* about how a caucus rule barred him from joining both the Congressional Black Caucus (CBC) and the Congressional Hispanic Caucus (CHC).[2] In it, he decried how this rule was out of touch:[3]

> The wall of separation between the CBC and CHC ignores the realities of racial identity, which feels especially tone-deaf in this present moment. You have to pick a side, so to speak. You can be either black or Latino, but never both. In real life, however, I am both. We Afro-Latinos refuse to be divided against ourselves by an arbitrary rule that bears no relation to how we experience identity in the real world.

In response, Democratic representative Karen Bass from California, then chair of the CBC, explained that the CBC did not have a formal rule barring members from joining the CHC; rather, refraining from membership to both caucuses has been a longstanding norm among CBC members.[4]

[1] Washington Post Live. 2021. Race in America: The Power of Reprsentation with Rep. Ritchie Torres (D-N.Y.) (Full Stream 6/28). June 28. https://www.youtube.com/watch?v=LhL9Pev5pkc, comments start at 20:06

[2] Torres, Ritchie. 2020. I'm Afro-Latino, but I can't join both the black and Hispanic caucuses in Congress. That must change. *The Washington Post.* July 19. https://www.washingtonpost.com/opinions/2020/07/19/im-afro-latino-i-cant-join-both-black-hispanic-caucuses-congress-that-must-change/

[3] Torres, Ritchie. 2020. I'm Afro-Latino, but I can't join both the black and Hispanic caucuses in Congress. That must change. *The Washington Post.* July 19. https://www.washingtonpost.com/opinions/2020/07/19/im-afro-latino-i-cant-join-both-black-hispanic-caucuses-congress-that-must-change/

[4] Barrón-López, Laura and Heather Caygle. 2020. CBC head: Nothing is stopping Afro-Latinos from joining both Black, Hispanic caucuses. July 22. https://www.politico.com/news/2020/07/22/bass-torres-black-hispanic-caucuses-379070

Doing Identity Labor. Danielle Casarez Lemi, Oxford University Press. © Oxford University Press (2025).
DOI: 10.1093/9780197816851.003.0005

This exchange was reminiscent of Adriano Espaillat's experience in 2017.[5] Espaillat is a Dominican American Democratic congressmember from New York. He defeated former Congressmember Charles Rangel, a founding member of the CBC who was Black and Puerto Rican, in the 2014 Democratic primary and sought to join both the CBC and the CHC. According to Congressmember G. K. Butterfield, a Democrat from North Carolina (who served as the chair of the CBC in the 114th Congress and presents as a white man)[6], membership to the CBC and the CHC posed challenges for caucus unity: "Even though our agendas are typically parallel, occasionally they are not. So it may be problematic if someone wants to belong to two ethnic caucuses."[7] These examples illuminate how ethnorace is done between members of Congress by showing how politicians enforce, question, or conform to norms about group membership (Moya and Markus 2010).

While we'll never know Torres's motivations for penning the op-ed, or how members of the CBC view particular Afro-Latinx representatives who wish to join both caucuses, it's clear that classification to more than one ethnoracial category presents political questions for descriptive representatives. Torres's view echoes comments in Chapter 3 from Mixed Legislator #5, who is Black and MENA, on the tendency for people to assign them to a "box." Like Mixed Legislator #5, Torres does not fit neatly into single boxes: he is *both* Black and Latino. At the heart of what Torres and mixed legislators experience is the confusion that others impose on them for belonging to more than one ethnoracial group—the multiple classification triggers perceptions of ambiguity on where they stand politically. As discussed in Chapter 1, multiple classification can create opportunities for a mixed politician to perform identity labor—more so than their non-mixed counterparts. One way to observe this indirectly is through differences in electoral support for mixed candidates. If a mixed candidate is less likely to collect votes from their communities than their non-mixed counterpart, then the mixed candidate may need to perform more identity labor to close that gap. Is there an electoral support gap?

So far, we've learned what identity labor is, its influences, and how different politicians perform it. In Chapter 2, we learned how familial socialization and the ethnoracial hierarchy structured how Kamala Harris narrated her

[5] Caygle, Heather. 2017. Black caucus chafes at Latino who wants to join. *Politico*. February 3. http://www.politico.com/story/2017/02/congressional-black-caucus-hispanic-adriano-espaillat-234575.

[6] Hearn, Josephine. 2007. "Rep. Butterfield is Black." *Politico*, May 1. http://www.politico.com/blogs/politico-now/2007/05/rep-butterfield-is-black-001235.

[7] Caygle, Heather. 2017. Black caucus chafes at Latino who wants to join. *Politico*. February 3. http://www.politico.com/story/2017/02/congressional-black-caucus-hispanic-adriano-espaillat-234575.

ethnoracial identity in her memoir. In Chapter 3, we saw how familial socialization, ethnoracial appearance, and the ethnoracial hierarchy each shaped how mixed politicians understood their identities and how they performed identity labor. In Chapter 4, we observed the interaction between mixed politicians and the press and how mixed politicians were called to perform identity labor. We've seen identity labor from the perspective of the politicians and the media by analyzing their words and newspaper coverage. The world does ethnorace to these politicians (Moya and Markus 2010), and they perform identity labor in response.

In this chapter, I evaluate whether an electoral support gap exists for Kamala Harris and hypothetical politicians of different ethnoracial backgrounds by testing how voters evaluate candidates assigned to two ethnoracial categories. Prior chapters suggest that mixed politicians are evaluated differently from their non-mixed counterparts, and they may use identity labor to bring themselves closer to their ethnoracial constituents. This chapter presents evidence that there's an electoral gap, and voters react differently to different kinds of mixed candidates according to the ethnoracial hierarchy. Mixed classification is *both* an electoral advantage and a disadvantage. I argue that this is also suggestive of an identity labor gap between mixed and non-mixed candidates, such that mixed candidates must perform more identity labor to close this gap.

Theorizing the Electoral Support Gap

Mixed classification is a double-edged sword. On one hand, mixed classification may pose challenges for descriptive representatives securing support from their own communities. Absent information about their self-identification, mixed classification may result in sanctions from group members by raising questions about where that individual stands in relation to the group (Hogg et al. 2012, 282). When a mixed candidate explains their ethnoracial identity through identity labor, voters may make inferences about their issue competencies (Masuoka 2015). Without that explanation, a mixed candidate's ethnoracial identity and competencies on issues relevant to the group might be called into question (Garay et al. 2019). A candidate's fit with a group category, in this case, an ethnoracial category, becomes a tool to secure votes (also see Harris 2020). People may be less supportive of a mixed candidate from their group than a non-mixed counterpart, especially people who strongly identify with their group or feel linked fate (e.g., Dawson 1995; Harris and Findley 2012; McConnaughy et al. 2010). Whether mixed candidates appeal to those with linked fate is an open question (e.g., Kinder and McConnaughy 2006, 159). Strong attachments to one's ethnoracial group and feelings of linked fate might influence the degree to which voters accept mixed candidates as members of their group (Wilkinson 2014; Jones-Correa et al. 2016; Jardina 2019, 2020; Nicholson et al. 2020; Lu 2020).

Voters' reactions to mixed and non-mixed candidates depend on the voters' and the candidates' positions in the ethnoracial hierarchy. When a candidate is classified into two ethnoracial categories, voters from different ethnoracial groups might react differently depending on the mixed candidate's ethnoracial combination. For example, in a study about Congressman Charles Rangel, Black voters reacted favorably to information about his background, while Latinx respondents' evaluations were more lukewarm (Adida et al. 2016). For mixed Black candidates generally, Black and non-Black voters' reactions reflect the legacy of the one-drop rule. All else considered, Black voters might not draw a strong distinction between a Black candidate and a mixed Black candidate based on classification alone. At the same time, non-Black voters might draw distinctions between candidates from their group who are also Black, as in the case of Black and white voters evaluating a mixed Black and white candidate (Ho et al. 2017, 763). Questions about group loyalty may be particularly pronounced for non-Black voters evaluating non-Black mixed candidates, like Asian American voters evaluating mixed Asian and white candidates (Chen et al. 2019).

Voters who oppose inter-ethnoracial marriage might apply those attitudes to mixed candidates. When I interviewed Mixed Legislator #5, who is Black and MENA, they explained how their grandmother cut their mother off for marrying outside of their ethnoracial group:

> My mother was disowned when she married my dad. And so that was a reality, you know, that we knew of growing up, my whole life, that because my mother had married someone of a different race, the consequence was that she lost most of her family over it, including her own mother.

Politicians like Mixed Legislator #5 may have constituents who oppose inter-ethnoracial marriage in their districts. Marrying outside of your ethnoracial group might violate group prototypes, and people who oppose inter-ethnoracial marriage with different groups may react negatively toward mixed candidates (see Dalmage 2000; Flores 2020). The relevance of attitudes toward mixed romantic relationships for evaluations of mixed politicians was confirmed in 2008 when white voters who expressed greater disapproval of a relative dating a Black person were less likely to support Barack Obama (Tesler 2013, 116). People from different ethnoracial groups may evaluate mixed candidates as a reflection of their group identity, a sense of linked fate, or their feelings about inter-ethnoracial marriage.

While mixed candidates may pay a penalty when appealing to their ethnoracial groups, on the other hand, mixed candidates' backgrounds may yield benefits. Some voters might apply the idea of the exceptional mixed person to mixed candidates and believe they represent fewer negative stereotypes attached to being a member of any group (Purdie-Vaughns and Eibach 2008, 382–383; Joseph 2013). Mixed candidates' multiple ethnoracial categories may interact to reduce the negative and amplify the positive stereotypes of each other (Hancock 2007; Bejarano 2013, 8, 39). Thus, voters across ethnoracial groups may generally prefer mixed candidates to outsider non-mixed candidates because they represent an exceptional novelty. This discussion leads me to two testable hypotheses about how voters evaluate mixed and non-mixed candidates:

The Electoral Support Gap Hypothesis (Hypothesis 1): Same-ethnorace non-mixed candidates are preferable to same-ethnorace mixed candidates, who are preferable to outsider non-mixed candidates. This means that in a contest between someone like Vice President Kamala Harris and Congressmember Pramila Jayapal, who is Indian American, Asian American voters might be less likely to support Harris, all else being considered.

The Exceptional Mixed Person Hypothesis (Hypothesis 2): Outsider mixed candidates will be preferable to outsider non-mixed candidates. This means that when mixed candidates are in the pool, like Kamala Harris, Latinx voters might prefer Harris over a Black or Asian American opponent if there's no Latinx candidate in the race.

The Role of Group Prototypes: I also explore how voters with stronger ethnoracial identities, based on psychological and political attachments to the group and attitudes toward inter-ethnoracial marriage, evaluate mixed and non-mixed candidates.

Because of the ethnoracial hierarchy, I also generally expect that non-Black voters will express ranked preferences, such that they tend to be less likely to vote for mixed Black candidates than non-Black mixed candidates.

Testing These Hypotheses

My argument is that classification of a candidate to at least two ethnoracial categories raises questions about how well a candidate adheres to group norms of ethnoracial identity, generating an electoral gap in support between mixed and non-mixed candidates. Classification may come from anyone, such as the media or pollsters. Voters react to candidates according to the candidates' ethnoracial backgrounds and their own ethnoracial backgrounds.

To test this argument, I draw on three data sources (see Chapter 5 Appendix for more details on data and methods). First, I return to the case of Vice President Kamala Harris. Whereas the analysis of news coverage of Harris in Chapter 2 focused on the contexts of depictions of Harris, here, I report the number of times specific demographic terms appeared in different news venues throughout Harris's career. This data shows how the media makes various demographic labels salient in articles that mention Harris.

Second, I use a split-sample test embedded in the 2016 National Asian American Post-election Survey (NAAS) to examine whether Harris had an electoral support gap in 2016. In 2016, the NAAS surveyed multiple ethnoracial groups around the country about politics. The NAAS asked Black and Asian Californians who they supported in the US Senate election between Democrats Kamala Harris and Loretta Sanchez. Harris is known as a Black politician (Sullivan 2019). We may assume that in the absence of information that she is Asian American, California voters recognized her as Black. The questionnaire structure allows me to measure how Black and Asian Californians treat Harris when they learn she is "Asian and African American," relative to an unspoken categorization as Black or African American. All respondents also were asked, "How important is being [respondent's ethnorace] to your identity?" and given the option to say *extremely important* to *not important at all*, as well as to decline to answer. This survey took place in the middle of Harris's 2016 US Senate election—years before voters nationwide were flooded with information about Harris—and it provides a window to observe how Black and Asian Californians evaluate a mixed politician.

Third, I use an original survey experiment, called a conjoint experiment, that I designed to capture the evaluations of Asian, Black, Hispanic, and white American voters (Hainmueller, Hopkins, and Yamamoto 2014).[8] The design

[8] This approach is consistent with recommendations from Sen and Wasow (2016, 509–512). The survey was programmed with *conjointSDT* (Strezhnev et al. 2014) and processed with *cjoint* (Barari et al. 2023). See Chapter 5 Appendix for more design details.

allows for comparisons between mixed and non-mixed candidates of specific combinations and provides a more demanding test of the electoral gap. Maybe mixed classification becomes irrelevant if a voter knows a candidate is a Democrat. Perhaps there's a gap even when the voters know a candidate's professional political experience. By building other candidate characteristics in addition to ethnorace into the design, I'm stacking the deck against finding effects of ethnoracial classification on vote choice.[9]

The conjoint experiment was conducted online in May 2016 on a sample of white, Black, Asian American, and Latinx respondents contracted through Qualtrics survey panels.[10] On average, this sample leans Democratic, relatively liberal, and relatively young. To examine how different notions of group identity bear on the identity labor gap, I asked questions about their feelings of linked fate (Sanchez and Vargas 2016). I also asked questions meant to tap into their psychological identification with their ethnoracial group (Mael and Tetrick 1992) and whether they approved or disapproved of a close relative of theirs marrying someone who was white, Black, Asian, or Hispanic (adapted from the General Social Survey and Schuman et al. 1985, 76).[11]

Respondents read a vignette about a congressional election for ten pairs of candidates pitted against each other.[12] After reviewing the candidate profiles, respondents were asked, "Which candidate would you vote for?" and selected between Candidate 1 and Candidate 2. Figure 5.1 is an example of what respondents saw. I note mixed categorization via the label of the candidate's ethnorace. These two surveys allow me to collect multiple pieces of evidence to test my argument by leveraging a real-world politician in the middle of a real-world election and hypothetical politicians who vary in ethnoracial classification.

[9] This experiment does not build candidate appearance or ancestry into the design, and it cannot speak to the effects of candidate appearance. As you can imagine, mixed and non-mixed candidates can appear in many ways that are more or less prototypical with their ethnoracial categories, and it's possible that a non-mixed person can perform more identity labor than a mixed person due to their appearance (see Sims 2025). A mixed person's parentage could also have many gender and ethnoracial combinations that could affect how voters view the candidate (see Flores 2020). The possibilities are endless, and for this reason, this chapter takes a "first cut" at testing whether there's an electoral gap, and implicitly an identity labor gap, between mixed and non-mixed candidates based on classification alone.

[10] See Chapter 5 Appendix for descriptive statistics and more details on question wording.

[11] Responses ranged from strongly approve to strongly disapprove. I am interested in people who approve or disapprove of interethnoracial marriage, so I collapsed this variable so that 1 = approve at all and 0 = disapprove at all.

[12] Research on conjoint experiments suggests up to 30 rating tasks may be asked without loss of data quality (Bansak et al., 2018).

Imagine it is election season and candidates are competing for a seat in Congress. Imagine further that the race has been narrowed down to two main competitive candidates, Candidate 1 and Candidate 2. Imagine that you must decide which candidate to support. The profiles below describe Candidate 1 and Candidate 2.

Please carefully review the options detailed below, then please answer the question below.

	Candidate 1	Candidate 2
Gender	Female	Female
Race	Black and White	White
Experience	Served in Congress	Served in the State Legislature
Party	Independent	Independent
Ideology	Liberal	Moderate
Nativity	Born Outside the US	Born Outside the US

Figure 5.1 Example of vignette

Findings

The electoral support gap for Kamala Harris in 2016

My analysis of news articles that mention Kamala Harris (see Chapter 5 Appendix) shows that there are trends in the dominance of specific terms related to Harris's ethnoracial background in various news venues. Although African American and Asian American newspapers highlight Harris's background more often than non-African/Asian American newspapers, each of these venues raises the salience of Harris's ethnoracial backgrounds. Does ethnoracial classification with two categories produce an electoral support gap?

In the 2016 NAAS, respondents were asked about their candidate preferences for the California US Senate election. Half of those surveyed received no information about Harris's background or the background of her US Senate opponent, Loretta Sanchez. In contrast, the other half received information about Harris as "of Asian and African American descent" and Sanchez as "of Latina descent." After reading these descriptions, survey respondents were asked who they would vote for if the election were held today: Harris or Sanchez.

Figure 5.2 visualizes the average support for Harris over Sanchez by ethnoracial group and the importance of identity. Overall, in the top panel of Figure 5.2, support for Harris is higher among Black Californians, at about 85 percent than among Asian Californians, at about 63 percent. Considering

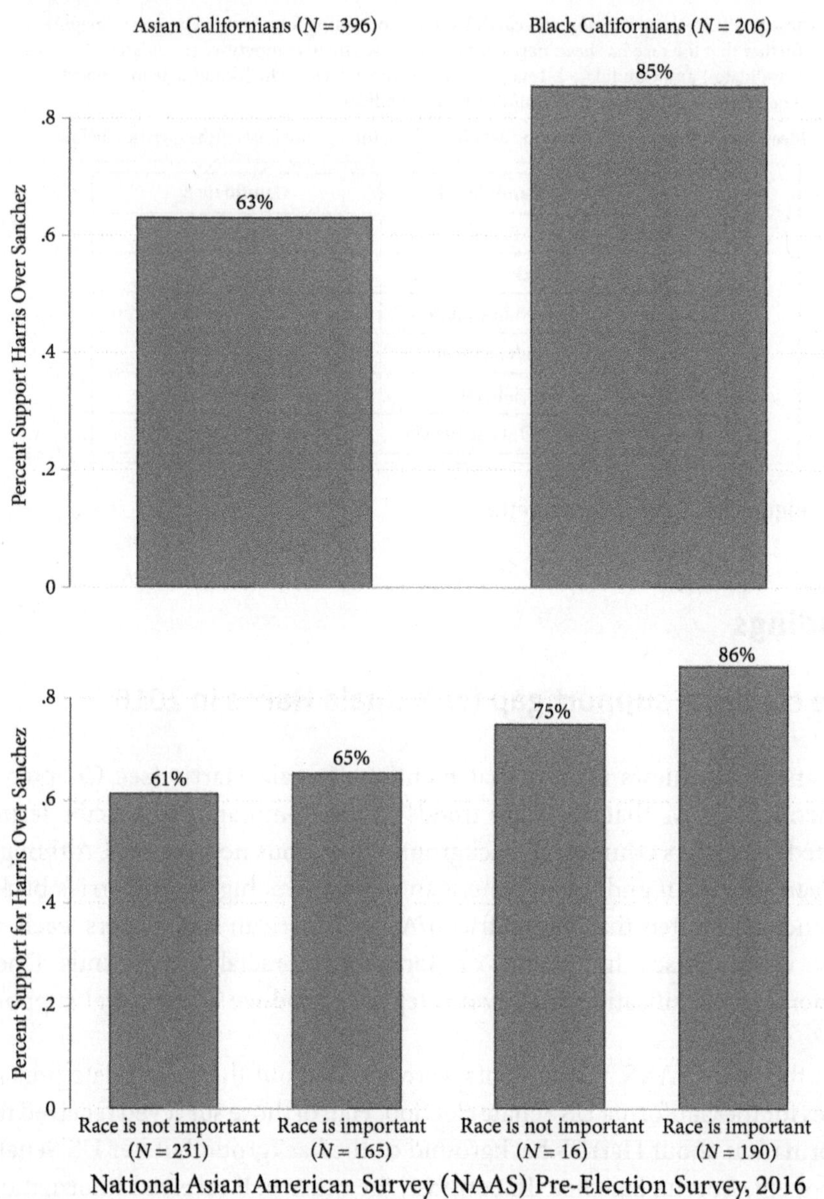

Figure 5.2 Support for Harris over Sanchez by ethnorace and importance of identity

the importance placed on identity, just over 60 percent of Asian Californians in either category support Harris over Sanchez, while about 75–86 percent of Black Californians in either category supported Harris over Sanchez. Notably, sixteen Black Californians did not place importance on their ethnoracial identity.

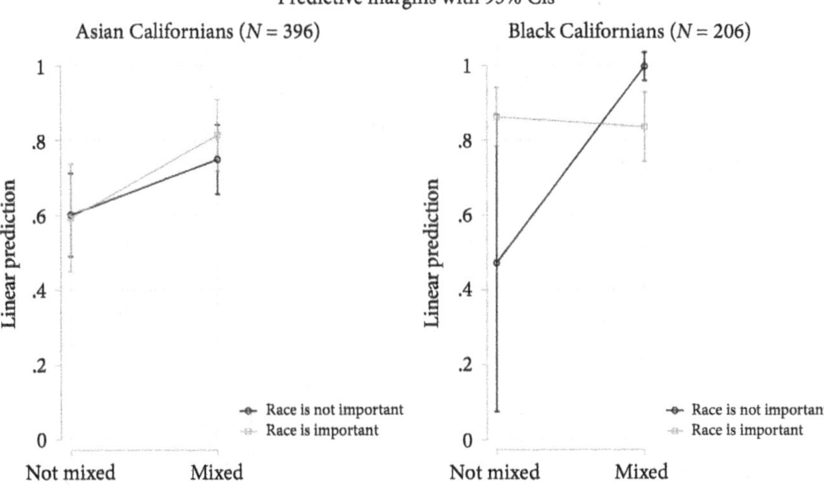

Figure 5.3 Testing the electoral support gap for Harris in 2016

Figure 5.3 illustrates the effect of framing Harris as mixed or non-mixed, accounting for shared Democratic partisanship with Harris/Sanchez and the importance placed on ethnoracial identity.[13] Among Black Californians, the effect of providing information on Harris's ethnoracial background interacts with the importance one places on their own ethnoracial identity. There is a statistically significant relationship between the two (−.552, $p = .010$). When Black Californians who do *not* place importance on their ethnoracial identities are given information about Harris's ethnoracial background, the average probability of voting for Harris over Sanchez increases from about 47 percent to nearly 100 percent. By contrast, the average probability of voting for Harris among Black Californians who placed importance on their ethnoracial identities and read about Harris's mixed background is about 84 percent. This 16 percentage point difference between these two groups is statistically significant (Wald test: F (1, 201) = 6.77, $Prob > F = .01$). This means that Black Californians with stronger identities were less likely to support Harris in the mixed condition than Black Californians with weaker identities in

[13] Output is from an OLS regression that interacts ethnorace with importance of identity and controls for shared partisanship with an indicator variable (1 = shared partisanship, 0 = else). The command "pweight" was used to call "pweight," or person weight, from the dataset, to account for the underlying sampling design of the NAAS. Regressing survey condition on ethnorace, party identification, and importance of identity shows no statistically significant relationship between these variables and question condition (see Table 5A.15 in the Appendix). See Gomila (2021) for a discussion on using OLS to estimate treatment effects for binary outcomes.

the mixed condition. However, these results should be interpreted cautiously and tentatively given the relatively small sample size of 206 Black Californians in the statistical model and the sixteen Black Californians who did not say identity was important. Moreover, the generally high level of support for Harris in either condition suggests that exposure to mixed classification may not do much to invite even more support among Black Californians with stronger identities. I do not find statistically significant differences among Asian Americans who place importance on their identities.

The findings above reflect the difference between Harris generally being viewed as a Black politician and being framed by pollsters as mixed. These findings suggest a pollster's external classification of a mixed candidate may shift voters' evaluations of that candidate. In the findings above, Black Californians with strong identities were already highly likely to support Harris regardless of the description they read, so classifying Harris as mixed may not meaningfully undermine support from these Black Californians. However, Mixed classification may only increase support among Black Californians with weaker identities, but in doing so, may create distance between Harris and some Black Californian voters with strong ethnoracial identities. Her identification as "African American and Asian" may not create the same differences among Asian Americans, perhaps because "Asian American" does not resonate with Asian Americans from different ethnic groups (see Junn and Masuoka 2008).[14] Again, given the small sample size of this analysis, these findings should be interpreted to be suggestive.

Overall, these findings suggest that support for someone as well-known as Harris could be manipulated by the mere association with two ethnoracial categories, regardless of their identity. The NAAS is particularly informative because the questions were asked in the middle of a real-world election. Candidates like Harris may need to make up for lost ground if the media presents them as mixed candidates, even if they do not identify as such. Importantly, these findings suggest that the media, advertisers, and public opinion pollsters may inadvertently manipulate support for a mixed candidate based on how the candidate is classified.

The electoral support gap for different mixed and non-mixed candidates

My analysis of the NAAS suggests an electoral gap for Harris when she was depicted as mixed. Does this trend occur for mixed candidates with different backgrounds? The results from my original conjoint experiment, which allows me to test and classify candidates to a variety of ethnoracial

[14] But see Lemi et al. (2022) for an analysis of Indian American evaluations of Kamala Harris.

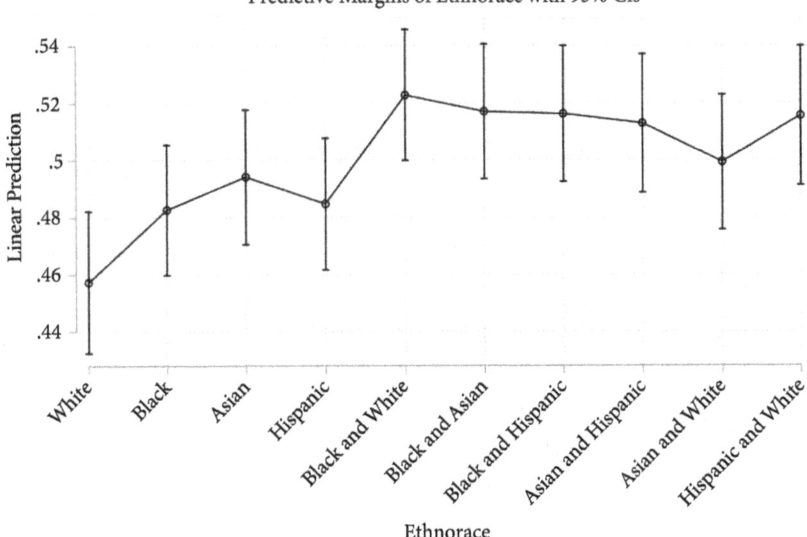

Figure 5.4 Average probability of selection by candidate ethnorace (Full Sample)
Bars are 95 percent confidence intervals, and results are clustered by the respondent

combinations and leverage a larger number of observations, suggest that an electoral gap does exist.

Figure 5.4 shows voters' general preferences for mixed and non-mixed candidates are consistent with the exceptional mixed person hypothesis.[15,16] There is a general upward tilt in the probability of voting for mixed candidates, ranging from about 46 percent to about 52 percent from white candidates to Hispanic and white candidates. There is a general advantage to being classified with two ethnoracial categories.

The electoral gap depends on a voter's position in the ethnoracial hierarchy relative to a mixed candidate. Figure 5.5 shows preferences for mixed and non-mixed candidates by the respondent's ethnorace. As each panel shows, voting patterns ebb and flow for each ethnoracial group according to whether the candidate shares an ethnoracial background with the respondent. For instance, for Asian Americans, the probability of selecting any Asian candidate ranges from about 53 percent to 60 percent. Support dips to 42

[15] I report these findings according to recommendations from Leeper et al. (2020) and Hainmueller et al. (2014) using Stata BE 17.0 and cluster robust standard errors by respondent. I report the marginal means of candidate ethnorace from a linear regression model with all other candidate attributes, clustered standard errors by respondent, and a control variable for shared partisanship (Merolla et al., 2017).

[16] These were calculated with the margins command in Stata. Plots were created with Bischof (2017). See Chapter 5 Appendix for full statistical output for each figure from the conjoint analysis. This analysis is not weighted (Mullinix et al., 2015).

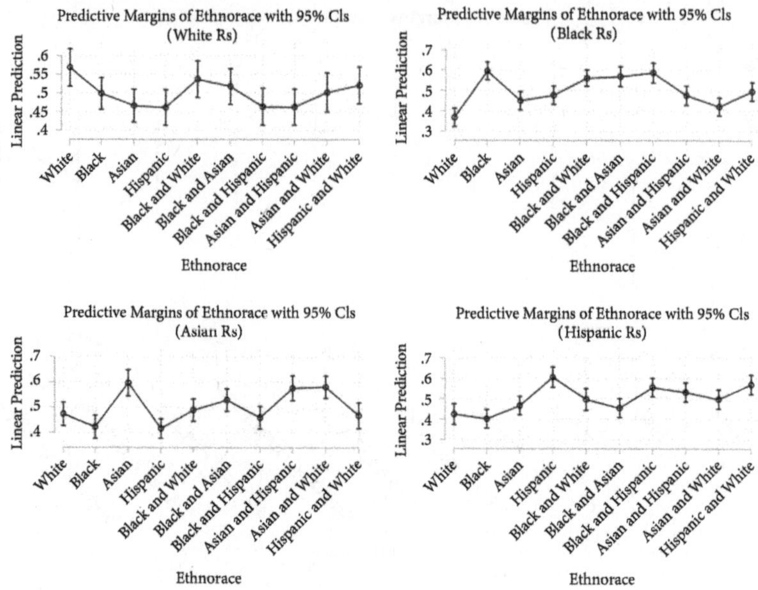

Figure 5.5 Average probability of selection by ethnorace of respondent
Bars are 95 percent confidence intervals, and results are clustered by respondent

percent for a non-mixed Black candidate and 47 percent for a non-mixed white candidate. Taken together, Figures 5.4 and 5.5 suggest some support for the exceptional mixed person hypothesis *and* the electoral gap hypothesis. Relative to all other non-mixed candidates, mixed candidates are favored, considering all voters pooled together. Considering each group of voters separately, they are *also* generally *disfavored.*

Testing the electoral gap and exceptional mixed person hypotheses

To test the electoral gap and exceptional mixed person hypotheses, in Figure 5.6, I collapsed the combinations of candidate ethnorace into same-ethnorace mixed, same-ethnorace non-mixed, outsider mixed, and outsider non-mixed based on the voter's ethnorace.[17] For example, a white candidate is a same-ethnorace non-mixed candidate for white respondents. Mixed Black

[17] Figures report the average marginal component effect (AMCE) of candidate ethnorace or the average change in the probability of being selected given a candidate's ethnorace. Confidence intervals that do not cross zero indicate statistically significant differences from the baseline category. These estimates are from a model that contains all the attributes, including an indicator variable for whether a voter shared partisanship with a candidate. Plots created with Jann (2005, 2007) and Bischof (2017).

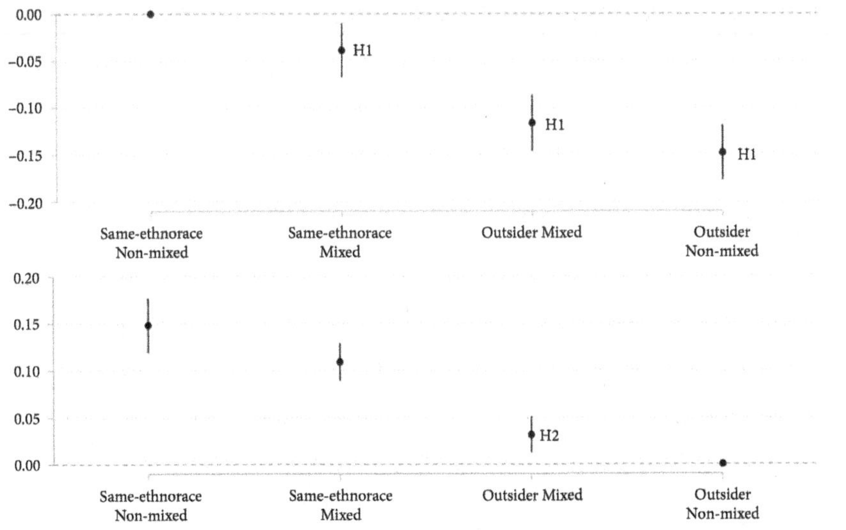

Figure 5.6 Average change in probability of selection by candidate ethnorace (Full Sample)

Bars are 95 percent confidence intervals, and results are clustered by respondent

and white, Asian and white, and Hispanic and white candidates are same-ethnorace mixed candidates for white respondents. All other candidates are either outsider non-mixed or outsider mixed candidates. Figure 5.6 shows the average change in percentage points that a candidate was more or less likely to be selected relative to a non-mixed candidate from the voter's group or a non-mixed candidate outside the voter's group. The top panel tests the electoral gap hypothesis, and the bottom panel tests the exceptional mixed person hypothesis.

In the top panel of Figure 5.6, mixed candidates experience an electoral gap. Compared to a non-mixed candidate who shares ethnoracial group membership with the voter, mixed candidates from the voter's group are about four percentage points less likely to be selected (p = .007). This finding reflects what one mixed representative in Chapter 3 told me about their time on the city council—a non-mixed candidate is "one of us." There is a penalty for being classified as mixed. At the same time, mixed candidates may experience the benefits of being stereotyped as the exceptional mixed person. In the bottom panel, compared to a non-mixed outsider, a mixed candidate who doesn't share the voter's ethnorace is more likely to be selected by about three percentage points (p = .001). This finding means that mixed candidates might have more appeal to voters outside their communities than their non-mixed counterparts. This finding brings to mind Alberto Torrico's comments to the

Average Marginal Component Effect of Candidate Ethnorace (By Ethnorace of Respondent)

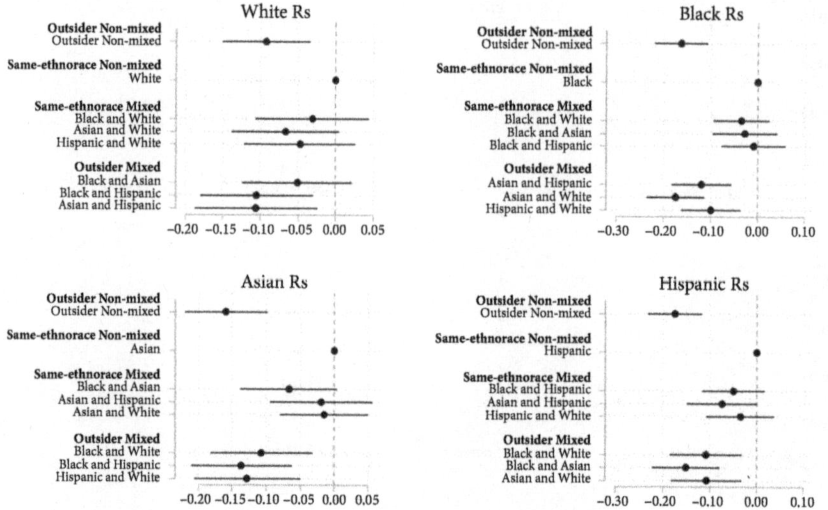

Figure 5.7 Average change in probability of selection by ethnorace of respondent and candidate ethnorace (Electoral Support Gap Hypothesis)

Markers at 0 are the base categories. Bars are 95 percent confidence intervals, and results are clustered by respondent

press about reflecting "the face of California":[18] mixed people are the so-called future—often fetishized by society.

Testing the electoral gap and exceptional mixed person hypotheses by ethnorace of voter

The ethnoracial hierarchy underpins the nature of the electoral gap. Two mixed candidates who are Asian American and white and Asian American and Black have different strategic opportunities to appeal to Asian American voters because they occupy different positions in the ethnoracial hierarchy. Testing the electoral gap and exceptional mixed person hypotheses as they relate to the ethnoracial hierarchy thus requires running the same tests in Figure 5.4, but disaggregating by the ethnorace of the voter and each ethnoracial combination for mixed and non-mixed candidates.

Figure 5.7 shows that there are differences among ethnoracial groups. Black voters in this sample do not systematically evaluate mixed Black candidates differently from non-mixed Black candidates. The estimates for mixed Black

[18] Contra Costa Times. 2006. *Capitol notebook: Times Sacramento Bureau*. April 2.

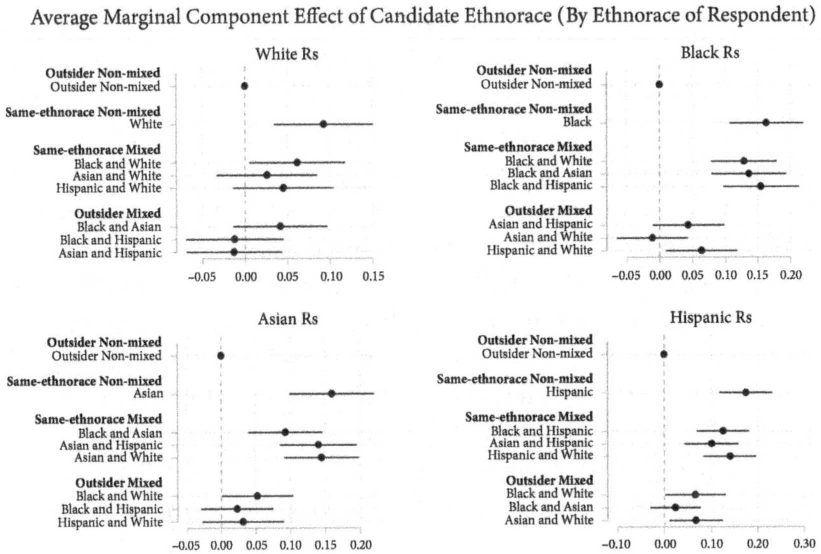

Average Marginal Component Effect of Candidate Ethnorace (By Ethnorace of Respondent)

Figure 5.8 Average change in probability of selection by ethnorace of respondent and candidate ethnorace (Exceptional Mixed Person Hypothesis)

Markers at 0 are the base categories. Bars are 95 percent confidence intervals, and results are clustered by respondent.

candidates are negative but do not reach statistical significance. The effect sizes for mixed Black candidates range from about 1 to 3 percentage points. These estimates indicate that any shifts in the average change in the probability of selection based on classification are minimal—perhaps owing to the historical legacy of the one-drop rule.

By contrast, white, Asian, and Latinx respondents reject specific mixed candidates from their ethnoracial groups, with marginally statistically significant differences. Relative to a white candidate, white respondents are less likely to select a mixed Asian and white candidate (−.07, $p = .067$). Relative to an Asian candidate, Asian American respondents are less likely to select a mixed Black and Asian candidate (−.07, $p = .066$). Relative to a Hispanic candidate, Latinx respondents are less likely to select a mixed Asian and Hispanic candidate (−.07, $p = .053$). These mixed candidates each pay about a 7-percentage point penalty, and these differences are marginally statistically significant.

Do mixed candidates yield the benefits of the exceptional mixed person trope? In Figure 5.8, specific outsider mixed candidates are preferable to outsider non-mixed candidates. The mixed candidates likely to benefit from the exceptional mixed person stereotype are at least white or relatively higher in the ethnoracial hierarchy. Among white respondents, the only outsider mixed candidate that trends positively is the mixed Black and Asian candidate (.04, p = .142), though this effect is not statistically significant. Among Black respondents, the mixed Hispanic and white candidate is preferable to Asian, white, and Hispanic candidates combined (.06, p = .022). Among Asian American respondents, the only outsider mixed candidate with a positive and statistically significant effect is the mixed Black and white candidate (.05, p = .047). Among Latinx respondents, mixed Black and white (.07, p = .043) and mixed Asian and white (.07, p = .020) candidates are more likely to be selected than outsider non-mixed candidates. Voters may not uniformly apply the exceptional mixed person trope to all mixed candidates. Mixed Black and Asian, Hispanic and white, Black and white, and Asian and white candidates might yield the benefits of this trope by appealing to voters outside their ethnoracial groups. Notably, preferences for the mixed Black and white candidate in particular are consistently positive across groups in Figure 5.8.

The Role of Group Prototypes

Linked Fate and Group Identity

People who strongly identify with their group might withhold support for mixed candidates because non-mixed candidates more strongly adhere to a dominant prototype—they are classified to a single ethnorace. Alternatively, people who strongly identify with their group might not distinguish between mixed and non-mixed candidates because they support any candidate from their ethnoracial group—mixed candidates are closer to the group prototype than total outsiders.[19]

I do not find that the presence of linked fate is statistically significantly consequential for assessing mixed and non-mixed candidates across ethnoracial groups (see Table 5A.9 in the Appendix). Regarding group identity, I find that assessments of non-mixed candidates and mixed candidates depend on whether one strongly identifies with their ethnoracial group (see Table 5A.9 in the Appendix). Figure 5.9 illustrates this, showing that both stronger and weaker identifiers tend to prefer non-mixed candidates from their group and that the probability of selection declines the further a candidate is from the non-mixed candidate. Among strong identifiers, the average probability of voting for a non-mixed outsider candidate is about 43 percent.

[19] Due to small sample sizes, I do not disaggregate these results by ethnoracial group. Linked fate is coded where 0 = else, 1 = reported linked fate. High group identity is coded where 0 = below the median of all identity scores and 1 = at or above the median.

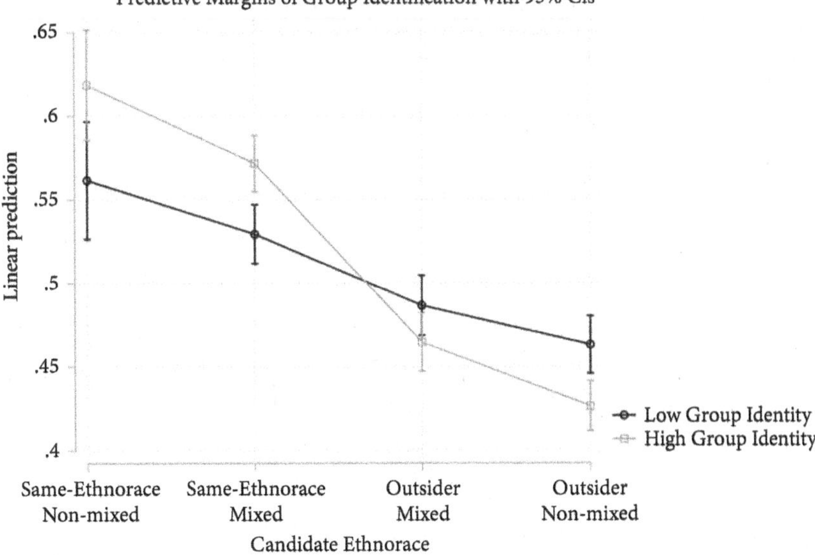

Figure 5.9 Average probability of selection by candidate ethnorace and respondent group identity
Bars are 95 percent confidence intervals, and results are clustered by respondent

A non-mixed candidate from one's group has about a 19-percentage point lead in the average probability of selection at about 62 percent. By contrast, for strong identifiers, a mixed candidate from one's group only has about a 14-percentage point lead over a non-mixed outsider at about 57 percent. Those with stronger identities are about 5.7 percentage points more likely than those with weaker identities to select non-mixed candidates from their group ($p = .020$). Those with stronger identities are also about 4.2 percentage points more likely than those with weaker group identities to select mixed candidates from their group ($p = .001$). Notably, voters with stronger identities do not distinguish between candidates from their own group, mixed or not (Wald test: $F(1, 785) = 26$, $Prob > F = .61$). These findings suggest that although voters with stronger ethnoracial identities prefer any candidate from their group, mixed candidates may not get the same average level of support as their counterparts, compared to a total outsider.

Attitudes toward inter-ethnoracial marriage

Beliefs about marriage with other ethnoracial groups are another dimension of how one thinks about group identity. If someone does not approve

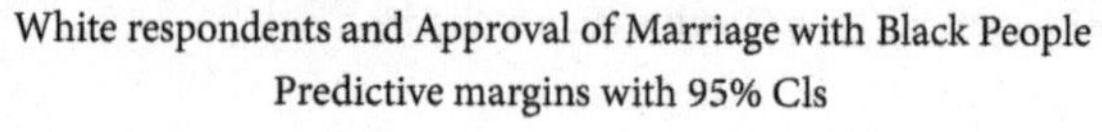

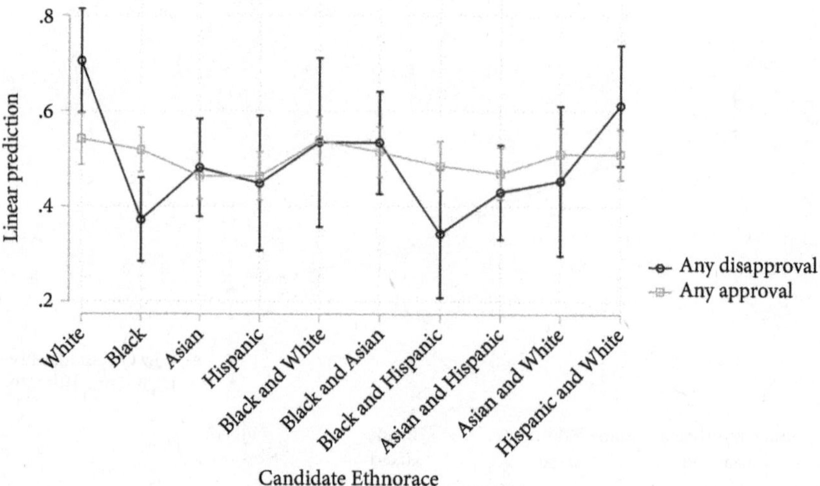

Figure 5.10 White respondents' average probability of selection of candidates by approval of marriage with Black people

Bars are 95 percent confidence intervals, and results are clustered by respondent

of marriage with an outsider, mixed candidates might have to work harder to win their vote. Because of the nature of the ethnoracial hierarchy, the relevance of attitudes toward inter-ethnoracial marriage to candidate evaluations likely varies by ethnoracial group. I find some evidence that attitudes toward inter-ethnoracial marriage influence evaluations of candidates from some ethnoracial groups (see Tables 5.A8–5.A11 in the Appendix). I find that approval of marriage between Black and Asian American people conditions the selection of Black and Asian candidates for white, Black, and Asian American voters.

In Figure 5.10, among white voters, expressing opposition to a relative marrying a Black person is associated with less support for a Black candidate (−.15, $p = .004$), compared to those who express approval (Table 5.A9). The average probability of voting for a Black candidate for those who express disapproval is about 37 percent. By contrast, it's about 53 percent for Black and Asian candidates—a 16-percentage-point difference. This difference between the two candidates is statistically significant (Wald test: $F(1,189) = 5.44$, $Prob > F = .0207$). White voters who oppose intermarriage with Black people might be more likely to vote for a mixed Black and Asian candidate than a non-mixed Black candidate.

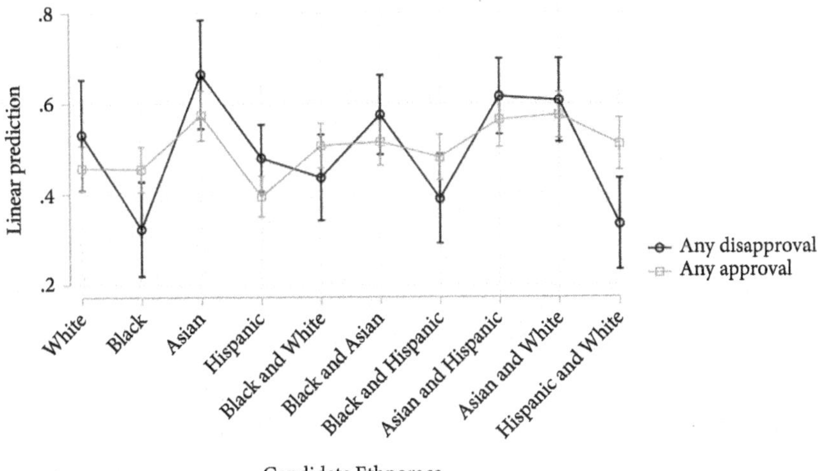

Figure 5.11 Asian American respondents' average probability of selection of candidates by approval of marriage with Black people
Bars are 95 percent confidence intervals, and results are clustered by respondent

A similar pattern exists among Asian American respondents in Figure 5.11 (see Table 5.A11 in the Appendix). Compared to those who approve of marriage with Black persons, those who disapprove are less likely to vote for a Black candidate (−.13, $p = .026$). The average probability of voting for a Black candidate when an Asian respondent opposes marriage with Black people is only about 32 percent. That average probability jumps to 57 percent for mixed Black and Asian candidates. This difference between the two candidates is statistically significant (Wald test: $F(1, 206) = 5.99$, $Prob > F = .0152$). In other words, Asian Americans in this sample who oppose marriage with Black people might be less likely to support a Black candidate but more likely to support a mixed Black and Asian candidate.

In Figure 5.12, among Black respondents, opposition to intermarriage with Asian Americans is not statistically significantly associated with evaluations of non-mixed Asian candidates (−.08, $p = .08$) (see Table 5A.12 in the Appendix). The average probability of selecting an Asian candidate, given opposition to intermarriage with Asian Americans, is about 38 percent. Among those who oppose marriage with Asian Americans, the average probability of selecting a mixed Black and Asian candidate is about 72 percent. The difference between the two candidates is statistically significant (Wald test: $F(1, 202) = 6.35$, $Prob > F = .0125$). This suggests that Black voters who

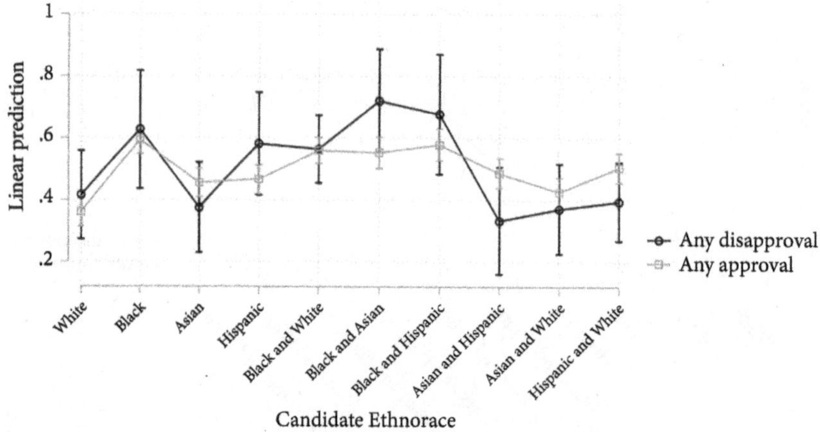

Figure 5.12 Black respondents' average probability of selection of candidates by approval of marriage with Asian people
Bars are 95 percent confidence intervals, and results are clustered by respondent

are less likely to vote for an Asian candidate might be more likely to vote for a mixed Black and Asian candidate.

Taken together, these findings suggest that mixed Black and Asian candidates may have particular appeal to Black, Asian, and white voters. For some, it's likely because mixed candidates are a part of those groups. For Asian and white voters in particular, it may be because these mixed candidates are perceived to be higher in the ethnoracial hierarchy than non-mixed Black candidates.

Discussion

Overall, the findings from this chapter suggest an electoral support gap between mixed and non-mixed candidates. Based on classification alone, voters seem to prefer candidates that fit more neatly into predominant ideas of prototypical ethnoracial boxes (e.g., Harris 2020). Compared to their non-mixed counterparts, mixed candidates are penalized by this preference by a gap in support. Compared to outsider non-mixed candidates, mixed classification positively affects vote choice across groups, perhaps because of the broader fetishizing of mixed people and because their communities extend support to them.[20] Preferences for specific mixed candidates may depend on the voter's ethnorace, identity attachments, and beliefs about inter-ethnoracial marriage. The patterns found here correspond to the American ethnoracial hierarchy and illustrate the legacy of the one-drop rule and contemporary anti-Blackness directed at mixed Black candidates. Strikingly, the hypothetical mixed candidates who performed best across groups and attitudes toward inter-ethnoracial marriage were the mixed Black and white candidate—like Barack Obama—and the mixed Black and Asian candidate—like Kamala Harris.

Mixed politicians navigate a system and voters who do ethnorace to them (Moya and Markus 2010). Voters do ethnorace to mixed candidates by evincing a gap in electoral support. I argue that this gap in electoral support is evidence that there may also be an identity labor gap—both for mixed and non-mixed candidates. I interpret these findings to mean that mixed candidates must engage in the kind of identity labor we saw from the legislators in previous chapters—they must explain their ethnoracial identities. As I discussed in Chapter 1, classification into multiple ethnoracial categories disrupts the ability to quickly interpret a mixed candidate as a member of one's own group because the classification itself flags the candidate as one who violates group prototypes. A voter cannot easily use ethnoracial classification to make inferences about the mixed candidate's group identity, group politics, or loyalty to the group. This disruption creates a gap in support for mixed candidates relative to their non-mixed counterparts. That gap suggests the need for mixed candidates to "drop hints," in the language of Mixed Legislator #18, to bring themselves closer to prototypicality and communicate that they are, in fact, a member of their ethnoracial groups. Mixed candidates must work harder—using identity labor—to court votes from members of their ethnoracial group. Mixed candidates hold this disadvantage because non-mixed candidates are advantaged based on a single classification. Classification into a single ethnoracial category *is* the prototype. Non-mixed candidates do not necessarily need to explain their identity based on classification alone—it's apparent.

By contrast, while mixed candidates may cultivate support from outside groups, their non-mixed counterparts may have to use identity labor to distinguish themselves as more desirable candidates. Non-mixed candidates hold this disadvantage *because* mixed candidates are advantaged. For voters from outsider groups, classification into multiple ethnoracial categories may

[20] Participants could also make inferences about mixed candidates' political ideologies, although candidate ideology was accounted for in the experimental design.

activate the exceptional mixed person trope and elevate mixed candidates above non-mixed candidates. As Chapter 4 showed, newspapers take an interest in mixed politicians' ethnoracial backgrounds. Classification into multiple ethnoracial categories is non-prototypical, but it may also be an interesting novelty to voters and the press. This dichotomy in electoral support for mixed and non-mixed candidates is consistent with research on the relationship between colorism and candidate evaluations—depending on the ethnorace of the voter (among other things), sometimes lighter-skinned (and possibly perceived as mixed) candidates are advantaged (e.g., Weaver 2012; Burge et al 2020; Lerman et al. 2015; Lemi and Brown 2019; Orey and Zhang 2019; Anderson et al. 2020; Chirco and Buchanan 2022). To summarize: The electoral gaps found here suggest that when appealing to their own groups, mixed candidates must do more identity labor than their non-mixed counterparts to gain electoral support because of the ambiguity their multiple classification causes. When appealing to outsiders, mixed candidates can do less because that same classification bestows privilege.

Identity labor is a manufactured performance between strategic politicians, newsrooms with strategic readership goals, and pollsters measuring public opinion throughout the election season. A mixed politician may have ideas about the persona they wish to leverage. Still, the goals of newsrooms and pollsters may clash with that politician's goals—inadvertently disadvantaging or advantaging the mixed politician relative to their non-mixed counterparts and creating identity labor gaps. What is the broader significance of identity labor for representation in American politics?

6
Conclusion

On a cold Tuesday in December of 2021, I was sitting on my couch, still in my jammies at 3 p.m., working on revisions for this book. Young Rock, the NBC sitcom about Dwayne Johnson, aka The Rock, was on TV. I don't follow The Rock that closely, but as a mixed celebrity who identified as Black and Samoan in a Tweet in 2019,[1] his public persona just happens to exemplify how identity labor operates. The show reminded me of his 2017 comedy sketch on Saturday Night Live with Tom Hanks, in which they announced they were going to run for office together in 2020. In detailing the strong points of their candidacy with Johnson for president, Johnson quipped: "I of course would get the minority vote…because everyone just assumes that I'm, well, whatever they are."[2] The joke is, of course, that he appears so ethnoracially ambiguous that he might be mistaken for a member of any non-white ethnoracial group—which could be advantageous when securing votes and forming political relationships. Johnson's public behavior is an example of identity labor.

Much like mixed celebrities and mixed politicians, all of us perform identity labor to some extent. In my own experiences, my performance of ethnoracial identity has evolved with age, geography, and social context. I haven't visited my hometown in nearly a decade, and my social network as an adult is far less Asian American and more Latinx now than it was as a kid. In the context of the Bay Area's large Asian American population, Asian Americans tended to interpret me as white. In predominantly white professional settings, I'm interpreted as Latina. In Texas, I'm Latina. And even when I'm covered in a hat, big sunglasses, and an N95 respirator mask (which I still wear as of the publication of this book), Latinx people approach me and speak Spanish. My gender presentation is implicated in how people interpret my ethnorace: my eyebrows are permanently tattooed with pointy arches, I slick my ponytails down with Tres Flores pomade, and I love a fresh set of acrylic

[1] Shropshire, Terry. 2019. "The Rock sets the record straight about his racial identity. Rollingout." March 22. https://rollingout.com/2019/03/22/the-rock-sets-the-record-straight-about-his-racial-identity/

[2] Doreen McCallister. "America needs us": Johnson and Hanks announce presidential bid on "SNL". National Public Radio, May 21 2017. URL http://www.npr.org/sections/thetwo-way/2017/05/21/529352459/america-needs-us-johnson-and-hanks-announce-presidential-bid-on-snl.

Doing Identity Labor. Danielle Casarez Lemi, Oxford University Press. © Oxford University Press (2025).
DOI: 10.1093/9780197816851.003.0006

nails (style cues taken from my Mexichino chola sister circa 1996). When I was younger, I often used stories about my relatives to defend myself against accusations that I was white or wasn't who I said I was. I didn't have the language to articulate how even though sometimes I *looked* white and had some European ancestry, *I* wasn't white. Back then, I didn't know how to connect politics to ethnoracial identity. Today, I draw on my family history to explore how my ancestors were coerced to assimilate into white American culture, as well as the vast diversity of our communities that we often forget about when talking about mixed people. There's no one way to look or be a member of an ethnoracial group. Although we're all performing ethnoracial identity in some manner, politicians are distinct in that, unlike celebrities or other public figures, they do it to win power that has the potential to affect the lives of millions of people. That's why identity labor matters.

———

What does it mean to be a descriptive representative of American communities of color in an increasingly diverse democracy? How might politicians use their ethnoracial identities strategically when engaging with different political stakeholders? What do these changes mean for how we think about and study representation? This book shows that the answers to these questions are nuanced.

As a step toward answering those questions, I have theorized the concept of identity labor—public identity management that politicians, especially mixed politicians, perform for the press, their colleagues, and voters. The previous chapters show the contours of identity labor—its influences, nature, and public depictions of it. Politicians' early socialization shapes how they perform identity labor: mixed politicians draw on lessons learned from family members about what it means to be a member of their ethnoracial group. Throughout the book, we've encountered how parents and grandparents shaped the way that mixed politicians understand themselves. For Vice President Kamala Harris, in Chapter 2, her mother was a key figure in socializing her into African American and Indian cultures.

People's interpretations of politicians' ethnoracial appearances constrain the nature of their identity labor. In Chapter 3, some mixed legislators explained the variety of tactics they use to head off questions about their identities because of how they look. The interviews in Chapter 3 also suggested that mixed politicians challenge the current structure of ethnoracial caucuses in legislatures around the country. When a mixed politician can join two ethnoracial caucuses, their presence may raise questions about strategic coordination within the caucuses. By joining multiple ethnoracial caucuses, individual mixed representatives may wield power to support their legislation—or be the reason a caucus fractures around an issue. The presence of mixed representatives within the ethnoracial caucuses brings into stark relief that the system was built on ethnoracial binaries and may force mixed legislators to choose their ethnoracial constituents on some issues.

Chapter 4 demonstrated that from the perspective of reporters, editors, and those who determine the final runs of printed news, mixed parentage inspires newspaper coverage. Someone who doesn't "look like" a member of an ethnoracial group must explain their ethnoracial identity to the public because society draws on biological essentialism to map people to ethnoracial categories. That mixed politicians must publicly explain their ethnoracial identities creates opportunities to exploit their backgrounds or more work to win votes, like we saw in Chapter 5.

The ethnoracial hierarchy shapes how candidates can strategically use their identities in American politics. In Chapter 2, Kamala Harris's experiences as a Black person informed some of the memorable parts of her memoir: her experience with busing, her mother's involvement in the Civil Rights Movement, and her time at Howard University. Chapter 3 showed that the experiences of mixed legislators tended to parallel their non-mixed counterparts and that Black legislators, mixed and non-mixed, had similar experiences with anti-Blackness from others in their lives. Chapter 4 showed that the media rehashes stereotypical tropes about mixed people in reporters' coverage of mixed politicians. Mixed Black politicians in Chapter 4 tended to be depicted with the tragic mixed person trope, while mixed Asian American politicians tended to be portrayed in terms of diversity and the exceptional mixed person trope. In Chapter 5, although mixed candidates had a broad advantage over their non-mixed counterparts, with the exception of Black voters, white, Hispanic, and Asian American voters tended to express weaker preferences for specific mixed candidates from their own groups. The experiences of performing identity labor for mixed politicians are thus situated in a political landscape characterized by the legacy of the one-drop rule, white supremacy broadly, and anti-Blackness in particular.

These findings have three implications for legislative politics, electoral politics, and the theorizing of descriptive representation in political science. First, the ethnoracial caucuses may need to adapt to the growing presence of mixed legislators. Mixed legislators can leverage their ethnoracial group memberships into ethnoracial caucus memberships that facilitate political support for their bills. Yet, the benefit of multiple memberships may come at the cost of questions of loyalty (e.g., Fine et al. 2022). As more mixed politicians enter office and join multiple ethnoracial caucuses, it's possible that ethnoracial caucuses may adjust their rules, coordination tactics, or overall strategies to account for having members in more than one ethnoracial caucus. The experiences of mixed legislators also illuminate the ethnoracial binaries and implicitly biological definitions of ethnorace that the ethnoracial caucus system is built on. As in everyday life, identity is a multidimensional process within the legislature—you may identify any way you wish, but others may not view you as a group member, sometimes because of how you look (also see Rockquemore and Brunsma 2002; Khanna 2004). Official membership in a caucus does not soften that.

Second, mixed candidates appear to occupy a paradoxical position in electoral politics. Mixed politicians may have an electoral advantage over non-mixed candidates, as shown in Chapter 5. Still, some mixed candidates are penalized by their ethnoracial groups, who may prefer candidates with more prototypical backgrounds. While the discourse on diversity focuses on intergroup diversity, growing intragroup diversity may lead to more internal conflicts that erupt in the candidacies of mixed politicians. Group identity boundaries may harden and challenge mixed people with political ambition.

Third, political scientists must move beyond the traditional definition of descriptive representation by ethnorace. The traditional definition holds that a descriptive representative is one who shares the "outward manifestations of belonging to their group" (Mansbridge 1999, 628). Mixed representatives may be confused as members of other groups and must sometimes make their identities explicit to their own communities, who can't always tell they share group membership. Mixed politicians may also face suspicion if they campaign with multiple ethnoracial identities or advocate for their multiple ethnoracial communities through the ethnoracial caucuses. Scholars of multiracial identity have long shown that mixed people's ethnoracial classification is often highly variable (e.g., Sims 2016) and that they face pressure to "choose one" (Townsend et al. 2009). Yet, scholars of descriptive representation have not considered how ethnoracial ambiguity and institutional structures built on ethnoracial binaries complicate what it means to be a legitimate descriptive representative. For some mixed representatives, the traditional definition of descriptive representative simply does not apply.

The Role of Identity in Descriptive Representation

An updated theory of descriptive representation should distinguish between representatives who 1) have some ethnoracial appearance, and 2) affirm their identity based on connections to their community (e.g., Dovi 2002, 735), often through ancestry and kinship. In some instances, those cases may not overlap, like the representatives discussed in this book whose appearances do not align with their identities.

I want to emphasize the importance of ethnoracial *identity*—not just one's appearance–for the substantive representation of groups in democracy. Iris Marion Young (1997, 393–398) saw group identities as representative of diverse, context-dependent "perspectives"—though not necessarily shared experiences—on political life and processes in a democracy. As a result, Young argues, group identities vis-à-vis different perspectives are resources for deliberative democracy, as individuals can offer their group-informed perspective without being an individual beneficiary of a proposed solution to an issue (Young 1997, 398–404). Within a deliberative democracy, then, the value of ethnoracial identity is not derived just from shared appearances or shared experiences (Mansbridge 1999); ethnoracial identities can represent diverse perspectives to draw on in the pursuit of justice. Mixed representatives do not need to look a particular way to advocate for their group, nor do they even need to have a particular set of experiences to advocate for their group—they only need to provide their group-informed perspective.

Black feminist thought and intersectionality underscore the role of identity in politics and facilitate my understanding of the role of identity for mixed representatives. In 1977, the Combahee River Collective (CRC), a group of Black feminists, delivered *A Black Feminist Statement*, a statement that outlined the collective's political principles (Taylor 2017, 18–27). The CRC put forth the notion of "identity politics," in which "the most profound and potentially radical politics come directly out of [their] own identity, as opposed to working to end somebody else's oppression" (Taylor 2017, 18).[3] This concept offers a different, more transformative alternative to how political scientists understand descriptive representation.

Action is key in identity politics. Regarding representation and political empowerment, "'identity politics' [is] not just about who you [are]; it [is] also about what you [can] do to confront the oppression you [are] facing," including "taking up campaigns not just to ensure the liberation of other people but also to guarantee your own freedom" (Taylor 2017, 11). To Patricia Hill Collins and Sirma Bilge (2020, 170), the CRC viewed "identity as a political location."[4] In other words, identity is not just a label, but a position in a broader system of power. While Pitkin (1967, 81) focuses on what one

[3] Notably, the concept of "identity politics" as the CRC defined it does not align with how academics nor public discourse treats it (Barbara Smith in Taylor 2017, 52–53; Barbara Smith and Taylor 2017, 53–54).

[4] In making this statement, Hill Collins and Bilge cite page 15 in Linda Alcoff's 2006 book *Visible Identities: Race, Gender, and the Self.*

"is like," and Mansbridge (1999, 628) focuses on how one looks, the CRC's concept of identity politics is about how one *acts*. Indeed, the CRC explicitly viewed "any type of biological determinism a particularly dangerous and reactionary basis upon which to build a politic" (Taylor 2017, 21). Traditional theorizing of descriptive representation bundles biology with one's politics.

Solidarity and coalitions are important aspects of identity politics (Taylor 2017, 12; Demita Frazier in Taylor 2017, 104). These components are missing in traditional theorizing of descriptive representation and of the concept itself, in which a representative is depicted as uniquely situated to advocate for their own marginalized group based on membership to a single group category (Demita Frazier, Taylor 2017, 98; but see Swain 1993 and Tyson 2016).

In identity politics, individuals derive political power from their position within hierarchies of identity categories. In political science, descriptive representation based on ethnorace aligns with the idea "that unless you suffer a particular kind of oppression, that you have no role in the struggle against it" (Barbara Smith in Taylor 2017, 52–53; Barbara Smith in Taylor 2017, 53–54). This shallow understanding of the role of ethnorace and representation may explain why then-candidate Kamala Harris was so controversial–she checked many boxes for descriptive representation, but as a California prosecutor,[5] she may have directly harmed Black Californians in her position as the San Francisco District Attorney (Jackson 2020; Bose 2020). Ideas from the CRC encourage us to challenge conventional thinking about descriptive representation. The potential for change, or substantive representation, comes not from "outward manifestations of belonging to a group" or "shared experiences" (Mansbridge 1999) or even what one "is like" (Pitkin 1967), but the extent to which one leans into one's identity and all that encompasses it to consciously fight against oppression of oneself and others.

I draw on Black feminist thought and intersectionality to point us toward a more transformative direction in representational politics through my analysis of mixed representatives. Patricia Hill Collins's (2000) *Black Feminist Thought: Knowledge, Consciousness and the Politics of Empowerment*, an accounting of the contours Black feminist thought, re-orients how we treat "experience" in representation. In drawing out the relationship between Black women's experiences in the United States and Black feminist thought, Hill Collins (2000, 25) writes, "this neither means that individual

[5] Demby, Gene. 2020. Let's Talk About Kamala Harris. *NPR Code Switch*. October 14. https://www.npr.org/2020/10/13/923369723/lets-talk-about-kamala-harris

African-American women have all had the same experiences nor that we agree on the significance of our varying experiences." Additionally, Hill Collins (2000, 28) emphasizes that while there is no single "Black woman experience," the diversity of Black women's experiences may form "a Black women's collective standpoint [that] eschews essentialism in favor of democracy."

Applied to representation, Hill Collins's points about recognizing individual experiences and collective experiences have two ramifications for how we theorize descriptive representation. First, whereas Mansbridge (1999, 638) simultaneously rejected essentialism and sought to mitigate it by emphasizing the contextual necessity of descriptive representation, Hill Collins re-orients our thinking entirely by emphasizing that Black women's experiences may overlap and still be individually distinct. Recognizing that individual experiences overlap group social categories changes the conversation about descriptive representation. A mixed representative who does not "appear" to be a member of a marginalized group can hold on, to the extent they wish (Hill Collins 2000, 25), to the experiences they do have as a member of that community, even if they lack exact shared experiences with another person from their group. Their experience is one part of a whole rather than *the* experience that qualifies them to represent their group (Hill Collins 2000, 28). What matters is their perspective as a member of the group (Young 1997). Importantly, Hill Collins's (2000) treatment of experience does not define a group's experience by biological characteristics that we assign to ethnoracial categories, but by the overlap of the vast experiences within a group.

Second, whereas traditional approaches puzzle over how and whether a member of a marginalized group legislates for that group because of the assumption of some shared experience derived from appearances, Hill Collins (2000, 25) explicitly recognizes that not all members of a group "agree" about their experiences. Therefore, a new theory of descriptive representation that centers identity should acknowledge that representatives within ethnoracial groups are not monolithic—leaving room for the presence of and exploration into mixed representatives.

Intersectionality offers a lens to theorize how mixed representatives can leverage their identities toward substantive representation (Crenshaw 1991; Taylor 2017, 7). Hill Collins and Bilge (2020, 186–188) name four ways in which identity is understood from an intersectional perspective: identities as strategically essential, identity as de facto coalitions, identities and intersecting power relations, and identities as having transformative potential.

The first is *identities as strategically essential*, in which individuals may treat identity categories as uniform when political moments warrant doing so. A mixed white and Asian representative, for example, may strategically reference their individual "Asian American perspective" in a room of white colleagues discussing a bill that may negatively affect Asian Americans. The second, drawn from Kimberlé Crenshaw (1991, 1299), is *identity as de facto coalitions*, which means that identity is a resource that individuals, within their own positions of power in their own groups, can use to build solidarity across groups. A mixed legislator may find themselves able to build relationships between caucuses and exploit the positive stereotypes attached to mixed people. A mixed Black and Asian American legislator can call on their Asian American identity in meetings with the Black Caucus and their Black identity in meetings with the Asian and Pacific Islander Caucus when discussing issues relevant to either community. A mixed legislator who is white and non-white may intentionally exploit their proximity to whiteness, and perhaps their lighter skin, to attract material support for their communities from liberal white representatives. This would not be a case of a representative superficially "shape-shifting" (Saward 2014), but drawing on politicized identities that are meaningful to the representative and acting toward the empowerment of their communities.

The third is *identities and intersecting power relations*, in which the process of identity acquisition is a function of politics that shape one's everyday life and politics that shape larger systems. For example, an Asian American and Latinx legislator may arrive at a Mexipino identity as a result of local contexts that encourage marriage between Mexicans and Filipinos (Guevarra 2012). But at a structural level, their identity is partially a function of Western imperialism and the exploitation of immigrants (Omi and Winant 1994; Ocampo 2016). This political position may prove valuable for a mixed representative who can draw on similarities between Asian Americans and Latinx people on an interpersonal level as well as distill how immigration policy intersects with foreign policy.

The fourth speaks to identities as having transformative potential to effect change. Identities, when conceived of as loci of power, become tangible resources to effect meaningful change. Fernando Tormos (2017, 712) has put forth the concept of *intersectional solidarity* to describe the "process of creating ties and coalitions across social group differences by negotiating power asymmetries." Mixed identity experiences vary by one's specific ethnoracial backgrounds and socioeconomic status (e.g., Lee and Bean 2010; Davenport 2016a) and present opportunities to question the broader nonsense of ethnoracial categories and the American racial order (Spencer 1999; Daniel 2001). In a representational context, this means focusing less on a representative's appearance and more on a representative's locus of power via identity categories. Taken together, focusing on identity, rather than descriptive characteristics, offers a sharper theorization of how representatives may leverage their group membership to advocate for marginalized people.

This discussion brings me to additional ideas put forth by scholars who explicitly politicize ethnorace (Guinier and Torres 2003; Davis 2006; Washington 2020). Rather than treat ethnorace as just a mere descriptive category, Lani Guinier and Gerald Torres (2003, 12–14) draw on the experiences of Black Americans and develop the concept of *political race*, an idea that centers the injustices experienced by communities of color and encourages us to develop action steps to rectify those injustices. Myra Washington's (2020) analysis of Meghan Markle shows how celebrities may demonstrate a politicized understanding of ethnorace. According to Washington (2020, 349, 352), Markle's way of publicly navigating Blackness and whiteness is a testament to "race as a political identity," or a conception of ethnorace that is decoupled from visible characteristics. Reconceptualizing ethnoracial identity as a political identity allows us to go beyond ethnorace as superficial labeling or association with biological characteristics.

A Proposal: Identity Representatives

Based on this discussion, I propose a type of representative that encompasses representatives whose shared identities with marginalized groups drive their relationships and their political commitments: *identity representatives.* I define identity representatives as those who share kinship, ancestry, and/or identities with constituents, and who leverage those identities to act for those communities and in solidarity with marginalized people against oppression from dominant groups. Sharing racialized biological characteristics that aid in ethnoracial ascription is not a requirement to be an identity representative. One may be both a descriptive representative and an identity representative. Yet, as this book shows, this is not always the case. While descriptive representatives and identity representatives may overlap in some instances, distinguishing between the two requires asking legislators how they identify (Hardy-Fanta et al. 2013; Lemi 2018), perhaps even tracing their life histories to understand the "weight" of their identities in their work (e.g., Brown 2014a), assessing the extent to which they *act* in solidarity with marginalized groups (also see Dovi 2002), and counting them accordingly. This conceptualization of representatives does not require that a representative look a certain way or have a certain experience. This definition emphasizes their political understanding of their identity and their motivation for substantive representation and solidarity with marginalized groups. This conceptualization is thus inclusive of some of the mixed representatives studied here that traditional descriptive representation theory would ignore.

Future Research

This book offers a number of new directions political scientists should explore regarding mixed politicians and identity labor. First, as Chapter 3 showed especially, people's reactions to mixed politicians depend partially on mixed politicians' ethnoracial appearances. Chapter 5 focused on the effect of mixed classification, and it is possible that by varying ethnorace, participants made inferences about the candidates' appearances or attractiveness (Terkildsen 1993; Lerman et al. 2015; Ahuja et al. 2016; Pauker et al. 2018; Abrajano et al. 2018). The mere perception of incongruence between how someone is classified and how they look could prompt the need to perform identity labor (see Sims 2025). Mixed candidates who "look" like they aren't mixed may not need to perform identity labor as much as mixed candidates whose appearances "look mixed" (Sims 2025). Future research should consider how a candidate's ethnoracial identity and appearance influence voter evaluations.

Second, future research should systematically explore how different manifestations of identity labor affect political outcomes in different contexts. This research raises a number of questions about how candidates may perform identity labor at different levels of office, for different kinds of electorates, and at different points in the campaign cycle. Exploring identity labor from the campaign's perspective may be fruitful, given that I spoke to legislators in this book on "state time," or in their capacity as elected officials, not as candidates.

Third, future research should examine how ethnorace, in combination with other identities, like gender, sexuality, class, and disability, shapes how mixed politicians perform identity labor within the context of broader systems of oppression. For instance, US Senator Tammy Duckworth, who is white and Asian American, is a disabled woman veteran. How does her status as a disabled woman veteran inform how she performs ethnorace? This book also raises questions for future work on whether various campaign strategies are available to mixed candidates. Society often treats mixed people as the epitome of "post-racial" America (e.g., Thornton 2009, 112–113). Are mixed politicians more successful at using "post-racial" language in their campaigns (e.g., Wamble and Laird 2020)? Do mixed women face specific constraints in appealing to their ethnoracial and gender constituents (e.g., Holman et al. 2016)?

Fourth, with the exception of Chapter 5, the story of this book was primarily told by my interpretation of an elite perspective—the voices of elected officials themselves. I invite political scientists to conduct in-depth qualitative research with voters, perhaps by holding focus groups around the country, to more deeply interrogate the mechanisms that underlie voter evaluations of mixed candidates. I had hoped to be able to do that for this book!

The Future of Representation in American Politics

What should we make of the findings in this book for the future of representation in American politics? Scholars have explored the potential for the mixed population to change ethnoracial discourse in the United States (Daniel 2001, 175; Hochschild et al. 2012, 11). Political scientists reading this should not ask whether mixed representatives will represent mixed people's supposed distinct political interests in the future. That is the wrong question to ask. Instead, political scientists should consider how the presence of mixed politicians reveals the faulty logic we've relied on in the study of descriptive representation. Analyzing the experiences of mixed representatives shows the limitations of current theory when we observe that mixed representatives can slip in and out of their descriptive representative status depending on the context. Society might allow a mixed representative that people interpret as white, or non-white and non-Black, to shift between whiteness and other categories. Society might not let a mixed descriptive representative that people interpret as Black do the same. Some mixed people can strategically turn their racialization on and off, and others cannot. The ability to shift one's racialization has ramifications for how we count descriptive representatives.

Although some mixed politicians might use terms like "biracial" to describe themselves, the politicians considered here perform identity labor within the constraints of traditional ethnoracial categories and group interests. As politicians, their experiences with the media, voters, other politicians, and their politics are intertwined with larger political structures and ethnoracial binaries undergirded by white supremacy. It is currently unclear what a "mixed-race agenda" would be to create a mixed ethnoracial caucus around (see Lee 2008; Hochschild and Weaver 2010, 750–752). However, mixed representatives, especially those who have dual non-white backgrounds, might be interlocutors between different ethnoracial caucuses. Mixed white legislators may not necessarily abandon their non-white counterparts. Yet as in broader society, diversifying state legislatures might grapple with heightened ethnoracial lines as more mixed representatives become legislators (Lee and Bean 2010). Whether Americans will use the growing number of these politicians as an opportunity to question the nonsense of ethnoracial classification or simply celebrate the diverse fabric of American life while ignoring pervasive racism in the United States is a longer-term question.

The prevalence of the genetic testing industry also raises normative and practical questions about the role of identity and descriptive representation in American democracy (see Roth et al. 2018). Genetic testing might open the door for representatives to "prove" their ethnorace and for others to "become" identity representatives of communities to which they have no significant ties. With these tests, some politicians may attempt to legitimately claim group membership to different ethnoracial groups, even for nefarious reasons. What is the difference between a mixed representative's claims to group membership based on parentage or grandparentage, and a person who claims to be a group member based on ancestry from generations ago? Does appearance matter here? Who decides?

The media often uses the mixed population to mark the supposed progress of ethnoracial relations in the United States (e.g., Squires 2007; Thornton 2009). As we become more mixed, ethnorace will cease to be relevant, so the familiar story goes. Scholars of mixed identity have arrived at similar conclusions: increased mixed identity may indicate growing inequalities in ethnoracial status *despite* increased diversity (Lee and Bean 2010; Davenport 2016a, 64). As the growing, post-Civil Rights Movement, post-Multiracial Category Movement, and post-Obama mixed population comes of age and runs for elected office, mixed candidates may encounter challenges to using their backgrounds strategically to secure their ethnoracial constituencies. Those challenges may intersect with how various stakeholders interpret their appearance. Ultimately, overcoming those challenges hinges on our collective ability to move beyond representation at face value alone.

Appendix

Chapter 2

The analyses in this chapter use qualitative and quantitative text analysis. These analyses are generally informed by previous text analyses of news coverage of the 2000 Census (Squires 2007; Thornton 2009) and the news coverage analysis in Chapter 4.

First, I explore how Harris contextualizes her ethnoracial identity in her memoir, *The Truths We Hold: An American Journey*. This analysis comes from a larger analysis I conducted with my coauthors, Sarah Virginia Hayes and Maricruz Ariana Osorio. We used discourse analysis (Hardy et al. 2004). We theorized Harris's political ideology within the context of broader developments in elite Black politics and her status as a mixed person (Lemi et al. 2023). We each read the memoir and inductively identified themes from the text as they emerged and then discussed our coding for agreement (Thomas 2006). Our analysis was interpretive, and we did not establish quantitative inter-coder reliability (Hardy et al. 2004, also see O'Connor and Joffe 2020).

Second, I analyzed how Harris has performed identity labor over time on her website by studying 132 archived versions of Harris's website biography from 2003 to 2009. I collected these archived versions in 2021 from WayBackMachine.com using the WayBackMachine Downloader (Khaleghy et al. 2015–2016). After dropping archived biography pages that no longer connected to a web archive and dropping non-biography snapshots that were pulled in the initial data collection, 132 archived biographies, including duplicates, remained.

Third, I conducted a qualitative analysis of news coverage of Harris over time, drawing from Nexis and Ethnic NewsWatch. Nexis is a database that holds archives of news media, such as newspapers. Similarly, Ethnic NewsWatch is a database that holds archives of news media specifically meant for ethnic group audiences. Rather than limit the analysis to a few newspapers, I downloaded articles from news sources returned by both Nexis and Ethnic NewsWatch to gather a holistic view of how reporters have portrayed Harris over time.

For articles downloaded from Nexis, I searched for news articles published from January 1, 2002, through December 31, 2019. In 2020, I downloaded the first 1000 news articles from Nexis that mentioned "Kamala Harris." Due to restrictions on downloading permissions, I could not download the entire set of articles that Nexis returned beyond 1000. Notably, a striking number of college or university newspapers were returned, especially from the period corresponding to the 2020 Democratic primary. I manually removed articles with duplicated headlines that made it past Nexis's group duplicates feature. This collection of articles is not meant to be "representative" of all coverage of Harris.

For articles from Ethnic NewsWatch, I searched for news articles specifically tagged as serving African American/Caribbean/African and Asian/Pacific Islander audiences. I searched for English language articles that mentioned "Kamala Harris," "Kamala D. Harris," or "Kamala Devi Harris" that corresponded to her periods of elected office, including campaign periods before entering office: San Francisco Attorney General (January 1, 2002, to December 31, 2010), California Attorney General (January 1, 2011, to December 31, 2016), California US Senator (January 1, 2017, to December 31, 2018), and her run as a Democratic candidate for President (January 1, 2019, to December 31, 2019). Due to the lack of an interpreter, these articles are necessarily limited to English. Table 2A.1 reports the sources and counts of articles from Nexis and Ethnic NewsWatch.

Table 2A.1 News articles that mention Kamala Harris

San Francisco Attorney General (up to 2010)					
Nexis (N = 58)		Ethnic NewsWatch, Asian/Pacific Islander (N = 138)		Ethnic NewsWatch, African American/ Caribbean/African (N = 174)	
American Banker	1	Asianweek	37	Caribbean Today	1
Christian Science Monitor	1	Filipino Reporter	4	Chicago Citizen	1
Daily Breeze	1	India—West	52	Hyde Park Citizen	2
Daily Breeze (Torrance, California)	1	India Abroad	32	Jackson Advocate	1
Daily Bruin: University of California—Los Angeles	1	News India—Times	12	Los Angeles Sentinel	34
KTLA-TV, Los Angeles	4	Northwest Asian Weekly	1	Michigan Chronicle	3
Monterey County Herald	1			New York Beacon	4
Palo Alto Daily News	4			Oakland Post	7
Sacramento Bee	3			Philadelphia Tribune	4
San Gabriel Valley Tribune	1			Precinct Reporter	4
San Mateo County Times	2			Sacramento Observer	25
Santa Cruz Sentinel	6			Sun Reporter	83
Small Business column	5			Take Pride! Community Magazine	1
The Bakersfield Californian	2			The Jacksonville Free Press	1
The Daily Titan: California State University—Fullerton	1			The Tennessee Tribune	1
The Forward Association	1			Westside Gazette	2
The Fresno Bee	1				
The Guardsman via U-Wire	1				
The Oakland Tribune	10				
The Press Democrat, Santa Rosa, Calif.	1				
The Record	2				
The Stanford Daily via U-Wire	1				
The Stanford Daily: Stanford University	2				
The Willits News	1				
Tri-Valley Herald (Pleasanton, California)	1				

San Francisco Attorney General (up to 2010)					
Nexis (*N* = 58)		Ethnic NewsWatch, Asian/Pacific Islander (*N* = 138)		Ethnic NewsWatch, African American/ Caribbean/African (*N* = 174)	
USA TODAY	2				
Wilkes Barre Times	1				

California Attorney General (2011–2016)					
Nexis (*N* = 526)		Ethnic NewsWatch, Asian/Pacific Islander (*N* = 137)		Ethnic NewsWatch, African American/ Caribbean/African (*N* = 389)	
Advertising Age	1	Eastern Eye	1	Afro—American	2
American Banker	26	India—West	76	Afro—American Red Star	5
American Medical News	1	India Abroad	29	Call & Post	3
Appeal-Democrat	19	News India—Times	30	Caribbean Today	1
bondbuyer.com	3	The Filipino Express	1	Chicago Citizen	2
Burbank Leader	1			Columbus Times	2
Business Insurance	1			Hyde Park Citizen	2
Caribbean News Now	1			India—West	1
Chester Progressive	1			Jackson Advocate	1
Collegian: Delta College	2			Los Angeles Sentinel	131
Corning Observer	2			Miami Times	2
Daily 49er: California State University—Long Beach	3			Michigan Chronicle	1
Daily Bruin: University of California—Los Angeles	14			Mississippi Link	1
Daily Californian: University of California—Berkeley	14			New Pittsburgh Courier	1
Daily Illini: University of Illinois at Urbana—Champaign	1			New York Amsterdam News	1
Daily Pilot	5			New York Beacon	3
Daily Press	14			Oakland Post	76
Daily Trojan: University of Southern California	3			Philadelphia Tribune	7
Emergency Management	1			Precinct Reporter	14
Feather River Bulletin	1			Sacramento Observer	49
Glendale News-Press	6			South Florida Times	2

continued

Table 2A.1 *continued*

California Attorney General (2011–2016)					
Nexis (*N* = 526)		Ethnic NewsWatch, Asian/Pacific Islander (*N* = 137)		Ethnic NewsWatch, African American/ Caribbean/African (*N* = 389)	
Government Technology	1			Sun Reporter	57
Harvard Political Review: Harvard University	1			The Charlotte Post	1
Independent Coast Observer	3			The Indianapolis Recorder	1
Indiana Daily Student: Indiana University	1			The Jacksonville Free Press	4
KSWB-TV	2			The Louisiana Weekly	6
KTLA-TV	2			The Tennessee Tribune	3
KTXL-TV	9			Tri—State Defender	1
La Canada Valley Sun	1			Washington Informer	4
Laguna Beach Coastline Pilot	2			Westside Gazette	5
Lassen County Times	3				
Lodi News	7				
Miami Student: Miami University	1				
Mustang Daily: California State Polytechnic University-Pomona	1				
New York Times	1				
North County Times	5				
Palo Alto Daily News	6				
Pasadena Sun (California)	1				
Pioneer Press	1				
Portola Reporter	2				
The Porterville Recorder (California)	2				
Santa Cruz Sentinel	15				
Sierra Star	1				
Small Business column	6				
Spartan Daily: San Jose State University	1				
Stateline	3				
Suffolk Voice: Suffolk University	1				

California Attorney General (2011–2016)			
Nexis (*N* = 526)		Ethnic NewsWatch, Asian/Pacific Islander (*N* = 137)	Ethnic NewsWatch, African American/Caribbean/African (*N* = 389)
The Bakersfield Californian	19		
The Bond Buyer	2		
The Brown Daily Herald: Brown University	1		
The California Aggie: University of California—Davis	4		
The Campanil: Mills College	1		
The Christian Science Monitor	12		
The Chronicle of Higher Education	1		
The Columbia Chronicle	4		
The Columbia Chronicle: Columbia College	3		
The Daily Aztec: San Diego State University	1		
The Daily Cardinal: University of Wisconsin—Madison	5		
The Daily Egyptian: Southern Illinois University	1		
The Daily Kent Stater: Kent State University	1		
The Daily Texan: University of Texas—Austin	2		
The Daily Titan: California State University—Fullerton	2		
The Daily Universe: Brigham Young University	1		
The Daily Vidette: Illinois State University	1		
The Depaulia: DePaul University	1		
The Dispatch	10		

continued

Table 2A.1 *continued*

California Attorney General (2011–2016)			
Nexis (N = 526)		Ethnic NewsWatch, Asian/Pacific Islander (N = 137)	Ethnic NewsWatch, African American/ Caribbean/African (N = 389)
The District Chronicles: Howard University	6		
The Foghorn: University of San Francisco	5		
The Free Lance-Star	2		
The Guardian: University of California—San Diego	4		
The Guardsman: City College of San Francisco	2		
The Hays Daily News	1		
The Highlander: University of California—Riverside	1		
The Iowa State Daily: Iowa State University	1		
The Johns Hopkins News-Letter: Johns Hopkins University	1		
The Lion's Pride: Saint Leo University	2		
The Northern Star: Northern Illinois University	15		
The Oakland Tribune	71		
The Observer: Case Western Reserve University	1		
The Orion: California State University—Chico	3		
The Pacifican: University of the Pacific	2		
The Panther: Chapman University	1		
The Press Democrat	52		
The Racquet: University of Wisconsin—LaCrosse	1		
The Record	39		
The Reporter	3		

California Attorney General (2011–2016)					
Nexis (*N* = 526)		Ethnic NewsWatch, Asian/Pacific Islander (*N* = 137)		Ethnic NewsWatch, African American/ Caribbean/African (*N* = 389)	
The Santa Fe New Mexican	1				
The Signal: California State University—Stanislaus	1				
The Stanford Daily: Stanford University	6				
The State Hornet: California State University—Sacramento	2				
The State Press: Arizona State University	1				
The Times-Herald	5				
The Union: El Camino College	1				
Times-Herald	1				
Tri-Valley Herald	1				
Tribune Regional News	1				
University Times: California State University—Los Angeles	2				
USA TODAY	19				
York Daily Record	1				

California US Senator (2017–2018)					
Nexis (*N* = 352)		Ethnic NewsWatch, Asian/Pacific Islander (*N* = 122)		Ethnic NewsWatch, African American/ Caribbean/African (*N* = 255)	
American Banker	5	Eastern Eye	2	Afro—American	3
Appeal-Democrat	3	India—West	69	Afro—American Red Star	18
Badger Herald: University of Wisconsin—Madison	1	India Abroad	18	Call & Post	2
CE Noticias Financieras English	40	News India—Times	30	Caribbean Today	2
Calvin College Chimes: Calvin College	1	Northwest Asian Weekly	1	Chicago Citizen	1

continued

Table 2A.1 *continued*

California US Senator (2017–2018)					
Nexis (*N* = 352)		Ethnic NewsWatch, Asian/Pacific Islander (*N* = 122)		Ethnic NewsWatch, African American/ Caribbean/African (*N* = 255)	
College Heights Herald: Western Kentucky University	2	The Filipino Express	2	Chicago Defender	1
College Media Network: Media network college	7			Chicago Weekend	1
Connect2Mason: George Mason University	1			Hyde Park Citizen	1
Daily Bruin: University of California—Los Angeles	9			Los Angeles Sentinel	41
Daily Californian: University of California—Berkeley	25			Miami Times	2
Daily Collegian: Pennsylvania State University	1			Michigan Chronicle	1
Daily Inter Lake, Kalispell, Mont.	1			Mississippi Link	9
Daily Mississippian: University of Mississippi	1			New York Amsterdam News	6
Daily Targum: Rutgers University	1			New York Beacon	2
Daily Trojan: University of Southern California	4			Oakland Post	9
Education Week	1			Philadelphia Tribune	27
Emory Wheel: Emory University	1			Precinct Reporter	9
Golden Gate Xpress Golden Gate Xpress: San Francisco State University	2			Sacramento Observer	14
High Point Enterprise (North Carolina)	1			South Florida Times	2
Hilltop: Howard University	1			Sun Reporter	24
Idaho Argonaut: University of Idaho	1			The Boston Banner	1
Independent Record (Helena, Montana)	1			The Charlotte Post	9
Indiana Daily Student: Indiana University	3			The Indianapolis Recorder	3

California US Senator (2017–2018)					
Nexis (N = 352)		Ethnic NewsWatch, Asian/Pacific Islander (N = 122)		Ethnic NewsWatch, African American/ Caribbean/African (N = 255)	
InsideSources.com	19			The Jacksonville Free Press	16
Loquitur: Cabrini College	1			The Louisiana Weekly	12
Metro Vartha	6			The Skanner	4
Michigan Daily: University of Michigan-Ann Arbor	2			The Tennessee Tribune	1
Minnesota Daily: University of Minnesota	1			Tri—State Defender	1
Nation State Times: SUNY College at Oneonta	1			Washington Informer	27
Northeast Mississippi Daily Journal (Tupelo)	1			Westside Gazette	6
Northwestern Missourian: Northwest Missouri State University	1				
Norwalk Reflector, Ohio	1				
Old Gold and Black: Wake Forest University	1				
Palo Alto Daily News (California)	1				
Philly.com	5				
Richland Chronicle: Richland College	1				
Santa Cruz Sentinel	1				
Stillman Advance: Stillman College	13				
The Acorn: Drew University	8				
The Anniston Star (Alabama)	2				
The Bakersfield Californian	6				
The Bates Student: Bates College	3				
The Bi-College News: Haverford College/Bryn Mawr College	1				
The Blade (Toledo, Ohio)	3				

continued

Table 2A.1 *continued*

California US Senator (2017–2018)			
Nexis ($N = 352$)		Ethnic NewsWatch, Asian/Pacific Islander ($N = 122$)	Ethnic NewsWatch, African American/ Caribbean/African ($N = 255$)
The Bond Buyer	2		
The Bottom Line: Frostburg State University	1		
The Breeze: James Madison University	3		
The California Aggie: University of California, Davis	4		
The Campanil: Mills College	1		
The Christian Science Monitor	2		
The Chronicle of Higher Education	2		
The Chronicle: College of Lake County	1		
The Chronicle: Hofstra University	1		
The Collegian: University of Richmond	1		
The Collegian: University of Tulsa	1		
The Columbian: Columbia College	1		
The Creightonian: Creighton University—The Creightonian	1		
The Daily Campus: University of Connecticut	2		
The Daily Cardinal: University of Wisconsin—Madison	1		
The Daily Free Press: Boston University	1		
The Daily Iowan: University of Iowa	6		
The Daily Item (Sunbury, Pennsylvania)	1		

California US Senator (2017–2018)			
Nexis (*N* = 352)		Ethnic NewsWatch, Asian/Pacific Islander (*N* = 122)	Ethnic NewsWatch, African American/ Caribbean/African (*N* = 255)
The Daily Kent Stater: Kent State University	3		
The Daily Titan: California State University—Fullerton	2		
The Daily Universe: Brigham Young University	1		
The Daily Vidette: Illinois State University	2		
The Daily Vidette: Illinois State University September	1		
The Daily World (Aberdeen, Washington)	1		
The Day (New London, Connecticut)	1		
The Fayetteville Observer (Fayetteville, North Carolina)	1		
The Foghorn: University of San Francisco	1		
The Gateway: University of Nebraska at Omaha	3		
The Good 5 Cent Cigar: University of Rhode Island	2		
The Hatchet: George Washington University	3		
The Hawk: Saint Joseph's University	1		
The Highlander: University of California—Riverside	1		
The Hoya: Georgetown University	1		
The Hoya: Georgetown University January	1		
The Ironton Tribune	1		
The Ironton Tribune, Ohio	1		

continued

Table 2A.1 *continued*

California US Senator (2017–2018)			
Nexis ($N = 352$)		Ethnic NewsWatch, Asian/Pacific Islander ($N = 122$)	Ethnic NewsWatch, African American/ Caribbean/African ($N = 255$)
The Joplin Globe (Missouri)	1		
The Journal: University of Illinois—Springfield	1		
The Justice: Brandeis University	2		
The Lariat: Baylor University	1		
The Lion's Pride: Saint Leo University	3		
The Marquette Tribune: Marquette University	1		
The Meridian Star (Mississippi)	1		
The Miscellany News: Vassar College	1		
The Monitor (McAllen, Texas)	1		
The Montana Standard (Butte)	1		
The News-Sentinel (Fort Wayne, Indiana)	1		
The Northern Iowan: University of Northern Iowa	2		
The Northern Star: Northern Illinois University	3		
The Oakland Post: Oakland University	4		
The Oberlin Review: Oberlin College	1		
The Observer: Case Western Reserve University	1		
The Observer: University of Notre Dame	2		
The Pan American: University of Texas—Pan American	1		

California US Senator (2017–2018)			
Nexis (*N* = 352)		**Ethnic NewsWatch, Asian/Pacific Islander (*N* = 122)**	**Ethnic NewsWatch, African American/ Caribbean/African (*N* = 255)**
The Panther: Chapman University	1		
The Pitt News: University of Pittsburgh—Pittsburgh Campus	1		
The Poly Post: California State Polytechnic University—Pomona	1		
The Post: Ohio University	1		
The Press Democrat	21		
The Rotunda: Longwood College	1		
The Salem State Log: Salem State College	1		
The Santa Clara: Santa Clara University	1		
The Scroll: Brigham Young University-Idaho	1		
The Shorthorn: University of Texas—Arlington	1		
The Stanford Daily: Stanford University	4		
The State Hornet: California State University—Sacramento	1		
The Student Printz: University of Southern Mississippi	1		
The Stute: Stevens Institute of Technology	1		
The Tartan: Carnegie Mellon University	1		
The Ticker: Baruch College	1		
The Times Leader (Wilkes-Barre, Pennsylvania)	1		

continued

Table 2A.1 *continued*

California US Senator (2017–2018)					
Nexis ($N = 352$)		Ethnic NewsWatch, Asian/Pacific Islander ($N = 122$)		Ethnic NewsWatch, African American/ Caribbean/African ($N = 255$)	
The Times-Tribune (Scranton, Pennsylvania)	2				
The Tower: Catholic University of America	3				
The Towerlight: Towson University	1				
The Tufts Daily Tufts Daily: Tufts University	1				
The University News: Saint Louis University	1				
The University Star: Texas State University—San Marcos	1				
The Valley Vanguard: Saginaw Valley State University	1				
The Viking News: Westchester Community College	1				
The Wesleyan Argus: Wesleyan University	2				
USA TODAY	16				
University Times: California State University—Los Angeles	1				
Victoria Advocate (Texas)	1				
Washington Square News: New York University	1				
Waterloo Courier (Iowa)	2				

US Democratic Primary (2019)					
Nexis ($N = 961$)		Ethnic NewsWatch, Asian/Pacific Islander ($N = 1$)		Ethnic NewsWatch, African American/ Caribbean/African ($N = 104$)	
Advocate: University of Colorado Denver	1	Eastern Eye	1	Afro—American Red Star	4
Aiken Standard (South Carolina)	1			Call & Post	10

US Democratic Primary (2019)				
Nexis (N = 961)		Ethnic NewsWatch, Asian/Pacific Islander (N = 1)	Ethnic NewsWatch, African American/Caribbean/African (N = 104)	
Albert Lea Tribune (Minnesota)	1		Caribbean Today	1
American Banker	3		Chicago Defender	1
Arkansas Traveler: University of Arkansas	1		Los Angeles Sentinel	1
Badger Herald: University of Wisconsin—Madison	2		Miami Times	4
Burbank Leader (Glendale, California)	2		Michigan Chronicle	3
CE Noticias Financieras English	139		New Pittsburgh Courier	2
Campus Times: University of Rochester	2		New York Amsterdam News	11
Cardinal Points: SUNY College at Plattsburgh	1		Oakland Post	6
Caribbean News Now, Grand Cayman, Cayman Islands	1		Philadelphia Tribune	16
Cavalier Daily: University of Virginia	1		Sacramento Observer	9
Cedar Falls Waterloo Courier (Iowa)	1		Sun Reporter	7
Chicago Maroon: University of Chicago	2		The Charlotte Post	6
Claflin Panther: Claflin University	1		The Jacksonville Free Press	5
Cleburne Times-Review (Texas)	1		The Louisiana Weekly	7
Clinton Herald (Iowa)	1		The Tennessee Tribune	6
College Heights Herald: Western Kentucky University	6		Washington Informer	5
College Media Network: Media network college	5			
Collegian: Delta College	1			
Colorado Daily: University of Colorado at Boulder	1			

continued

Table 2A.1 *continued*

US Democratic Primary (2019)			
Nexis (N = 961)		Ethnic NewsWatch, Asian/Pacific Islander (N = 1)	Ethnic NewsWatch, African American/Caribbean/African (N = 104)
Columbia Daily Tribune (Missouri)	1		
Commonwealth Journal (Somerset, Kentucky)	1		
Commonwealth Times: Virginia Commonwealth University	4		
Connect2Mason: George Mason University	3		
Connecticut Post (Bridgeport)	4		
Cornell Daily Sun: Cornell University	1		
Cumberland Times-News (Maryland)	1		
Daily 49er: California State University—Long Beach	1		
Daily Bruin: University of California—Los Angeles	2		
Daily Californian: University of California—Berkeley	18		
Daily Collegian: Pennsylvania State University	11		
Daily Collegian: University of Massachusetts—Amherst	2		
Daily Eastern News: Eastern Illinois University	2		
Daily Gamecock: University of South Carolina—Columbia	1		
Daily Princetonian: Princeton University	2		
Daily Targum: Rutgers University	1		
Daily Trojan: University of Southern California	6		

US Democratic Primary (2019)			
Nexis (*N* = 961)		Ethnic NewsWatch, Asian/Pacific Islander (*N* = 1)	Ethnic NewsWatch, African American/ Caribbean/African (*N* = 104)
Dominican Star: Dominican University	1		
Driftwood: University of New Orleans	1		
East Carolinian: East Carolina University	1		
Education Week	5		
Emory Wheel: Emory University	2		
Enid News & Eagle (Oklahoma)	1		
Flat Hat: College of William and Mary	2		
Golden Gate Xpress: San Francisco State University	1		
Government Technology	3		
Grand Forks Herald (North Dakota)	1		
Harvard Political Review: Harvard University	1		
High Point Enterprise (North Carolina)	1		
Hilltop News: St. Edward's University	1		
Hilltop: Howard University	4		
Idaho Argonaut: University of Idaho	3		
Indiana Daily Student: Indiana University	4		
Inside Vandy: Vanderbilt University	1		
InsideSources.com	70		
Investor's Business Daily	2		
Knight News: Queens College	2		
Lubbock Avalanche-Journal (Texas)	2		

continued

Table 2A.1 *continued*

US Democratic Primary (2019)			
Nexis (*N* = 961)		Ethnic NewsWatch, Asian/Pacific Islander (*N* = 1)	Ethnic NewsWatch, African American/ Caribbean/African (*N* = 104)
Massachusetts Daily Collegian: University of Massachusetts—Amherst	1		
Metro Vartha	2		
Miami Student: Miami University	1		
Michigan Daily: University of Michigan-Ann Arbor	17		
Minnesota Daily: University of Minnesota	1		
Newton Daily News, Iowa	1		
Northeast Mississippi Daily Journal (Tupelo)	2		
Oklahoma Daily: University of Oklahoma Norman Campus	1		
Old Gold and Black: Wake Forest University	2		
Pacific Index: Pacific University	3		
Philly.com	47		
Post-Bulletin (Rochester, Minnesota)	1		
Princetonian: Princeton University	1		
Reflector: Mississippi State University	1		
Richland Chronicle: Richland College	1		
Rocky Mountain Collegian: Colorado State University	1		
San Francisco Daily Californian: University of California—Berkeley	1		
Six Mile Post: Georgia Highlands College	1		

US Democratic Primary (2019)			
Nexis (*N* = 961)		Ethnic NewsWatch, Asian/Pacific Islander (*N* = 1)	Ethnic NewsWatch, African American/ Caribbean/African (*N* = 104)
Sonoma State Star: Sonoma State University	1		
Southern Digest: Southern University-Baton Rouge	2		
Spartan Daily: San Jose State University	2		
St. Joseph News-Press (Missouri)	2		
State Times: SUNY College at Oneonta	2		
Statesman: University of Minnesota-Duluth	1		
Stillman Advance: Stillman College	58		
Stillwater NewsPress (Oklahoma)	1		
Tahlequah Daily Press (Oklahoma)	1		
The Acorn: Drew University	6		
The Albany Student Press: SUNY at Albany	2		
The Anniston Star (Alabama)	1		
The Athenaeum: Acadia University	2		
The Augsburg Echo: Augsburg College	1		
The BG News: Bowling Green State University	1		
The Bates Student: Bates College	1		
The Beacon: Wilkes University	2		
The Blade (Toledo, Ohio)	5		
The Bottom Line: Frostburg State University	4		

continued

Table 2A.1 *continued*

US Democratic Primary (2019)			
Nexis (N = 961)		Ethnic NewsWatch, Asian/Pacific Islander (N = 1)	Ethnic NewsWatch, African American/ Caribbean/African (N = 104)
The Bradley Scout: Bradley University	2		
The Branding Iron: University of Wyoming	1		
The Breeze: James Madison University	6		
The Brown Daily Herald: Brown University	1		
The Brunswick News (Georgia)	1		
The Bullet: Mary Washington	2		
The Butler Collegian: Butler University	1		
The California Aggie: University of California, Davis	1		
The Campanil: Mills College	1		
The Campus: Allegheny College	1		
The Campus: City College of New York	3		
The Capital (Annapolis, Maryland)	1		
The Catalyst: Colorado College	3		
The Christian Science Monitor	18		
The Chronicle of Higher Education	2		
The Citizens' Voice (Wilkes-Barre, Pennsylvania)	2		
The Clause: Azusa Pacific University	3		
The College Voice: Connecticut College	1		
The Collegian: University of Tulsa	4		

US Democratic Primary (2019)			
Nexis (*N* = 961)		Ethnic NewsWatch, Asian/Pacific Islander (*N* = 1)	Ethnic NewsWatch, African American/ Caribbean/African (*N* = 104)
The Columbian: Columbia College	9		
The Concordian: Concord College February	1		
The Current: Nova Southeastern University	2		
The Current: University of Missouri—St. Louis	2		
The Daily Campus: University of Connecticut	9		
The Daily Cardinal: University of Wisconsin—Madison	1		
The Daily Cardinal: University of Wisconsin—Madison January	1		
The Daily Cougar: University of Houston	4		
The Daily Egyptian: Southern Illinois University, Carbondale	1		
The Daily Free Press: Boston University	1		
The Daily Gamecock: University of South Carolina—Columbia	5		
The Daily Iowan: University of Iowa	49		
The Daily Kent Stater: Kent State University	4		
The Daily Texan: University of Texas—Austin	1		
The Daily Universe: Brigham Young University	3		
The Daily Utah Chronicle: University of Utah	1		

continued

Table 2A.1 *continued*

US Democratic Primary (2019)			
Nexis (N = 961)		Ethnic NewsWatch, Asian/Pacific Islander (N = 1)	Ethnic NewsWatch, African American/ Caribbean/African (N = 104)
The Daily Vidette: Illinois State University	5		
The Dartmouth: Dartmouth College	4		
The Decatur Daily (Alabama)	1		
The Depaulia: DePaul University	1		
The Derry News (New Hampshire)	2		
The Duke Chronicle: Duke University	6		
The Famuan: Florida Agricultural and Mechanical University	4		
The Forward Association	1		
The Free Press (Mankato, Minnesota)	1		
The Gateway: University of Nebraska at Omaha	1		
The Georgetown Voice: Georgetown University	1		
The Griffen: Canisius College	1		
The Guardian: University of California—San Diego	1		
The Guardsman: City College of San Francisco	2		
The Gulfordian: Guilford College	2		
The Harvard Crimson: Harvard University	1		
The Hatchet: George Washington University	2		
The Highlander: University of California—Riverside	4		
The Hillsdale Collegian: Hillsdale College	4		

US Democratic Primary (2019)			
Nexis ($N = 961$)		Ethnic NewsWatch, Asian/Pacific Islander ($N = 1$)	Ethnic NewsWatch, African American/ Caribbean/African ($N = 104$)
The ISU Bengal: Idaho State University	1		
The Ionian: Iona College	1		
The Ironton Tribune, Ohio	1		
The Johns Hopkins News-Letter: Johns Hopkins University	2		
The Justice: Brandeis University	2		
The Keene Sentinel (New Hampshire)	14		
The Kentucky Kernel: University of Kentucky	3		
The Lanthorn: Grand Valley State University	1		
The Lariat: Baylor University	3		
The Leader: SUNY at Fredonia	1		
The Main Campus: University of Maine	2		
The Marquette Tribune: Marquette University	2		
The Mass Media: University of Massachusetts—Boston	2		
The Mesa Press: San Diego Mesa College	1		
The Michigan Journal: University of Michigan—Dearborn	1		
The Mirror: Fairfield University	2		
The Miscellany News: Vassar College	3		
The Nevada Sagebrush: University of Nevada—Reno	2		

continued

Table 2A.1 *continued*

US Democratic Primary (2019)			
Nexis ($N = 961$)		Ethnic NewsWatch, Asian/Pacific Islander ($N = 1$)	Ethnic NewsWatch, African American/ Caribbean/African ($N = 104$)
The New Hampshire: University of New Hampshire	1		
The Northern Iowan: University of Northern Iowa	2		
The Northern Star: Northern Illinois University	14		
The Nubian Message: North Carolina State University	2		
The Oberlin Review: Oberlin College	2		
The Observer: Case Western Reserve University	3		
The Observer: University of Notre Dame	3		
The Oracle: Oral Roberts University	2		
The Oracle: University of South Florida	1		
The Pace Press: Pace University	1		
The Pacifican: University of the Pacific	1		
The Pitt News: University of Pittsburgh—Pittsburgh Campus	8		
The Point News: St. Mary's College of Maryland	2		
The Post: Ohio University	3		
The Press Democrat	3		
The Prodigy: University of California—Merced	1		
The Quad: West Chester University	3		

US Democratic Primary (2019)			
Nexis (N = 961)		Ethnic NewsWatch, Asian/Pacific Islander (N = 1)	Ethnic NewsWatch, African American/ Caribbean/African (N = 104)
The Record-Eagle (Traverse City, Michigan)	2		
The Recorder: Central Connecticut University	1		
The Register Guard (Eugene, Oregon)	4		
The Reveille: Louisiana State University	4		
The Rocket: Slippery Rock University	1		
The Rotunda: Longwood College	1		
The Salem News (Beverly, MA)	2		
The Sandspur: Rollins College	1		
The Santa Clara: Santa Clara University	1		
The Scarlet: Clark University	3		
The Shorthorn: University of Texas—Arlington	4		
The Slate: Shippensburg University	2		
The Snapper: Millersville University	1		
The Spectator: University of Wisconsin—Eau Claire	3		
The Spinnaker: University of North Florida	1		
The Stanford Daily: Stanford University	9		
The State Hornet: California State University—Sacramento	1		
The Student Life: Pomona College	4		

continued

Table 2A.1 *continued*

US Democratic Primary (2019)			
Nexis (N = 961)		Ethnic NewsWatch, Asian/Pacific Islander (N = 1)	Ethnic NewsWatch, African American/ Caribbean/African (N = 104)
The Student Life: Washington University—St. Louis	1		
The Stute: Stevens Institute of Technology	1		
The Tack: Buena Vista Universit	1		
The Tartan: Carnegie Mellon University	1		
The Telegraph (Nashua, New Hampshire)	4		
The Ticker: Baruch College	4		
The Times Leader (Wilkes-Barre, Pennsylvania)	1		
The Times and Democrat (Orangeburg, South Carolina)	8		
The Tower: Catholic University of America	3		
The Trail: University of Puget Sound	2		
The Tripod: Trinity College	2		
The Troubadour: Franciscan University—Steubenville	1		
The Tufts Daily Tufts Daily: Tufts University	1		
The Tufts Daily: Tufts University April	1		
The University Leader: Fort Hays State University	1		
The University News: Saint Louis University	1		
The Whit: Rowan University	2		
The Whitman College Pioneer: Whitman College	1		

US Democratic Primary (2019)			
Nexis (N = 961)		Ethnic NewsWatch, Asian/Pacific Islander (N = 1)	Ethnic NewsWatch, African American/ Caribbean/African (N = 104)
The Will (Nigeria)	2		
The Yale Herald: Yale University	1		
Tufts Daily: Tufts University	1		
US Daily Mississippian: University of Mississippi	1		
USA TODAY	42		
University News: University of Missouri—Kansas City	1		
Vermont Cynic: University of Vermont	1		
Walla Walla Union-Bulletin (Washington)	1		
Washington Square News: New York University	3		
Waterloo Courier (Iowa)	7		
Waterloo Waterloo Courier (Iowa)	1		
Watertown Daily Times (New York)	1		
Wellesley News: Wellesley College	1		
Western Courier: Western Illinois University	5		

For the quantitative analyses of the website in Chapter 2 and the news coverage of Harris in Chapter 5, I used several R packages that aid in cleaning and analyzing text data (Feinerer et al. 2020, 2020; Miratrix 2018; Kim 2020; Huang et al. 2021; Grün et al. 2021; Ooms 2022; Benoit et al. 2022; Vaughan et al. 2022; Gruber 2021; Welbers et al. 2017). For news articles from Nexis, clean.text() was used to clean the text. term_stats() was used to identify word counts for both Nexis and Ethnic Newswatch sources, and I only report the counts of the exact string of characters. For instance, counts for "Jamaican," "jamaican," and "jamaican-american" constitute separate strings. I did this because it would be impractical to differentiate many similar strings (including strings with typos) across thousands of documents, but also because an argument can be made that "jamaican-american" is not substantively the same as "jamaican american." Therefore, these word counts may be considered a blunt count. Word counts constitute instances of words in articles that mention Harris, not necessarily words that describe Harris. I only reported instances of the words I am focused on in the chapter, not their related words. These tools also facilitated my qualitative analysis of news coverage of Harris, as I used what I learned from the analysis in Chapter 4 to search for key terms in the texts and scanned the articles in an iterative fashion to identify instances of identity labor in action.

Chapter 3

In 2018 and 2019, I conducted nationwide interviews in-person and by phone with thirty seven state legislators' offices around the country. Some interviews occurred with staff present, some occurred with the legislator and staff separately, and some just with staff. I chose a nationwide sample because identification patterns vary with regional context (Brunsma 2006, 69–71, 73–4), and likely how ethnorace becomes salient in the legislature.

One challenge in studying the mixed population is that it comprises a small percentage of the general population, and it can be difficult to recruit a large enough sample size to analyze data from different kinds of mixed people. The challenge of a small population exists among politicians as well. I purposefully sampled known mixed legislators so I could learn directly from them about their legislative experiences (Creswell and Plano Clark 2017, 228–229). Like other political scientists (e.g., Lien and Filler 2022), I took a broad approach to finding mixed politicians. I located mixed officials using what I had learned about some politicians, third-party lists, webpages (e.g., NALEO 2019; Center for American Women in Politics), and a separate survey I had conducted in 2018. In some cases, sources that identified legislators as mixed led me to legislators who were not mixed. I used snowball sampling to find additional mixed interviewees by asking mixed legislators if they knew other legislators like them.

I originally intended to compare mixed legislators to their non-mixed counterparts with similar characteristics such as gender and partisanship (Gerring 2007, 131–139; Lemi 2018). I encountered severe logistical challenges that prevented me from doing this. I had designated the summer as my primary time to collect data, and legislators had different personal and legislative schedules across the country. Securing interviews is more challenging when a researcher cannot travel to all locations. Close comparisons became futile due to logistical challenges in securing interviews with appropriately matched groups, so when I did make comparisons, I analyzed the data by making looser comparisons between mixed and non-mixed legislators based on ethnoracial backgrounds.

The average interview length was about thirty four minutes. The shortest interview was about five minutes, and the longest interview was about one hour and twenty-six minutes. Securing interviews with legislators is notoriously difficult, and the ability to do so depends on the legislator's schedule, the campaign cycle, the researcher's schedule, and the legislator's trust in the researcher and interest in participating. As researchers, our recruitment emails may be sent to spam or to a staff member responsible for prioritizing a legislator's schedule, and we're not always high on that prioritization. Sometimes it's easier to just show up at their offices and see if they can get you in. In one case, I was leaving the Capitol for the day and just so happened to see a legislator I wanted to interview walk past me. I then turned around and headed to their office to see if they wanted to chat with me, and successfully secured the interview—for five minutes. As I held the interviews, I sought to balance asking follow-up questions at certain points with keeping a quick interview pace since I knew some legislators were squeezing me in and that the conversation could end at any moment if something came up.

Because I was interested in obtaining information that is not readily available—legislators' thoughts about ethnorace and their professional relationships—I used in-depth, semi-structured interviews for data collection (Beamer 2002, 87; Marshall et al. 2022, 147–150).

I traveled to some states to interview legislators in their Capitol or district offices, and other interviews were held over the phone. As I held these interviews, I purposely chose not to keep field notes on what their offices looked like, shifts in body language and mannerisms, and when on the phone, nuances in tone. At the time, I worried that my memory would be faulty, and I'd find it difficult to "verify" what I'd written, whether I accurately time-marked the notes to the audio to track voices to gestures, and whether I'd accurately or adequately captured what I was quickly noting in the moment. I also recognized that keeping a notebook of handwritten notes would present a data security risk as I walked around state capitol buildings, and typing vigorously on a laptop during the interview would likely be quite distracting for both myself and the interviewee. I wanted to devote all of my attention to the conversation. My analysis in this book relies wholly on the transcripts of the recordings.

The questions I asked reflect a life-history approach (Marshall and Rossman 2010), and they were adopted, adapted, and derived from previous research on ethnorace and descriptive representation (e.g., Fenno 1978, 2003; Swain 1993; Geron 2005; Casellas 2010; Rouse 2013; Brown 2014a). I used the same questions for staff when I interviewed staff about their legislator. Due to the fast-paced nature of the legislature and natural flows of conversation, some questions were paraphrased, or were not or could not be asked of interviewees.

In collecting data nationwide, I also learned how using a standardized questionnaire had drawbacks. The questions I used were situated within previous research and meant to align with Masuoka and Junn's (2013) ethnoracial hierarchy framework. Yet as I collected data, I realized my questionnaire could not dive into the nuances of the experiences of different groups, particularly Indigenous legislators (see Cuizon Villazor 2008). This mismatch reflects dominant approaches in the field that neglect Indigenous people (e.g., Ferguson 2016), as well as a positivist norm of standardization over nuance. In fact, a staff member for a mixed Indigenous legislator explained that from their perspective, "being [Indigenous] isn't limited to an ethnic or racial definition because of the treaties we have with the federal government, [Indigenous] people are a legal definition." If I could do this again, I would create tailored questionnaires that touch on specific group political histories and cultural contexts of being mixed. A sample of the questionnaire I used in 2018 and 2019 is reproduced below.

1) Tell me about yourself and your background—your family, growing up, your ethnic background, how you identify and why, etc. What has your experience been as a [RACE OF LEGISLATOR] person (as an adult, as an adolescent, as a young adult)?
2) Has your background contributed to your political views? In what ways? Can you give an example? Is there anything unique about being [SPECIFIC RACIAL GROUPS, ATTEMPT TO MIRROR RESPONDENT]?
3) Who would you say you represent? What is your district like at home? With whom do you usually work on legislation?
4) How would you say people perceive you? What about racially? Under what circumstances is your ethnic background an advantage? A disadvantage? What role does it play during the campaign? What about in news interviews? What about when you work with colleagues? Has anyone ever treated you differently because of your race? How often do you work with White, Black, Hispanic, and Asian American legislators?
5) There's a lot of talk about increasing diversity in America. Where do you think we are headed? Is there something unique about being [RACE CATEGORIES OF LEGISLATOR, or perhaps Multiracial] in America today? Would you support a "Multiracial" category on demographic forms?

We're at the end of the interview now. Do you know any other elected officials with multiracial backgrounds who would be willing to discuss this with me? (for multiracial interviewees)

My goal was to conduct an interview that felt informal and conversational. I used race and ethnicity interchangeably to encourage participants to take the conversation in their own direction and to reflect how many people use the two concepts. Indeed, one participant stated, "So my ethnic background is multiracial." Still, some explicitly distinguished between race and "culture" in our conversations. I also found it useful to ask participants how people would classify them on the street (López et al. 2018).

A research assistant I worked with in 2018–2019 and I transcribed the interviews. Because these individuals are elected officials, I deleted the recordings when the transcripts were finalized to mitigate the risk of identification in the event of a data breach. Identifiable information was stripped, and names of people and places were replaced. In at least two instances, driven by concern from the participants, I chose to remove data from the transcript in one and not save a specific segment of the conversation in the other that I felt could damage the participants' reputations if my transcripts were ever breached.

As I iterated on the analysis in Chapter 3, I found it helpful to have Small and Calarco's (2022) *Qualitative Literacy: A Guide to Evaluating Ethnographic Interview Research* handy to remind me to show, not tell. Keeping in mind their recommendation to establish cognitive empathy in qualitative reports, I aimed to strike the balance between conveying what participants shared with me, how they felt about it, and their vulnerability, without devolving into voyeurism of trauma from racism. I analyzed this data in a circular fashion as I collected it, transcribed it, thought about it, and read the transcripts (see Brown 2014a). I coded the transcripts using NViVo 12. The questions in the interview were tied to previous research on descriptive representatives and the semi-structured nature of the interview facilitated sorting their responses into categories. Because of this, the transcripts generally coded themselves and did not require a wholly grounded theory approach (Deterding and Waters 2021). Ultimately, I adapted procedures outlined by Deterding and Waters (2021). Because I was a research team of one with a full-time non-academic job and producing this book largely without research assistants, I combined coding based on indexing and analytical constructs to optimize my time. My coding structure landed on five buckets to organize large chunks of text: 1) family and earlier life, 2) the ethnoracial hierarchy, 3) ethnoracial appearance, 4) identity performance, and 5) the "multiracial" category. From there, I drilled down into more specific coding (e.g., reference to the one-drop rule, parental influence, etc.). While the first, third, and fifth categories easily mapped to the questionnaire, the second and fourth were more distributed throughout the conversation and tended to overlap with other categories. In the writing process, I flipped back and forth to the transcripts and dug in deeper as I wrote. I did not assess reliability because each participant did not receive the exact same questions in the exact same order, either because of time constraints, because they answered my questions in the natural course of conversation, or because it didn't make sense to pivot in the middle of a topic (Deterding and Waters 2021, 730–732). I'm less interested in the predominance of a theme based on how many legislators spoke about it and more interested in how participants described how familial socialization, the ethnoracial hierarchy, and ethnoracial appearances contribute (or don't contribute) to their identity performances. The coding offered high-level structure to the analysis, but in reality, the analysis involved combing through the transcripts multiple times.

Chapter 4

As with Chapter 2, the analysis in this chapter is informed by previous text analyses of multiracialism, work on Barack Obama's campaign strategy, and news coverage of non-white members of Congress (Grose 2006; Squires 2007; Thornton 2009; McIlwain 2013). In these studies, news articles were collected and quantitatively and qualitatively analyzed.

Because I am interested in studying a specific phenomenon—the nuances of the nature of identity labor in the press coverage of mixed politicians—I opted to use a purposive sampling approach (Onwuegbuzie and Leech 2007, 242). To find mixed representatives, I browsed the internet, Wikipedia articles, and conducted web searches. At some point back in 2014, I landed upon a blog that listed mixed public figures, which regrettably, I can no longer find to properly credit. I purposefully selected cases of mixed politicians in a sub-group design, where all cases represent sub-groups of types of mixed politicians by ethnorace (Onwuegbuzie and Leech 2007, 244–246). In building this sample, I am interested in what Onwuegbuzie and Leech (2007, 240) call "case-to-case transfer," or the extent to which what I find here generalizes to cases similar to the politicians I studied in this chapter. These politicians were selected as cases that belong to ethnoracial sub-groups of mixed politicians, and they also vary in gender and the level of office held (state or federal). With the exception of Alberto Torrico, I also omit multiethnic Latinx representatives from this analysis because of the challenges of separating race from ethnicity (e.g., Alcoff 2005). For example, although Ted Cruz is multiethnic with one Latinx parent and one non-Latinx parent, he's also arguably considered *just* white rather than "mixed-race." Due to the structural constraints on candidate emergence, party support, and winning elections (e.g., Silva and Skulley 2019; Brown and Lemi 2021), most of the mixed politicians in the sample are men, and all are Democrats.

The politicians I ultimately selected are interesting because they occupy a middle space in politics. At the time of the research, they had amassed public careers long enough to analyze news coverage over time. Yet, they were not so longstanding or high-profile in American politics that news coverage would be unique to them as individuals rather than as instances of mixed politicians. I focus on contemporary politicians who served in the post-Civil Rights and post-Multiracial Category Movement eras. I also opted to focus my analysis on politicians with mixed parentage rather than grandparentage, as individuals with mixed parentage were the focus of the Multiracial Category Movement. This decision excludes politicians like Representative Bobby Scott and former Senator John Ensign, who both have Filipino grandparents.

To obtain the data in 2014, I downloaded newspaper articles from LexisNexis and Ethnic NewsWatch from around the beginning of politicians' elected careers through November 2014 if candidates ran for re-election. As in Chapter 2, I downloaded all available articles as permitted if they mentioned the candidate's name. The initial batch of news articles was downloaded in 2014 and contained a larger selection of politicians than those analyzed here, for a total of 9483 articles.

To code the news articles, this chapter uses content analysis within a discourse analytic approach (Hardy et al. 2004). For each representative, I scanned each article and coded whether it mentioned (1) the representative's race at all (e.g. Asian, Asian American, Black, African American or specific ethnicity, such as Thai or Bolivian), (2) the candidate as a non-white person (e.g. only Black, only Asian, etc.), (3) the representative's racial or ethnic combination (e.g. Black and white, Filipino and white, etc.), (4) the representative's parentage with respect to race (e.g. Mother is Thai, Father is American, etc.), (5) culture (e.g. languages, customs, religions, etc.), (6) a representative's self-description of their race, and 7) diversity (e.g. The "changing face" of America; changing demographics statistics, etc.); all of which are derived from the literature on media coverage of non-white candidates and the literature on multiracial identity (e.g, Rockquemore and Brunsma 2002; Squires 2007; Thornton 2009; McIlwain and Caliendo 2011; Renn 2012). Articles that discussed the candidates in substantive terms, either by mentioning issues or bills/events in legislative sessions were also coded. The ways in which non-white media venues categorized candidates, either as non-whites or mixed, were used to assess non-white groups "claiming" a candidate. Articles that contained testimonies of non-white constituents expressing happiness about a same-ethnorace candidate in office, or articles that highlighted the candidate as a "first," were used to capture non-white group pride. In 2015, one research assistant that had no knowledge of the objective of the study coded a random sample (N = 1450) of the entire dataset. The assistant was first trained in a one-hour session, in which they were provided a list of coding directions and shown examples of each type of coding. The assistant practiced and was instructed to code 100 articles alone before proceeding. After the assistant coded 100 articles, inter-coder reliability was checked. Where reliability was substantially low and the assistant expressed confusion, I clarified instructions and had another training session with the assistant and offered additional guidance as needed. The research assistant also had access to my original coding. Across categories, preliminary Cohen's Kappa statistics ranged from .78 to .98. The percentage of articles in the entire sample that mention race at all is quite small (5.95 percent), which is consistent with McIlwain and Caliendo's (2011, 103) finding that almost 75 percent of 2024 news articles in elections between whites and non-whites for the US House and Senate from 1992–2006 *did not* discuss ethnorace. As such, while inter-coder reliability is preliminary and based on a single coder, the overall pattern of whether race is mentioned at all is consistent with past research. In 2015, I updated the collection of articles to include articles through November 2014 and I hand-coded those articles myself. For the analysis in this chapter, in 2021, I downloaded new articles from Ethnic NewsWatch in html form to facilitate using R to re-explore the text.

Although I primarily downloaded newspaper articles, occasionally other forms of media were returned, such as newswires and magazine articles. News sources that may serve specific ethnic group audiences also occasionally came through via LexisNexis. Table 4A.1 summarizes the counts and news sources for each politician in this chapter.

Table 4A.1 Sources of News Articles

Anthony G. Brown			
LexisNexis (1999–2014) N = 1194	***N***	**Ethnic NewsWatch, African American/ Caribbean/African (1998–2014) N = 225**	***N***
American Medical News	1	Afro-American	91
Cumberland Times-News (Maryland)	1	Afro-American Red Star	38
Daily Deal/The Deal	1	Chicago Defender	1
Daily the Pak Banker	1	Los Angeles Sentinel	1
India Investment News	1	Miami Times	2
India Pharma News	6	Mississippi Link	1
International New York Times	1	New York Amsterdam News	1
Legal Monitor Worldwide	12	New York Beacon	6
Maryland Gazette	1	Philadelphia Tribune	7
Newsday (New York)	1	Precinct Reporter	2

Anthony G. Brown			
LexisNexis (1999–2014) N = 1194	N	**Ethnic NewsWatch, African American/ Caribbean/African (1998–2014) N = 225**	N
Progressive Media—Company News	1	Sacramento Observer	4
Richmond Times Dispatch (Virginia)	1	Sun Reporter	3
The Aegis, Bel Air, MD	1	The Charlotte Post	1
The Baltimore Sun	206	The Jacksonville Free Press	1
The Capital (Annapolis, MD)	38	The Louisiana Weekly	2
The Christian Science Monitor	1	The Weekly Gleaner	4
The Daily Record (Baltimore, MD)	165	Washington Informer	44
The Maryland Gazette	13	Afro—American	6
The New York Times	9	Afro—American Red Star	2
The Washington Post	715	Caribbean Today	1
US Official News	17	Chicago Defender	1
WMI Company News	1	Miami Times	3
		New York Beacon	1
		The Louisiana Weekly	1
		Washington Informer	1

Hansen Clarke					
LexisNexis (1999–2014) N = 207		**Ethnic NewsWatch, African American/ Caribbean/African (1990–2014) N = 285**		**Ethnic NewsWatch, Asian/Pacific Islander (2004–2014) N = 65**	
Aberdeen American News (South Dakota)	1	Call & Post	1	Asianweek	1
BBC Monitoring South Asia—Political Supplied by BBC Worldwide Monitoring	1	Chicago Defender	2	Filipino Reporter	1
bondbuyer.com	2	Los Angeles Sentinel	2	Hmong Times	1
Charleston Daily Mail (West Virginia)	1	Michigan Chronicle	162	India—West	25

continued

Table 4A.1 *continued*

Hansen Clarke					
LexisNexis (1999–2014) $N = 207$		**Ethnic NewsWatch, African American/ Caribbean/African (1990–2014) $N = 285$**		**Ethnic NewsWatch, Asian/Pacific Islander (2004–2014) $N = 65$**	
Chicago Daily Herald	1	Michigan Citizen	96	India Abroad	12
Crain's Detroit Business	29	New York Amsterdam News	1	News India—Times	24
Daily Deal/The Deal	1	New York Beacon	4	Northwest Asian Weekly	1
Detroit Free Press (Michigan)	53	Oakland Post	1		
Herald-Times (Bloomington, Indiana)	1	Precinct Reporter	1		
Michigan Lawyers Weekly	3	Sacramento Observer	5		
National Mortgage News	1	Sun Reporter	2		
Pittsburgh Post-Gazette (Pennsylvania)	2	The Jacksonville Free Press	1		
Providence Journal	1	The Louisiana Weekly	2		
Right Vision News	1	The Tennessee Tribune	1		
Roll Call	19	The Weekly Gleaner	1		
San Bernardino Sun (California)	1	Washington Informer	1		
South Bend Tribune (Indiana)	6	Westside Gazette	2		
St. Louis Post-Dispatch (Missouri)	2				
The Bismarck Tribune	1				
The Blade (Toledo, Ohio)	1				
The Bond Buyer	3				
The Capital (Annapolis, MD)	1				
The Christian Science Monitor	3				
The Daily Telegraph (London)	1				
The Financial Express (Bangladesh)	3				
The Hill	13				

Hansen Clarke					
LexisNexis (1999–2014) $N = 207$		Ethnic NewsWatch, African American/ Caribbean/African (1990–2014) $N = 285$		Ethnic NewsWatch, Asian/Pacific Islander (2004–2014) $N = 65$	
The Irish Times	1				
The New Nation (Bangladesh)	3				
The New York Times	5				
The Philadelphia Daily News	1				
The Salt Lake Tribune	1				
The Times of India (TOI)	1				
The Toronto Star	1				
The Washington Post	14				
The West Australian (Perth)	1				
Times of India (Electronic Edition)	2				
Tulsa World (Oklahoma)	2				
US Official News	1				
USA TODAY	9				
Windsor Star (Ontario)	13				

Tammy Duckworth			
LexisNexis (2012–2014) $N = 805$		Ethnic NewsWatch, Asian/Pacific Islander (2012–2014) $N = 27$	
Australian Financial Review	1	Filipino Reporter	2
Bangor Daily News (Maine)	1	Hmong Times	1
bondbuyer.com	1	India—West	12
Buffalo News (New York)	3	India Abroad	1
Canberra Times (Australia)	1	News India—Times	11
Charleston Daily Mail (West Virginia)	1		
Chicago Daily Herald	458		

continued

Table 4A.1 *continued*

Tammy Duckworth		
LexisNexis (2012–2014) $N = 805$		Ethnic NewsWatch, Asian/Pacific Islander (2012–2014) $N = 27$
Chicago Tribune (Illinois)	2	
Daily Gazette (Sterling, Illinois)	2	
Daily News (New York)	6	
Daily Today's Muslim Peshawar	1	
Dayton Daily News (Ohio)	3	
Denver Post	1	
Deseret Morning News (Salt Lake City)	2	
El Paso Times (Texas)	1	
Farmington Daily Times (New Mexico)	1	
Free Press Journal (India)	1	
Guardian.com	6	
Hartford Courant (Connecticut)	1	
Herald-Times (Bloomington, Indiana)	1	
Hobart Mercury (Australia)	1	
India Pharma News	2	
Investor's Business Daily	1	
Irish Independent	1	
Kirkus Reviews	1	
Korea Times	2	
Legal Monitor Worldwide	2	
Library Journal Reviews	1	
Los Angeles Times	4	
Monterey County Herald (California)	1	
MX Brisbane (Queensland, Australia)	1	
New Indian Express	1	
Philippines Daily Inquirer	1	

Tammy Duckworth		
LexisNexis (2012–2014) $N = 805$		Ethnic NewsWatch, Asian/Pacific Islander (2012–2014) $N = 27$
Pittsburgh Post-Gazette	4	
Pittsburgh Tribune Review	1	
Pocono Record, Stroudsburg, Pa.	1	
Post-Bulletin (Rochester, Minnesota)	1	
Reboot Illinois	4	
Richmond Times Dispatch (Virginia)	1	
Right Vision News	2	
Roll Call	6	
San Gabriel Valley Tribune (California)	1	
San Jose Mercury News (California)	2	
Spokesman Review (Spokane, WA)	4	
St. Louis Post-Dispatch (Missouri)	3	
St. Paul Pioneer Press (Minnesota)	2	
Star-News (Wilmington, NC)	2	
Stars and Stripes	2	
Tampa Bay Times	1	
Telegraph Herald (Dubuque, IA)	3	
The Advocate (Burnie)	1	
The Augusta Chronicle (Georgia)	1	
The Australian	1	
The Baltimore Sun	2	
The Bangkok Post (Thailand)	2	
The Bismarck Tribune	1	

continued

Table 4A.1 *continued*

Tammy Duckworth		
LexisNexis (2012–2014) *N* = 805		Ethnic NewsWatch, Asian/Pacific Islander (2012–2014) *N* = 27
The Capital (Annapolis, MD)	4	
The Christian Science Monitor	7	
The Columbian (Vancouver, Washington)	2	
The Daily Oklahoman (Oklahoma City, OK)	4	
The Daily Telegraph (London)	2	
The Fayetteville Observer (Fayetteville, North Carolina)	1	
The Forward	1	
The Globe and Mail (Canada)	1	
The Guardian (London)	1	
The Herald-Palladium, St. Joseph, Mich.	1	
The Hill	8	
The Honolulu Star-Advertiser	11	
The International Herald Tribune	3	
The Nation (Thailand)	4	
The National	1	
The New Hampshire Union Leader, Manchester	1	
The New York Post	2	
The New York Times	22	
The New Zealand Herald	2	
The Pantagraph (Bloomington, Illinois)	2	
The Philadelphia Daily News	1	

Tammy Duckworth			
LexisNexis (2012–2014) $N = 805$		**Ethnic NewsWatch, Asian/Pacific Islander (2012–2014) $N = 27$**	
The Salt Lake Tribune	2		
The State Journal-Register (Springfield, IL)	17		
The Tampa Tribune (Florida)	1		
The Telegraph (Alton, Illinois)	2		
The Times (London)	3		
The Times & Transcript (New Brunswick)	1		
The Times of India (TOI)	2		
The Toronto Star	1		
The Washington Post	33		
Times of India (Electronic Edition)	1		
Today's Zaman (Turkey)	1		
Tribune-Review (Greensburg, PA)	1		
Tulsa World (Oklahoma)	4		
US Official News	76		
USA TODAY	16		
Waterloo Region Record	1		
WGN-TV, Chicago	1		

Laura Richardson			
LexisNexis (2004–2014) $N = 328$		**Ethnic NewsWatch, African American/ Caribbean/African (1998–2013) $N = 291$**	
Aljazeera.net	1	Afro—American Red Star	5
American Banker	1	Call & Post	3
BBC Monitoring Asia Pacific—Political	1	Chicago Defender	1
BBC Monitoring Latin America—Political	1	Chicago Weekend	1

continued

Table 4A.1 *continued*

Laura Richardson			
LexisNexis (2004–2014) *N* = 328		**Ethnic NewsWatch, African American/ Caribbean/African (1998–2013) *N* = 291**	
BBC SUMMARY WORLD BROADCAST	1	Hyde Park Citizen	1
Buffalo News (New York)	2	Jackson Advocate	2
Chicago Daily Herald	1	Los Angeles Sentinel	225
Colorado Springs Business Journal (Colorado Springs, CO)	1	Michigan Chronicle	1
Contra Costa Times (California)	6	New Pittsburgh Courier	1
Daily Breeze (Torrance, California)	2	New York Beacon	7
Daily News (New York)	2	Oakland Post	3
Deseret Morning News (Salt Lake City)	2	Philadelphia Tribune	1
Facts on File World News Digest	3	Precinct Reporter	5
Gazette (Long Beach, California)	1	Sacramento Observer	22
Grunion Gazette (Long Beach, California)	16	South Florida Times	2
Independent Coast Observer (Gualala, California)	1	Sun Reporter	6
India Pharma News	1	The Charlotte Post	1
Inland Valley Daily Bulletin (Ontario, CA)	2	The Jacksonville Free Press	3
Intelligencer Journal/New Era (Lancaster, Pennsylvania)	1	The Skanner	1
Investment News	1		
Investor's Business Daily	3		
Journal of Commerce	13		
Lowell Sun (Massachusetts)	1		
Marin Independent Journal (California)	1		
McClatchy Washington Bureau	2		

Laura Richardson		
LexisNexis (2004–2014) $N = 328$		Ethnic NewsWatch, African American/ Caribbean/African (1998–2013) $N = 291$
Metropolitan News Enterprise (Los Angeles, California)	1	
Monterey County Herald (California)	6	
Orange County Register (California)	4	
Pasadena Star-News (California)	4	
Pittsburgh Post-Gazette (Pennsylvania)	3	
Press-Telegram (Long Beach, California)	12	
Roll Call	71	
Sacramento Bee (California)	1	
San Gabriel Valley Tribune (California)	10	
San Jose Mercury News (California)	6	
Sarasota Herald Tribune (Florida)	1	
St. Louis Post-Dispatch (Missouri)	1	
St. Paul Pioneer Press (Minnesota)	3	
The Atlanta Journal-Constitution	1	
The Augusta Chronicle (Georgia)	3	
The Bismarck Tribune	1	
The Blade (Toledo, Ohio)	2	
The Bond Buyer	2	
The Christian Science Monitor	1	
The Daily News of Los Angeles	35	
The Forward	1	

continued

Table 4A.1 *continued*

Laura Richardson					
LexisNexis (2004–2014) *N* = 328				Ethnic NewsWatch, African American/ Caribbean/African (1998–2013) *N* = 291	
The Globe and Mail (Canada)	1				
The Herald-Sun (Durham, N.C.)	1				
The Hill	34				
The Hour (Norwalk, Connecticut)	1				
The Independent (London)	1				
The International Herald Tribune	1				
The New York Times	16				
The Orange County Register (California)	1				
The Philadelphia Inquirer	1				
The Record (Stockton, California)	1				
The Sun (Lowell, Massachusetts)	1				
The Times (London)	1				
The Washington Post	24				
Tulsa World (Oklahoma)	4				
USA TODAY	3				
Wall Street Journal Abstracts	1				

Alberto Torrico					
LexisNexis (2003–2013) *N* = 511		Ethnic NewsWatch, Asian/Pacific Islander (2003–2010) *N* = 58		Ethnic NewsWatch, Hispanic (2007–2010) *N* = 7	
Chico Enterprise-Record (California)	5	Asianweek	27	La Prensa San Diego	6
Contra Costa Times (California)	162	India—West	19	El Chicano Weekly	1
Daily News, Los Angeles, Calif.	1	India Abroad	10		
Eureka Times Standard (California)	3	News India—Times	2		

Alberto Torrico			
LexisNexis (2003–2013) $N = 511$		Ethnic NewsWatch, Asian/Pacific Islander (2003–2010) $N = 58$	Ethnic NewsWatch, Hispanic (2007–2010) $N = 7$
Inland Valley Daily Bulletin (Ontario, CA)	7		
Inside Bay Area (California)	108		
Investment Management Weekly	1		
Investor's Business Daily	1		
Korea Times	1		
Marin Independent Journal (Marin, CA)	2		
Metropolitan News Enterprise (Los Angeles, California)	1		
Monterey County Herald (California)	14		
Orange County Register (California)	3		
Orland Press Register (California)	1		
Palo Alto Daily News (California)	1		
Pasadena Star-News (California)	3		
Pensions and Investments	1		
Right Vision News	1		
Roll Call	1		
Sacramento Bee (California)	6		
San Bernardino Sun (California)	7		
San Gabriel Valley Tribune (California)	10		
San Jose Mercury News (California)	114		
San Mateo County Times, Calif.	2		
Santa Cruz Sentinel (California)	2		
Southeast Texas Record	1		

continued

Table 4A.1 *continued*

Alberto Torrico			
LexisNexis (2003–2013) $N = 511$		Ethnic NewsWatch, Asian/Pacific Islander (2003–2010) $N = 58$	Ethnic NewsWatch, Hispanic (2007–2010) $N = 7$
The Argus (Fremont, California)	1		
The Bakersfield Californian	4		
The Bond Buyer	7		
The Christian Science Monitor	1		
The Daily News of Los Angeles	9		
The Forward	1		
The International Herald Tribune	1		
The Jerusalem Post	1		
The Modesto Bee (California)	1		
The New York Times	5		
The Orange County Register (California)	1		
The Record	1		
The Washington Post	1		
USA TODAY	1		
Vallejo Times Herald (California)	2		
Valley Times	7		

Chapter 5

Analysis of News Coverage of Kamala Harris

To create an identity labor gap, someone, like the media, makes a mixed candidate's ethnoracial identities salient. To explore words that describe demographic categories in articles that mention Kamala Harris, I analyzed the news articles I collected in Chapter 2. I grouped coverage into four different stages of her career:[1]

[1] I also manually removed articles with duplicated headlines. Some counts in tables are slightly inconsistent with counts in plots due to stray duplicates.

- As San Francisco District Attorney up until 2010 (2002–2010)
- As the California Attorney General up to 2016 (2011–2016)
- As California US Senator (2017–2018)
- As a Democratic primary presidential contender (2019)

San Francisco District Attorney (2002–2010)

In Figure 5A.1, I analyze news coverage of Harris from 2002 to 2010, from just before she was elected San Francisco District Attorney until when she was elected as California Attorney General. In 2010, the city of San Francisco was about 6 percent non-Latinx Black or African American, about 33 percent non-Latinx Asian American, about 42 percent non-Latinx white, and about 15 percent Latinx.[2] During this period, relatively few pieces mentioned terms associated with demographic categories in non-African/Asian American news. "Indian" appears twenty-seven times in two articles about Indian Americans. Two of the seven instances of "Black" describe black objects, a gun and an Obama beanie.[3,4] One article described Harris as "the daughter of an Indian mother and black father."[5] "African" was used in two articles, each of which described Harris as "African-American" and "African American."[6,7]

There are differences between non-Asian/African American newspapers and African American and Asian American newspapers. Just over half of all 138 articles from Asian American newspapers used "Indian" and "Asian." The term "mixed" was used twice in two articles, one of which was used to note Harris's "mixed Indian and African American heritage."[8] In African American news articles, over fifty percent mention "Black" and "African."

California Attorney General (2011–2016)

Figure 5A.2 summarizes news articles covering the five years when Harris was the California Attorney General and running for California US Senator. The year she began her term in 2011, California was about 6 percent non-Latinx Black or African American, 13 percent non-Latinx Asian American, about 40 percent non-Latinx white, and about 38 percent Hispanic.[9] In non-African/Asian American news, the terms "Indian" and "Asian" are mentioned in less than 5 percent of all 527 articles. In the 137 articles collected from Asian American newspapers, over 75 percent of all articles mention "India" and "Indian." In contrast to both other sources, "Black" occurs in over 40 percent of news articles and "African" occurs in about 40 percent of African American news articles.

California US Senator (2017–2018)

Figure 5A.3 summarizes news coverage of Harris as a US Senator from 2017 through 2018. In 2017, California was about 5 percent non-Latinx Black or African American, 14 percent

[2] U.S. Census Bureau. "HISPANIC OR LATINO ORIGIN BY RACE." *American Community Survey, ACS 1-Year Estimates Detailed Tables, Table B03002*, https://data.census.gov/table/ACSDT1Y2010.B03002?q=ACSDT1Y2010.B03002&g=160XX00US0667000. Accessed on 26 Aug 2025.

[3] Melvin, Joshua. 2010. Antioch shuttle driver charged with robbing Daly City bank on break. *San Mateo County Times, Calif. Small Business Column*. August 3.

[4] Paik, Neil. 2010. President Obama visits USC to ask attendees to vote. *Daily Bruin: University of California-Los Angeles*. October 25.

[5] Schouten, Fredreka. 2010. Candidates of Indian ancestry on the increase; Spring from most affluent, educated immigrant groups. *USA Today*. September 13.

[6] The Stanford Daily: Stanford University. 2010. Obama to fundraise in Palo Alto today. *The Stanford Daily: Stanford University*. October 21.

[7] Hecht, Peter. 2009. Contenders line up for attorney general. *Sacramento Bee (California)*. May 16.

[8] Tsering, L. 2004. TiE forum empowers women. *India—West*. April 9.

[9] As of publication, this table (B03002 for the 2011 American Community Survey 1-year estimates) cannot be located on the Census website: https://data.census.gov/table?q=california+race+and+hispanic+origin&tid=ACSDT1Y2011.B03002

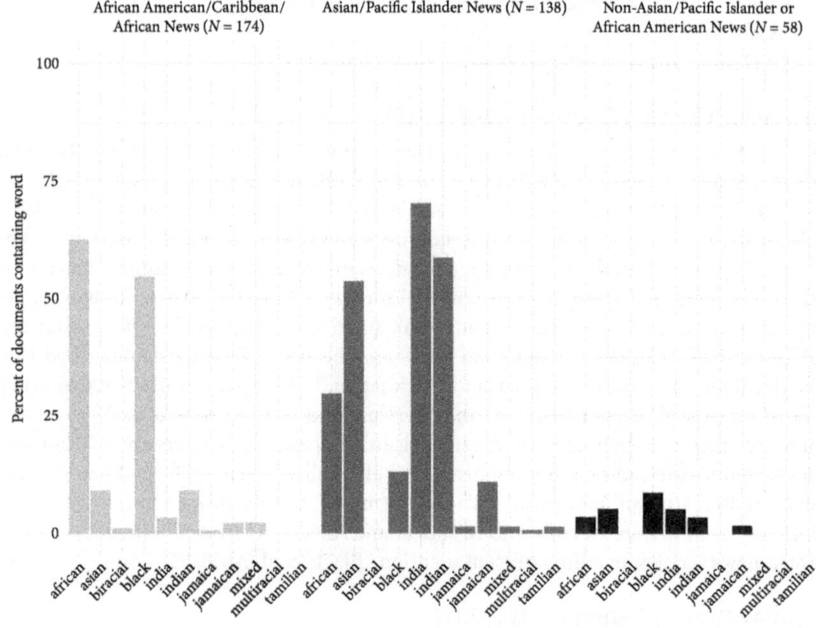

Figure 5A.1 Distribution of Words in Articles Mentioning Kamala Harris: San Francisco District Attorney (2002–2010)

non-Latinx Asian American, 37 percent non-Latinx white, and about 39 percent Latinx.[10] In non-Asian/African American news, the instances of these terms are relatively rare. There are differences between non-Asian/African American newspapers and Asian American and African American newspapers in words used and the patterns are similar to those during her California Attorney General stage.

Democratic Primary (2019)

Figure 5A.4 summarizes news coverage from the Democratic Presidential Primary in 2019. In 2019, the United States was about 12 percent non-Latinx Black or African American, 6 percent non-Latinx Asian American, 60 percent non-Latinx white, and 18 percent Latinx.[11] By the time Harris was running for president, in the 961 non-Asian/African American articles collected, only two articles that mentioned "Kamala Harris" used the term "multiracial," and they were not about her background.[12,13] 142 articles, or about 15 percent of all articles mentioned

[10] U.S. Census Bureau. "ACS DEMOGRAPHIC AND HOUSING ESTIMATES." *American Community Survey, ACS 1-Year Estimates Data Profiles, Table DP05*, https://data.census.gov/table/ACSDP1Y2017.DP05?q=california&y=2017. Accessed on 26 Aug 2025.

[11] U.S. Census Bureau. "ACS DEMOGRAPHIC AND HOUSING ESTIMATES." *American Community Survey, ACS 1-Year Estimates Data Profiles, Table DP05*, https://data.census.gov/table/ACSDP1Y2019.DP05. Accessed on 26 Aug 2025.

[12] Thiessen, Marc. 2019. Marc Thiessen: Biden's problem with Democrats is that he doesn't hate Republicans. *The Register Guard (Eugene, Oregon)*. June 21.

[13] CE Noticias Financieras English. 2019. Democratic debate reveals deep internal divisions to confront Trump. *CE Noticias Financieras English*. August 1.

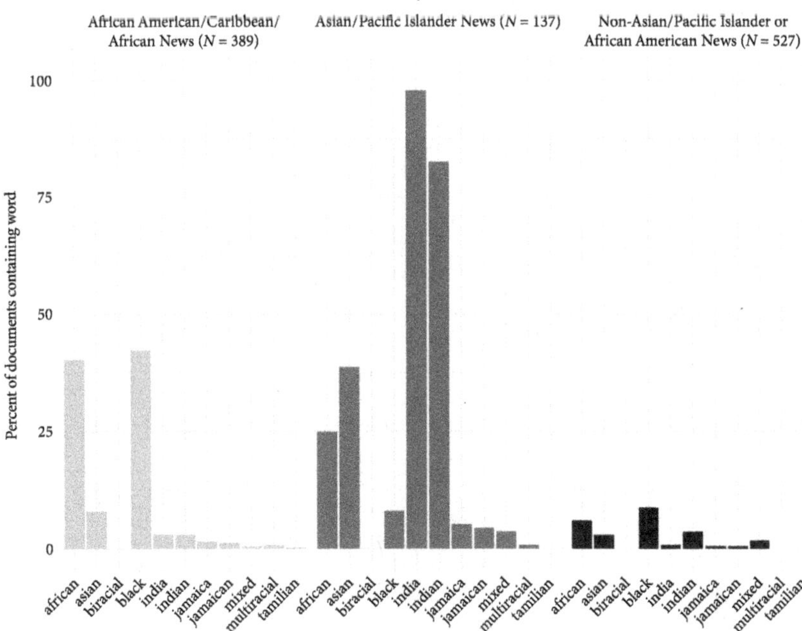

Figure 5A.2 Distribution of Words in Articles Mentioning Kamala Harris: California Attorney General (2011–2016)

"African" 251 times. "Black" was used 670 times in 208 documents, or about 22 percent of all articles. In African American newspapers, "Black" occurred in 65 percent of all news articles.

Ethnic NewsWatch returned one news article from Asian American/Pacific Islander newspapers in 2019 that mentioned Harris. The news article described her as someone who "is seeking to become the first mixed race woman to hold the office of US president" and as someone "who is of Indian and African heritage."[14]

The 2016 National Asian American Survey

The 2016 National Asian American Pre-election Survey is a nationally representative phone survey of adults who self-identify as Asian or Asian American from numerous ethnic groups, as well as Native Hawaiians, Pacific Islanders, white, Black, Latinx, and mixed Americans (Ramakrishnan et al. 2017). This survey is often used to examine Asian American political attitudes due to its large sample of Asian Americans and the diversity of ethnic groups included in the sample. The specific questions used for the analysis in Chapter 5, and how they were coded, can be found at the end of this appendix.

[14] Eastern Eye. 2019. Indian American senator joins race to be US President. *Eastern Eye*. January 25.

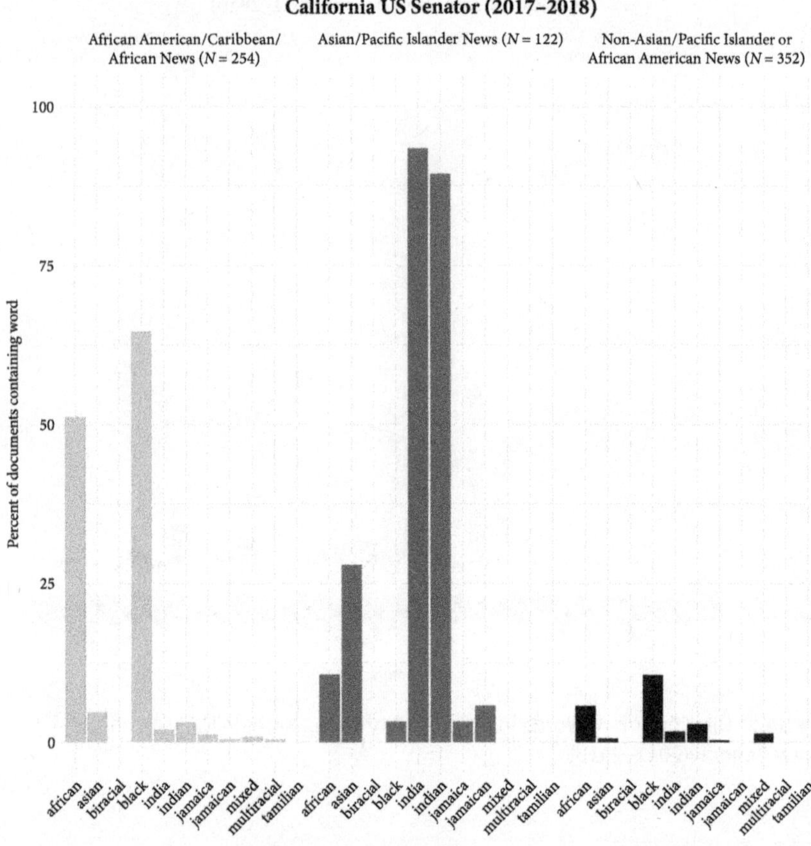

Figure 5A.3 Distribution of Words in Articles Mentioning Kamala Harris: California US Senator (2017–2018)

The Conjoint Experiment

The conjoint experiment was conducted online in May 2016 on a sample of white, Black, Asian, and Latinx respondents contracted through Qualtrics survey panels (see a summary of the sample in Table 5A.1). To examine how different notions of group identity bear on the identity labor gap, I asked questions about their feelings of linked fate (Sanchez and Vargas 2016; Gay et al. 2016). I also questions meant to tap into their psychological attachment to their ethnoracial group (Mael and Tetrick 1992) and whether they approved or disapproved of a close relative of theirs marrying someone who was white, Black, Asian, or Hispanic (adapted from the General Social Survey and Schuman et al. 1985, 76). These specific survey questions are reproduced at the end of this appendix.

Specific candidate attributes (ethnorace, gender, partisanship, political experience, nativity, party, ideology, and experience) were included in the conjoint because they are correlated with ethnorace (Lee 2008). For example, candidates of color tend to be liberal and Democrats (Lee 2008), and may have less political experience due to their general underrepresentation

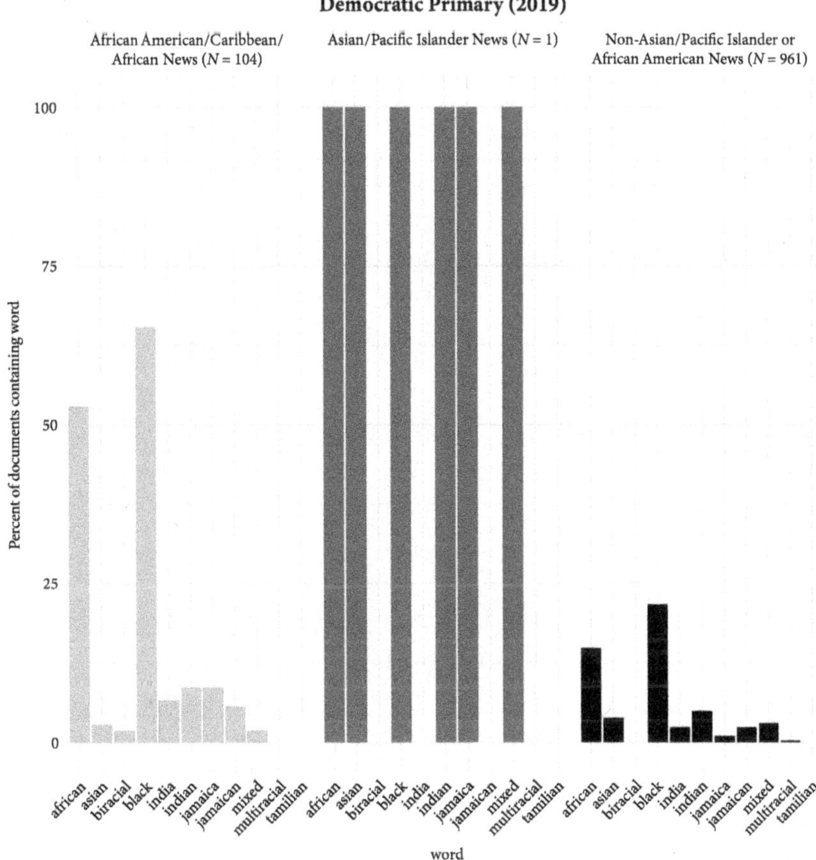

Figure 5A.4 Distribution of Words in Articles Mentioning Kamala Harris: Democratic Primary (2019)

in political institutions. Women with inter-ethnoracial parentage are more likely to disclose mixed identities than men with inter-ethnoracial parentage (Davenport 2016a). Candidates of color, particularly Asian and Hispanic candidates, may also raise questions about nativity (Masuoka and Junn 2013), as they may not be immediately read as "real Americans." All of these attributes are thus relevant to adequately capture the effect of race on the outcome because they are directly related to race. The primary treatment of interest, ethnorace, was completely randomized in the conjoint, such that there were no constraints on when or how many times each ethnoracial category/combination could appear. Table 5A.2 shows that ethnorace was distributed roughly evenly, with each profile being displayed for about 10 percent of all candidate profiles shown to the respondents.

Respondents entered the survey and provided consent before filling out demographic questions and attitudinal questions. They then answered an attention filter before rating candidate profiles and giving permission to use their data. There is little evidence that experiments on convenience samples are less valid than nationally representative samples (e.g., Coppock and McClellan 2019). At least 200 participants per ethnoracial group were targeted

Table 5A.1 Descriptive Statistics (Means)

	White Respondents (N = 190)	Black Respondents (N = 203)	Asian Respondents (N = 207)	Hispanics Respondents (N = 186)	All (N = 786)
Gender					
Male	51.05	50.74	51.21	50.54	50.89
Female	48.95	49.26	48.79	49.46	49.11
English is first language	98.42	97.04	79.71	77.96	88.30
Age	38.58	34.66	33.51	31.19	34.48
Party ID					
Democrats	40.00	75.86	48.79	48.39	53.56
Republicans	29.47	4.93	22.22	15.59	17.94
Independents	23.68	14.78	23.67	28.49	22.52
Something else	6.84	4.43	5.31	7.53	5.98
Region					
West	.23	.12	.49	.41	.31
Midwest	.23	.22	.12	.10	.17
South	.37	.48	.21	.35	.35
Northeast	.16	.18	.18	.15	.17
Identification with racial group (Min: 10; Max: 70)	40.70	46.88	45.63	45.81	44.80
Linked Fate (1 = Yes; 0 = Else)	.63	.77	.71	.69	.70
Approval of marriage with...					
Asian or Pacific Islander people	.93	.92	.97	.91	.93
Black people	.85	.99	.76	.84	.86
Hispanic people	.90	.94	.83	.97	.91
white people	.98	.86	.91	.92	.92

for sub-group analysis (Orme 2010, 65). After dropping mixed people and respondents who did not provide permission to use their data, 190 White, 203 Black, 186 Hispanic/Latino, and 207 Asian or Pacific Islander (API) respondents remained for a total sample size of 786.

Candidate profiles were created with *conjointsdt* (Strezhnev et al. 2014) and completely randomly generated and varied in ethnorace (Black, White, Asian, Hispanic, Black and White,

Table 5A.2 Distribution of Candidate Ethnorace Profiles by Ethnorace of Respondent

	Ethnorace of Respondent				
	Full sample	White	Black	Asian	Hispanic
Ethnorace of Candidate					
White	1,598	386	401	423	388
	(10.17%)	(10.16%)	(9.88%)	(10.22%)	(10.43%)
Black	1,620	402	429	425	364
	(10.31%)	(10.58%)	(10.57%)	(10.27%)	(9.78%)
Asian	1,560	385	398	390	387
	(9.92%)	(10.13%)	(9.80%)	(9.42%)	(10.40%)
Hispanic	1,616	366	443	444	363
	(10.28%)	(9.63%)	(10.91%)	(10.72%)	(9.76%)
Black and White	1,606	376	453	422	355
	(10.22%)	(9.89%)	(11.16%)	(10.19%)	(9.54%)
Black and Asian	1,605	402	384	437	382
	(10.21%)	(10.58%)	(9.46%)	(10.56%)	(10.27%)
Black and Hispanic	1,562	371	396	411	384
	(9.94%)	(9.76%)	(9.75%)	(9.93%)	(10.32%)
Asian and Hispanic	1,543	386	368	415	374
	(9.82%)	(10.16%)	(9.06%)	(10.02%)	(10.05%)
Asian and White	1,534	358	413	407	356
	(9.76%)	(9.42%)	(10.17%)	(9.83%)	(9.57%)
Hispanic and White	1,476	368	375	366	367
	(9.39%)	(9.68%)	(9.24%)	(8.84%)	(9.87%)
Total	15,720	3,800	4,060	4,140	3,720
	(100%)	(100%)	(100%)	(100%)	(100%)

Asian and White, Hispanic and White, Black and Asian, Asian and Hispanic, Black and Hispanic) and attributes correlated with ethnorace: gender (male, female), party (Democrat, Republican, Independent), ideology (liberal, moderate, conservative), and political experience (served in city council, served in the state legislature, served in Congress) (e.g., Sigelman et al. 1995; Lee 2008; Sen and Wasow 2016; Davenport 2016b).

A challenge scholars face in studying ethnorace is articulating what "ethnorace" is (e.g., Sen and Wasow 2016; Roth 2016). While the study could have only included labels for candidate ethnorace, absent all other information, by manipulating ethnorace, perhaps we are manipulating party (e.g., Lee 2008; White et al. 2014), nativity (e.g., Visalvanich 2017), or gender (e.g., Davenport 2016b). This design provides this information and ethnorace, so there is little question about these other attributes. This design makes finding the effects of mixed classification more challenging. If, after including these attributes, mixed categorization still has statistically significant effects on vote choice, the evidence for the argument will be more robust. I use a similar logic from Merolla et al. (2017) applied to the study of gender and representation.

Survey questions

Questions for National Asian American Survey

Not mixed (q4_8a): Thinking about the upcoming November election for **the U.S. Senate** in California ... [ROTATE ORDER] Kamala Harris and [ROTATE] Loretta Sanchez are Democrats and both will be on the ballot in November. If the election were being held today, who would you vote for?

1) Harris
2) Sanchez
3) DO NOT READ Someone else
88) DO NOT READ Don't know
99) DO NOT READ Refused

Mixed (q4_9a): Thinking about the upcoming November election for **the U.S. Senate** in California[ROTATE ORDER] Kamala Harris who is of Asian and African American descent and [ROTATE] Loretta Sanchez who is of Latina descent, are both Democrats and running against each other. If the election were being held today, who would you vote for?

1) Harris
2) Sanchez
3) DO NOT READ Someone else
88) DO NOT READ Don't know
99) DO NOT READ Refused

Identity (q2_2a): How important is being RACE to your identity? Would you say it is extremely important, very important, moderately important, a little important, or not important at all?

1) Not at all Important
2) Somewhat Important
3) Very Important
4) Extremely Important
88) Don't Know

Party ID (pid4): Generally speaking, do you usually think of yourself as a {READ CATEGORIES}, an independent, or in terms of some other party? [ROTATE 1 AND 2] 1) Democrat 2) Republican

3) Independent

Coded so that selected Harris Over Sanchez=1 if q4_8a=1 or q4_9a=1; 0 if q4_8a=2 or q4_9a=2

Coded so that identity is Important=1 if q2_2a=2, 3, or 4; 0 if else

Although they were not given a formal option to give these answers, 441 survey respondents volunteered someone else, said don't know, or refused to answer question q4_8a/q4_9a. I dropped them from the analysis so that it reflects only those who selected the given response options of Harris or Sanchez. This analysis is necessarily conditional on giving a response that was uniformly offered in each condition so as to compare groups of individuals who selected from the available response options (see Coppock 2019 for a discussion of post-treatment bias in audit experiments).

Questions for Conjoint Experiment

What is your age?

Is English your first language?

Yes
No

What is the highest level of education you have completed?

Less than High School
High School/GED
Some College
2-year College Degree
4-year College Degree
Masters Degree
Doctoral Degree
Professional Degree (JD, MD)

What is your combined annual household income?

Less than 30,000
30,000–39,999
40,000–49,999
50,000–59,999
60,000–69,999
70,000–79,999
80,000–89,999
90,000–99,999
100,000 or more

What racial or ethnic group(s) best describe you?

White
Black/African American
Hispanic/Latino
Asian or Pacific Islander[15]

[15] Although this label uses "Asian or Pacific Islander," Asian Americans were specifically targeted through Qualtrics for this survey.

Native American
Middle Eastern
Other

In which state do you currently reside?

Generally speaking, do you think of yourself as a Democrat, a Republican, an Independent, or something else?

Democrat
Republican
Independent
Something else

Thinking about politics these days, how would you describe your own political viewpoint?

Very liberal
Liberal
Moderate/Middle-of-the-Road
Conservative
Very conservative
Not Sure

Linked Fate (Dawson 1994):

Do you think that what happens to [R'S GROUP] people in this country will have something to do with what happens in your life?

Yes
No

Identity (Mael and Tertrick 1992):

When someone criticizes R'S RACE, it feels like a personal insult.
I don't act like the typical R'S RACE person. (REVERSE CODED)
I'm very interested in what others think about R'S RACE.
The limitations associated with R'S RACE apply to me also.
When I talk about R'S RACE, I usually say "we" rather than "they."
I have a number of qualities typical of R'S RACE.
The successes of R'S RACE are my successes.
If a story in the media criticized R'S RACE, I would feel embarrassed.
When someone praises R'S RACE, it feels like a personal compliment.
I act like a White person to a great extent.

Strongly disagree
Disagree
Somewhat disagree
Neither agree nor disagree

Somewhat agree
Agree
Strongly agree

Items were summed for each group so that higher values reflect greater identity with group. A new variable was then created to merge the scores into one variable. The scale for the entire sample was split at the median, where 1 = individual score was 44 or greater, 0 = else.

Attitudes toward Interracial Marriage (General Social Survey and Schuman et al. 1985, 76):

Do you approve or disapprove of a close relative of yours marrying someone who is [White, Black, Hispanic, Asian]?

Strongly approve
Approve
Somewhat approve
Somewhat disapprove
Disapprove
Strongly Disapprove

Coded so that 1 = any approval, 0 = any disapproval

Table 5A.3: Figure 5.3: Testing the Electoral Support Gap for Harris in 2016 (OLS interaction)

	Asian Californians		Black Californians	
Not mixed	0	[0,0]	0	[0,0]
Mixed	0.148*	[0.00266,0.293]	0.526*	[0.126,0.925]
Race is not important	0	[0,0]	0	[0,0]
Race is important	−0.00770	[−0.189,0.174]	0.390	[−0.0156,0.796]
Not mixed × Race is not important	0	[0,0]	0	[0,0]
Not mixed × Race is important	0	[0,0]	0	[0,0]
Mixed × Race is not important	0	[0,0]	0	[0,0]
Mixed × Race is important	0.0726	[−0.153,0.298]	−0.552**	[−0.970,−0.134]
Not R's Party	0	[0,0]	0	[0,0]
R's Party	0.0878	[−0.0244,0.200]	0.101	[−0.0575,0.260]
Constant	0.551***	[0.427,0.676]	0.403*	[0.00510,0.801]
Observations	396		206	
r2	0.0482		0.0757	

95% confidence intervals in brackets
$^{*}p < 0.05$, $^{**}p < 0.01$, $^{***}p < 0.001$

Table 5A.4: Figure 5.4: Average Change in Probability of Selection by Candidate Ethnorace (Full Sample)

	Full Sample	
Male	0	[0,0]
Female	0.0235**	[0.00699,0.0400]
White	0	[0,0]
Black	0.0254	[−0.0111,0.0618]
Asian	0.0368*	[0.00104,0.0726]
Hispanic	0.0274	[−0.00735,0.0621]
Black and White	0.0654***	[0.0298,0.101]
Black and Asian	0.0596**	[0.0236,0.0956]
Black and Hispanic	0.0589**	[0.0219,0.0959]
Asian and Hispanic	0.0555**	[0.0182,0.0927]
Asian and White	0.0419*	[0.00644,0.0773]
Hispanic and White	0.0581**	[0.0213,0.0948]
Born in the U.S.	0	[0,0]
Born Outside the U.S.	−0.121***	[−0.140,−0.102]
Democrat	0	[0,0]
Republican	−0.0765***	[−0.101,−0.0516]
Independent	0.0339**	[0.0115,0.0563]
Liberal	0	[0,0]
Moderate	0.00456	[−0.0170,0.0261]
Conservative	−0.0769***	[−0.102,−0.0514]
Served in Congress	0	[0,0]
Served in City Council	−0.0699***	[−0.0906,−0.0491]
Served in the State Legislature	−0.0222*	[−0.0412,−0.00323]
Not R's Party	0	[0,0]
R's Party	0.143***	[0.123,0.164]
Constant	0.531***	[0.492,0.570]
Observations	15708	
r2	0.0544	

95% confidence intervals in brackets
$^{*}p < 0.05$, $^{**}p < 0.01$, $^{***}p < 0.001$

Table 5A.5: Figure 5.5: Average Change in Probability of Selection by Ethnorace of Respondent

	White Rs		Black Rs		Asian Rs		Hispanic Rs	
Male	0	[0,0]	0	[0,0]	0	[0,0]	0	[0,0]
Female	0.0500**	[0.0144,0.0857]	0.0159	[−0.0152,0.0470]	−0.000530	[−0.0336,0.0326]	0.0274	[−0.00516,0.0599]
White	0	[0,0]	0	[0,0]	0	[0,0]	0	[0,0]
Black	−0.0698*	[−0.137,−0.00217]	0.228***	[0.159,0.297]	−0.0508	[−0.123,0.0215]	−0.0226	[−0.0973,0.0521]
Asian	−0.102**	[−0.172,−0.0326]	0.0821*	[0.0167,0.148]	0.123**	[0.0499,0.197]	0.0423	[−0.0306,0.115]
Hispanic	−0.107**	[−0.180,−0.0345]	0.109***	[0.0448,0.173]	−0.0567	[−0.121,0.00740]	0.181***	[0.113,0.250]
Black and White	−0.0311	[−0.107,0.0444]	0.194***	[0.131,0.256]	0.0159	[−0.0498,0.0816]	0.0733	[−0.00482,0.151]
Black and Asian	−0.0512	[−0.124,0.0215]	0.201***	[0.131,0.271]	0.0565	[−0.0149,0.128]	0.0308	[−0.0388,0.100]
Black and Hispanic	−0.105**	[−0.180,−0.0301]	0.220***	[0.148,0.291]	−0.0133	[−0.0800,0.0535]	0.132***	[0.0569,0.207]
Asian and Hispanic	−0.106*	[−0.187,−0.0244]	0.109**	[0.0402,0.177]	0.104**	[0.0349,0.173]	0.108**	[0.0331,0.183]
Asian and White	−0.0666	[−0.138,0.00471]	0.0538	[−0.0128,0.120]	0.108**	[0.0396,0.177]	0.0744*	[0.00364,0.145]
Hispanic and White	−0.0476	[−0.121,0.0263]	0.129***	[0.0628,0.195]	−0.00485	[−0.0789,0.0692]	0.147***	[0.0704,0.223]
Born in the U.S.	0	[0,0]	0	[0,0]	0	[0,0]	0	[0,0]
Born Outside the U.S.	−0.162***	[−0.201,−0.123]	−0.113***	[−0.148,−0.0788]	−0.0864***	[−0.121,−0.0515]	−0.126***	[−0.168,−0.0842]
Democrat	0	[0,0]	0	[0,0]	0	[0,0]	0	[0,0]
Republican	−0.0335	[−0.0812,0.0142]	−0.159***	[−0.217,−0.102]	−0.0516*	[−0.0990,−0.00413]	−0.0785**	[−0.129,−0.0275]
Independent	0.0500*	[0.00675,0.0932]	0.00465	[−0.0412,0.0505]	0.0180	[−0.0258,0.0617]	0.0538*	[0.00581,0.102]

continued

Table 5A.5: *continued*

	White Rs		Black Rs		Asian Rs		Hispanic Rs	
Liberal	0	[0,0]	0	[0,0]	0	[0,0]	0	[0,0]
Moderate	0.00891	[−0.0362,0.0540]	−0.00495	[−0.0447,0.0348]	0.0307	[−0.0144,0.0759]	−0.0172	[−0.0609,0.0265]
Conservative	−0.0493	[−0.103,0.00450]	−0.104***	[−0.149,−0.0592]	−0.0826**	[−0.138,−0.0269]	−0.0720**	[−0.121,−0.0233]
Served in Congress	0	[0,0]	0	[0,0]	0	[0,0]	0	[0,0]
Served in City Council	−0.0638**	[−0.105,−0.0221]	−0.0537**	[−0.0939,−0.0136]	−0.0893***	[−0.132,−0.0468]	−0.0753***	[−0.117,−0.0340]
Served in the State Legislature	−0.00234	[−0.0423,0.0376]	−0.0410*	[−0.0753,−0.00668]	−0.0276	[−0.0669,0.0116]	−0.0147	[−0.0531,0.0238]
Not R's Party	0	[0,0]	0	[0,0]	0	[0,0]	0	[0,0]
R's Party	0.149***	[0.108,0.190]	0.120***	[0.0724,0.167]	0.155***	[0.117,0.192]	0.109***	[0.0657,0.151]
Constant	0.604***	[0.527,0.680]	0.496***	[0.426,0.566]	0.538***	[0.458,0.619]	0.512***	[0.429,0.596]
Observations	3800		4060		4140		3708	
r2	0.0629		0.0931		0.0634		0.0645	

95% confidence intervals in brackets
$^{*}p < 0.05$, $^{**}p < 0.01$, $^{***}p < 0.001$

Table 5A.6: Figure 5.6: Average Change in Probability of Selection by Candidate Ethnorace (Full Sample)

	H2		H1	
Male	0	[0,0]	0	[0,0]
Female	0.0222**	[0.00571,0.0387]	0.0222**	[0.00571,0.0387]
Outsider non-mixed	0	[0,0]	−0.148***	[−0.177,−0.119]
Same-race non-mixed	0.148***	[0.119,0.177]	0	[0,0]
Same-race mixed	0.109***	[0.0892,0.129]	−0.0394**	[−0.0679,−0.0108]
Outsider mixed	0.0316**	[0.0122,0.0510]	−0.117***	[−0.146,−0.0867]
Born in the U.S.	0	[0,0]	0	[0,0]
Born outside the U.S.	−0.120***	[−0.139,−0.101]	−0.120***	[−0.139,−0.101]
Democrat	0	[0,0]	0	[0,0]
Republican	−0.0763***	[−0.101,−0.0514]	−0.0763***	[−0.101,−0.0514]
Independent	0.0351**	[0.0128,0.0574]	0.0351**	[0.0128,0.0574]
Liberal	0	[0,0]	0	[0,0]
Moderate	0.00632	[−0.0152,0.0278]	0.00632	[−0.0152,0.0278]
Conservative	−0.0763***	[−0.102,−0.0509]	−0.0763***	[−0.102,−0.0509]
Served in Congress	0	[0,0]	0	[0,0]
Served in City Council	−0.0713***	[−0.0920,−0.0507]	−0.0713***	[−0.0920,−0.0507]
Served in the State Legislature	−0.0224*	[−0.0413,−0.00352]	−0.0224*	[−0.0413,−0.00352]
Not R's Party	0	[0,0]	0	[0,0]
R's Party	0.143***	[0.122,0.164]	0.143***	[0.122,0.164]
Constant	0.516***	[0.484,0.549]	0.665***	[0.626,0.703]
Observations	15708		15708	
r2	0.0641		0.0641	

95% confidence intervals in brackets
*$p < 0.05$, **$p < 0.01$, ***$p < 0.001$
0s are base categories

Table 5A.7: Figure 5.7: Average Change in Probability of Selection by Ethnorace of Respondent and Candidate Ethnorace (Electoral Support Gap Hypothesis)

	White		Black		Asian		Hispanic	
Male	0	[0,0]	0	[0,0]	0	[0,0]	0	[0,0]
Female	0.0499**	[0.0143,0.0855]	0.0163	[−0.0150,0.0475]	−0.000434	[−0.0335,0.0326]	0.0269	[−0.00568,0.0595]
Outsider Non-mixed	−0.0926**	[−0.151,−0.0345]						
White	0	[0,0]						
Black and White	−0.0311	[−0.107,0.0444]						
Asian and White	−0.0666	[−0.138,0.00468]						
Hispanic and White	−0.0475	[−0.121,0.0263]						
Black and Asian	−0.0511	[−0.124,0.0216]						
Black and Hispanic	−0.105**	[−0.180,−0.0301]						
Asian and Hispanic	−0.106*	[−0.187,−0.0244]						
Born in the U.S.	0	[0,0]	0	[0,0]	0	[0,0]	0	[0,0]
Born Outside the U.S.	−0.162***	[−0.201,−0.123]	−0.113***	[−0.147,−0.0783]	−0.0866***	[−0.122,−0.0517]	−0.126***	[−0.168,−0.0840]
Democrat	0	[0,0]	0	[0,0]	0	[0,0]	0	[0,0]
Republican	−0.0336	[−0.0813,0.0141]	−0.159***	[−0.216,−0.101]	−0.0523*	[−0.0996,−0.00494]	−0.0790**	[−0.130,−0.0281]
Independent	0.0496*	[0.00635,0.0928]	0.00497	[−0.0408,0.0508]	0.0186	[−0.0252,0.0623]	0.0528*	[0.00491,0.101]
Liberal	0	[0,0]	0	[0,0]	0	[0,0]	0	[0,0]
Moderate	0.00864	[−0.0365,0.0538]	−0.00324	[−0.0425,0.0361]	0.0304	[−0.0145,0.0754]	−0.0165	[−0.0604,0.0275]
Conservative	−0.0496	[−0.103,0.00429]	−0.103***	[−0.148,−0.0577]	−0.0833**	[−0.139,−0.0276]	−0.0712**	[−0.120,−0.0223]

Served in Congress	0	[0,0]	0	[0,0]	0	[0,0]	0	[0,0]
Served in City Council	−0.0640**	[−0.106,−0.0224]	−0.0543**	[−0.0944,−0.0142]	−0.0891***	[−0.132,−0.0465]	−0.0750***	[−0.116,−0.0338]
Served in the State Legislature	−0.00304	[−0.0431,0.0370]	−0.0405*	[−0.0750,−0.00608]	−0.0277	[−0.0671,0.0116]	−0.0145	[−0.0530,0.0239]
Not R's Party	0	[0,0]	0	[0,0]	0	[0,0]	0	[0,0]
R's Party	0.149***	[0.108,0.190]	0.120***	[0.0727,0.167]	0.155***	[0.117,0.192]	0.109***	[0.0660,0.152]
Outsider Non-mixed			−0.163***	[−0.220,−0.106]				
Black			0	[0,0]				
Black and White			−0.0345	[−0.0943,0.0253]				
Black and Asian			−0.0271	[−0.0961,0.0418]				
Black and Hispanic			−0.00850	[−0.0771,0.0601]				
Asian and Hispanic			−0.119***	[−0.183,−0.0559]				
Asian and White			−0.174***	[−0.236,−0.113]				
Hispanic and White			−0.0993**	[−0.163,−0.0360]				
Outsider Non-mixed					−0.160***	[−0.221,−0.0985]		
Asian					0	[0,0]		

continued

Table 5A.7: *continued*

	White		Black		Asian		Hispanic	
Black and Asian					−0.0669	[−0.138,0.00438]		
Asian and Hispanic					−0.0193	[−0.0949,0.0563]		
Asian and White					−0.0152	[−0.0800,0.0497]		
Black and White					−0.107**	[−0.182,−0.0326]		
Black and Hispanic					−0.137***	[−0.211,−0.0624]		
Hispanic and White					−0.128**	[−0.206,−0.0501]		
Outsider Non-mixed							−0.174***	[−0.232,−0.117]
Hispanic							0	[0,0]
Black and Hispanic							−0.0494	[−0.116,0.0174]
Asian and Hispanic							−0.0735	[−0.148,0.00106]
Hispanic and White							−0.0345	[−0.107,0.0382]
Black and White							−0.108**	[−0.185,−0.0315]
Black and Asian							−0.151***	[−0.223,−0.0786]
Asian and White							−0.107**	[−0.182,−0.0318]
Constant	0.604***	[0.528,0.681]	0.722***	[0.646,0.798]	0.662***	[0.582,0.742]	0.694***	[0.613,0.775]
Observations	3800		4060		4140		3708	
r2	0.0626		0.0905		0.0626		0.0636	

95% confidence intervals in brackets
* $p < 0.05$, ** $p < 0.01$, *** $p < 0.001$
0s are base categories

Table 5A.8: Figure 5.8: Average Change in Probability of Selection by Ethnorace of Respondent and Candidate Ethnorace (Exceptional Mixed Person Hypothesis)

	White Rs		Black Rs		Asian Rs		Hispanic Rs	
Male	0	[0,0]	0	[0,0]	0	[0,0]	0	[0,0]
Female	0.0499**	[0.0143,0.0855]	0.0163	[−0.0150,0.0475]	−0.000434	[−0.0335,0.0326]	0.0269	[−0.00568,0.0595]
Outsider Non-mixed	0	[0,0]						
White	0.0926**	[0.0345,0.151]						
Black and White	0.0615*	[0.00510,0.118]						
Asian and White	0.0259	[−0.0333,0.0851]						
Hispanic and White	0.0451	[−0.0141,0.104]						
Black and Asian	0.0414	[−0.0140,0.0969]						
Black and Hispanic	−0.0125	[−0.0702,0.0451]						
Asian and Hispanic	−0.0133	[−0.0697,0.0432]						
Born in the U.S.	0	[0,0]	0	[0,0]	0	[0,0]	0	[0,0]
Born Outside the U.S.	−0.162***	[−0.201,−0.123]	−0.113***	[−0.147,−0.0783]	−0.0866***	[−0.122,−0.0517]	−0.126***	[−0.168,−0.0840]
Democrat	0	[0,0]	0	[0,0]	0	[0,0]	0	[0,0]
Republican	−0.0336	[−0.0813,0.0141]	−0.159***	[−0.216,−0.101]	−0.0523*	[−0.0996,−0.00494]	−0.0790**	[−0.130,−0.0281]
Independent	0.0496*	[0.00635,0.0928]	0.00497	[−0.0408,0.0508]	0.0186	[−0.0252,0.0623]	0.0528*	[0.00491,0.101]
Liberal	0	[0,0]	0	[0,0]	0	[0,0]	0	[0,0]

continued

Table 5A.8: *continued*

	White Rs		Black Rs		Asian Rs		Hispanic Rs	
Moderate	0.00864	[−0.0365,0.0538]	−0.00324	[−0.0425,0.0361]	0.0304	[−0.0145,0.0754]	−0.0165	[−0.0604,0.0275]
Conservative	−0.0496	[−0.103,0.00429]	−0.103***	[−0.148,−0.0577]	−0.0833**	[−0.139,−0.0276]	−0.0712**	[−0.120,−0.0223]
Served in Congress	0	[0,0]	0	[0,0]	0	[0,0]	0	[0,0]
Served in City Council	−0.0640**	[−0.106,−0.0224]	−0.0543**	[−0.0944,−0.0142]	−0.0891***	[−0.132,−0.0465]	−0.0750***	[−0.116,−0.0338]
Served in the State Legislature	−0.00304	[−0.0431,0.0370]	−0.0405*	[−0.0750,−0.00608]	−0.0277	[−0.0671,0.0116]	−0.0145	[−0.0530,0.0239]
Not R's Party	0	[0,0]	0	[0,0]	0	[0,0]	0	[0,0]
R's Party	0.149***	[0.108,0.190]	0.120***	[0.0727,0.167]	0.155***	[0.117,0.192]	0.109***	[0.0660,0.152]
Outsider Non-mixed			0	[0,0]				
Black			0.163***	[0.106,0.220]				
Black and White			0.128***	[0.0777,0.179]				
Black and Asian			0.136***	[0.0782,0.193]				
Black and Hispanic			0.154***	[0.0960,0.213]				
Asian and Hispanic			0.0435	[−0.0109,0.0979]				
Asian and White			−0.0113	[−0.0656,0.0430]				
Hispanic and White			0.0636*	[0.00932,0.118]				
Outsider Non-mixed					0	[0,0]		
Asian					0.160***	[0.0985,0.221]		
Black and Asian					0.0926***	[0.0390,0.146]		

Asian and Hispanic					0.140***	[0.0845,0.196]		
Asian and White					0.144***	[0.0907,0.198]		
Black and White					0.0521*	[0.000610,0.104]		
Black and Hispanic					0.0229	[−0.0297,0.0755]		
Hispanic and White					0.0313	[−0.0275,0.0902]		
Outsider Non-mixed							0	[0,0]
Hispanic							0.174***	[0.117,0.232]
Black and Hispanic							0.125***	[0.0688,0.181]
Asian and Hispanic							0.101***	[0.0429,0.159]
Hispanic and White							0.140***	[0.0831,0.196]
Black and White							0.0661*	[0.00226,0.130]
Black and Asian							0.0237	[−0.0304,0.0778]
Asian and White							0.0673*	[0.0109,0.124]
Constant	0.512***	[0.447,0.577]	0.559***	[0.498,0.621]	0.502***	[0.435,0.570]	0.519***	[0.450,0.588]
Observations	3800		4060		4140		3708	
r2	0.0626		0.0905		0.0626		0.0636	

95% confidence intervals in brackets
$^{*}p < 0.05$, $^{**}p < 0.01$, $^{***}p < 0.001$
0s are base categories

Table 5A.9: Figure 5.9: Average Change in Probability of Selection by Candidate Ethnorace and Respondent Group Identity

	Linked Fate		IDPG	
Male	0	(.)	0	(.)
Female	0.0221*	(0.00841)	0.0224*	(0.00842)
Same-race non-mixed	0.116**	(0.0279)	0.0983**	(0.0217)
Same-race mixed	0.0944**	(0.0179)	0.0662**	(0.0149)
Outsider mixed	0.0494*	(0.0190)	0.0235	(0.0145)
Outsider non-mixed	0	(.)	0	(.)
No linked fate	0	(.)		
Linked fate	−0.00662	(0.0127)		
Same-race non-mixed × No linked fate	0	(.)		
Same-race non-mixed × Linked fate	0.0463	(0.0329)		
Same-race mixed × No linked fate	0	(.)		
Same-race mixed × Linked fate	0.0209	(0.0216)		
Outsider mixed × No linked fate	0	(.)		
Outsider mixed × Linked fate	−0.0248	(0.0222)		
Outsider non-mixed × No linked fate	0	(.)		
Outsider non-mixed × Linked fate	0	(.)		
Born in the U.S.	0	(.)	0	(.)
Born outside the U.S.	−0.120**	(0.00953)	−0.120**	(0.00954)
Democrat	0	(.)	0	(.)
Republican	−0.0762**	(0.0126)	−0.0766**	(0.0126)
Independent	0.0352*	(0.0114)	0.0351*	(0.0114)
Liberal	0	(.)	0	(.)
Moderate	0.00634	(0.0110)	0.00615	(0.0109)
Conservative	−0.0763**	(0.0129)	−0.0765**	(0.0129)
Served in Congress	0	(.)	0	(.)
Served in City Council	−0.0717**	(0.0105)	−0.0715**	(0.0105)
Served in the State Legislature	−0.0228*	(0.00964)	−0.0231*	(0.00963)
Not R's Party	0	(.)	0	(.)
R's Party	0.143**	(0.0106)	0.143**	(0.0106)
Low group identity			0	(.)
High group identity			−0.0366*	(0.0116)
Same-race non-mixed × Low group identity			0	(.)
Same-race non-mixed × High group identity			0.0937*	(0.0296)

	Linked Fate		IDPG	
Same-race mixed × Low group identity			0	(.)
Same-race mixed × High group identity			0.0787**	(0.0200)
Outsider mixed × Low group identity			0	(.)
Outsider mixed × High group identity			0.0147	(0.0198)
Outsider non-mixed × Low group identity			0	(.)
Outsider non-mixed × High group identity			0	(.)
Constant	0.521**	(0.0189)	0.537**	(0.0177)
Observations	15708		15708	
r2	0.0645		0.0655	

Standard errors in parentheses
$^{+}p < 0.10$, $^{*}p < 0.05$, $^{**}p < 0.001$

Table 5A.10: Figure 5.10: White Respondents' Average Change in Probability of Selection of Candidates by Approval of Marriage with Black People

	w/Black people		w/Asian people		w/Hispanic people	
Male	0	(.)	0	(.)	0	(.)
Female	0.0516*	(0.0181)	0.0494*	(0.0181)	0.0497*	(0.0181)
White	0.0231	(0.0364)	0.0937*	(0.0372)	0.181	(0.111)
Black	0	(.)	0.0314	(0.0350)	−0.0656	(0.124)
Asian	−0.0548	(0.0363)	0	(.)	−0.0165	(0.104)
Hispanic	−0.0547	(0.0375)	−0.0139	(0.0366)	0	(.)
Black and White	0.0200	(0.0342)	0.0677+	(0.0366)	0.143	(0.132)
Black and Asian	−0.00424	(0.0376)	0.0531	(0.0369)	0.0510	(0.125)
Black and Hispanic	−0.0333	(0.0359)	0.00421	(0.0375)	−0.105	(0.125)
Asian and Hispanic	−0.0491	(0.0384)	−0.00158	(0.0361)	−0.132	(0.109)
Asian and White	−0.00779	(0.0389)	0.0456	(0.0366)	−0.0260	(0.153)
Hispanic and White	−0.00910	(0.0402)	0.0404	(0.0366)	0.179	(0.130)
Any disapproval	−0.146*	(0.0506)				
Any approval	0	(.)				
White × Any disapproval	0.310**	(0.0826)				
White × Any approval	0	(.)				
Black × Any disapproval	0	(.)				
Black × Any approval	0	(.)				
Asian × Any disapproval	0.164+	(0.0859)				

Asian × Any approval	0	(.)				
Hispanic × Any disapproval	0.131	(0.0970)				
Hispanic × Any approval	0	(.)				
Black and White × Any disapproval	0.142	(0.102)				
Black and White × Any approval	0	(.)				
Black and Asian × Any disapproval	0.166*	(0.0711)				
Black and Asian × Any approval	0	(.)				
Black and Hispanic × Any disapproval	0.00423	(0.0938)				
Black and Hispanic × Any approval	0	(.)				
Asian and Hispanic × Any disapproval	0.107	(0.0840)				
Asian and Hispanic × Any approval	0	(.)				
Asian and White × Any disapproval	0.0899	(0.101)				
Asian and White × Any approval	0	(.)				
Hispanic and White × Any disapproval	0.249*	(0.0825)				
Hispanic and White × Any approval	0	(.)				
Born in the U.S.	0	(.)	0	(.)	0	(.)
Born Outside the U.S.	−0.164**	(0.0197)	−0.162**	(0.0198)	−0.163**	(0.0199)
Democrat	0	(.)	0	(.)	0	(.)
Republican	−0.0338	(0.0243)	−0.0336	(0.0243)	−0.0336	(0.0243)
Independent	0.0489*	(0.0218)	0.0491*	(0.0219)	0.0498*	(0.0219)
Liberal	0	(.)	0	(.)	0	(.)

continued

Table 5A.10: *continued*

	w/Black people		w/Asian people		w/Hispanic people	
Moderate	0.00807	(0.0230)	0.00750	(0.0229)	0.00739	(0.0229)
Conservative	−0.0498^{+}	(0.0273)	−0.0495^{+}	(0.0272)	−0.0496^{+}	(0.0273)
Served in Congress	0	(.)	0	(.)	0	(.)
Served in City Council	−0.0671*	(0.0213)	−0.0651*	(0.0211)	−0.0661*	(0.0212)
Served in the State Legislature	−0.00336	(0.0203)	−0.00345	(0.0201)	−0.00319	(0.0201)
Not R's Party	0	(.)	0	(.)	0	(.)
R's Party	0.149**	(0.0208)	0.150**	(0.0208)	0.150**	(0.0209)
Any disapproval			−0.0138	(0.0680)		
Any approval			0	(.)		
White × Any disapproval			0.0881	(0.115)		
White × Any approval			0	(.)		
Black × Any disapproval			0.0145	(0.129)		
Black × Any approval			0	(.)		
Asian × Any disapproval			0	(.)		
Asian × Any approval			0	(.)		
Hispanic × Any disapproval			0.131	(0.100)		
Hispanic × Any approval			0	(.)		
Black and White × Any disapproval			0.0580	(0.142)		
Black and White × Any approval			0	(.)		
Black and Asian × Any disapproval			−0.0178	(0.0824)		
Black and Asian × Any approval			0	(.)		
Black and Hispanic × Any disapproval			−0.105	(0.119)		

Black and Hispanic × Any approval			0	(.)		
Asian and Hispanic × Any disapproval			−0.0304	(0.109)		
Asian and Hispanic × Any approval			0	(.)		
Asian and White × Any disapproval			−0.117	(0.111)		
Asian and White × Any approval			0	(.)		
Hispanic and White × Any disapproval			0.219^{+}	(0.131)		
Hispanic and White × Any approval			0	(.)		
Any approval					−0.0165	(0.0926)
White × Any approval					−0.0858	(0.117)
Black × Any approval					0.111	(0.129)
Asian × Any approval					0.0233	(0.111)
Hispanic × Any approval					0	(.)
Black and White × Any approval					−0.0729	(0.138)
Black and Asian × Any approval					0.00486	(0.130)
Black and Hispanic × Any approval					0.119	(0.131)
Asian and Hispanic × Any approval					0.147	(0.115)
Asian and White × Any approval					0.0736	(0.158)
Hispanic and White × Any approval					−0.130	(0.135)
Constant	0.556^{**}	(0.0403)	0.504^{**}	(0.0386)	0.514^{**}	(0.0922)
Observations	3800		3800		3800	
r2	0.0672		0.0654		0.0657	

Standard errors in parentheses
$^{+}p < 0.10$, $^{*}p < 0.05$, $^{**}p < 0.001$

Table 5A.11: Figure 5.11: Asian American Respondents' Average Change in Probability of Selection of Candidates by Approval of Marriage with Black People

	w/White people		w/Black people		w/Hispanic people	
Male	0	(.)	0	(.)	0	(.)
Female	−0.000884	(0.0168)	−0.00233	(0.0169)	−0.00200	(0.0169)
White	0	(.)	0.00180	(0.0384)	0.0438	(0.0349)
Black	−0.0474	(0.0371)	0	(.)	0.0117	(0.0349)
Asian	0.108*	(0.0369)	0.118*	(0.0413)	0.163**	(0.0377)
Hispanic	−0.0678*	(0.0334)	−0.0605+	(0.0361)	0	(.)
Black and White	0.00942	(0.0340)	0.0510	(0.0378)	0.0778*	(0.0340)
Black and Asian	0.0439	(0.0364)	0.0593+	(0.0358)	0.0945*	(0.0349)
Black and Hispanic	−0.0176	(0.0349)	0.0252	(0.0387)	0.0541	(0.0341)
Asian and Hispanic	0.0909*	(0.0361)	0.108*	(0.0410)	0.170**	(0.0366)
Asian and White	0.0932*	(0.0358)	0.118*	(0.0390)	0.154**	(0.0345)
Hispanic and White	−0.00364	(0.0389)	0.0543	(0.0388)	0.0798*	(0.0385)
Any disapproval	−0.0790	(0.107)				
Any approval	0	(.)				
White × Any disapproval	0	(.)				
White × Any approval	0	(.)				
Black × Any disapproval	−0.0223	(0.157)				
Black × Any approval	0	(.)				
Asian × Any disapproval	0.159	(0.177)				

Asian × Any approval	0	(.)				
Hispanic × Any disapproval	0.121	(0.129)				
Hispanic × Any approval	0	(.)				
Black and White × Any disapproval	0.0681	(0.139)				
Black and White × Any approval	0	(.)				
Black and Asian × Any disapproval	0.139	(0.157)				
Black and Asian × Any approval	0	(.)				
Black and Hispanic × Any disapproval	0.0341	(0.127)				
Black and Hispanic × Any approval	0	(.)				
Asian and Hispanic × Any disapproval	0.143	(0.140)				
Asian and Hispanic × Any approval	0	(.)				
Asian and White × Any disapproval	0.174	(0.131)				
Asian and White × Any approval	0	(.)				
Hispanic and White × Any disapproval	−0.0552	(0.136)				
Hispanic and White × Any approval	0	(.)				
Born in the U.S.	0	(.)	0	(.)	0	(.)
Born Outside the U.S.	−0.0863**	(0.0177)	−0.0832**	(0.0176)	−0.0842**	(0.0176)
Democrat	0	(.)	0	(.)	0	(.)
Republican	−0.0519*	(0.0240)	−0.0516*	(0.0238)	−0.0519*	(0.0238)
Independent	0.0188	(0.0222)	0.0199	(0.0222)	0.0178	(0.0222)

continued

Table 5A.11: *continued*

	w/White people		w/Black people		w/Hispanic people	
Liberal	0	(.)	0	(.)	0	(.)
Moderate	0.0309	(0.0229)	0.0298	(0.0229)	0.0305	(0.0230)
Conservative	−0.0831*	(0.0282)	−0.0854*	(0.0282)	−0.0839*	(0.0282)
Served in Congress	0	(.)	0	(.)	0	(.)
Served in City Council	−0.0881**	(0.0216)	−0.0880**	(0.0216)	−0.0893**	(0.0215)
Served in the State Legislature	−0.0268	(0.0199)	−0.0270	(0.0201)	−0.0275	(0.0199)
Not R's Party	0	(.)	0	(.)	0	(.)
R's Party	0.153**	(0.0191)	0.154**	(0.0188)	0.154**	(0.0189)
Any disapproval			−0.132*	(0.0588)		
Any approval			0	(.)		
White × Any disapproval			0.206*	(0.101)		
White × Any approval			0	(.)		
Black × Any disapproval			0	(.)		
Black × Any approval			0	(.)		
Asian × Any disapproval			0.223*	(0.0915)		
Asian × Any approval			0	(.)		
Hispanic × Any disapproval			0.216*	(0.0785)		
Hispanic × Any approval			0	(.)		

Black and White × Any disapproval	0.0619	(0.0837)		
Black and White × Any approval	0	(.)		
Black and Asian × Any disapproval	0.192*	(0.0784)		
Black and Asian × Any approval	0	(.)		
Black and Hispanic × Any disapproval	0.0407	(0.0850)		
Black and Hispanic × Any approval	0	(.)		
Asian and Hispanic × Any disapproval	0.183*	(0.0848)		
Asian and Hispanic × Any approval	0	(.)		
Asian and White × Any disapproval	0.165*	(0.0789)		
Asian and White × Any approval	0	(.)		
Hispanic and White × Any disapproval	−0.0443	(0.0867)		
Hispanic and White × Any approval	0	(.)		
Any disapproval			−0.00586	(0.0482)
Any approval			0	(.)
White × Any disapproval			0.0794	(0.0957)
White × Any approval			0	(.)
Black × Any disapproval			−0.0337	(0.0930)
Black × Any approval			0	(.)
Asian × Any disapproval			0.0999	(0.0978)

continued

Table 5A.11: *continued*

	w/White people		w/Black people		w/Hispanic people	
Asian × Any approval					0	(.)
Hispanic × Any disapproval					0	(.)
Hispanic × Any approval					0	(.)
Black and White × Any disapproval					−0.0281	(0.0756)
Black and White × Any approval					0	(.)
Black and Asian × Any disapproval					0.108	(0.0770)
Black and Asian × Any approval					0	(.)
Black and Hispanic × Any disapproval					−0.0672	(0.0766)
Black and Hispanic × Any approval					0	(.)
Asian and Hispanic × Any disapproval					−0.0546	(0.0731)
Asian and Hispanic × Any approval					0	(.)
Asian and White × Any disapproval					0.0785	(0.0899)
Asian and White × Any approval					0	(.)
Hispanic and White × Any disapproval					−0.166*	(0.0778)
Hispanic and White × Any approval					0	(.)
Constant	0.545**	(0.0401)	0.520**	(0.0416)	0.483**	(0.0386)
Observations	4140		4140		4140	
r2	0.0652		0.0697		0.0671	

Standard errors in parentheses
$^{+}p < 0.10$, $^{*}p < 0.05$, $^{**}p < 0.001$

Table 5A.12: Figure 5.12: Black Respondents' Average Change in Probability of Selection of Candidates by Approval of Marriage with Asian People

	w/White people		w/Asian people		w/Hispanic people	
Male	0	(.)	0	(.)	0	(.)
Female	0.0164	(0.0158)	0.0152	(0.0157)	0.0158	(0.0158)
White	0	(.)	−0.0935*	(0.0347)	−0.114**	(0.0338)
Black	0.247**	(0.0377)	0.137**	(0.0364)	0.113*	(0.0345)
Asian	0.101*	(0.0360)	0	(.)	−0.0326	(0.0359)
Hispanic	0.120**	(0.0348)	0.0117	(0.0361)	0	(.)
Black and White	0.218**	(0.0347)	0.105*	(0.0339)	0.0839*	(0.0339)
Black and Asian	0.206**	(0.0386)	0.0981*	(0.0343)	0.0785*	(0.0371)
Black and Hispanic	0.244**	(0.0375)	0.123**	(0.0352)	0.100*	(0.0373)
Asian and Hispanic	0.129**	(0.0371)	0.0313	(0.0346)	−0.00675	(0.0337)
Asian and White	0.0745*	(0.0372)	−0.0290	(0.0362)	−0.0522	(0.0340)
Hispanic and White	0.158**	(0.0359)	0.0496	(0.0354)	0.0224	(0.0348)
Any disapproval	0.111*	(0.0554)				
Any approval	0	(.)				
White × Any disapproval	0	(.)				
White × Any approval	0	(.)				
Black × Any disapproval	−0.112	(0.102)				
Black × Any approval	0	(.)				

continued

Table 5A.12: *continued*

	w/White people		w/Asian people		w/Hispanic people	
Asian × Any disapproval	−0.109	(0.0931)				
Asian × Any approval	0	(.)				
Hispanic × Any disapproval	−0.0499	(0.0957)				
Hispanic × Any approval	0	(.)				
Black and White × Any disapproval	-0.150^{+}	(0.0802)				
Black and White × Any approval	0	(.)				
Black and Asian × Any disapproval	−0.00767	(0.0994)				
Black and Asian × Any approval	0	(.)				
Black and Hispanic × Any disapproval	−0.158	(0.123)				
Black and Hispanic × Any approval	0	(.)				
Asian and Hispanic × Any disapproval	−0.121	(0.107)				
Asian and Hispanic × Any approval	0	(.)				
Asian and White × Any disapproval	−0.124	(0.0859)				
Asian and White × Any approval	0	(.)				
Hispanic and White × Any disapproval	-0.187^{*}	(0.0930)				
Hispanic and White × Any approval	0	(.)				
Born in the U.S.	0	(.)	0	(.)	0	(.)
Born Outside the U.S.	-0.113^{**}	(0.0175)	-0.112^{**}	(0.0174)	-0.113^{**}	(0.0175)
Democrat	0	(.)	0	(.)	0	(.)

Republican	−0.161**	(0.0292)	−0.159**	(0.0293)	−0.160**	(0.0291)
Independent	0.00357	(0.0231)	0.00331	(0.0233)	0.00438	(0.0233)
Liberal	0	(.)	0	(.)	0	(.)
Moderate	−0.00573	(0.0202)	−0.00552	(0.0201)	−0.00409	(0.0201)
Conservative	−0.104**	(0.0227)	−0.104**	(0.0228)	−0.104**	(0.0229)
Served in Congress	0	(.)	0	(.)	0	(.)
Served in City Council	−0.0535*	(0.0203)	−0.0526*	(0.0205)	−0.0547*	(0.0204)
Served in the State Legislature	−0.0415*	(0.0175)	−0.0407*	(0.0175)	−0.0417*	(0.0174)
Not R's Party	0	(.)	0	(.)	0	(.)
R's Party	0.120**	(0.0241)	0.120**	(0.0241)	0.119**	(0.0241)
Any disapproval			−0.0796	(0.0775)		
Any approval			0	(.)		
White × Any disapproval			0.134	(0.118)		
White × Any approval			0	(.)		
Black × Any disapproval			0.114	(0.147)		
Black × Any approval			0	(.)		
Asian × Any disapproval			0	(.)		
Asian × Any approval			0	(.)		
Hispanic × Any disapproval			0.194	(0.124)		
Hispanic × Any approval			0	(.)		

continued

Table 5A.12: *continued*

	w/White people		w/Asian people		w/Hispanic people	
Black and White × Any disapproval			0.0841	(0.0929)		
Black and White × Any approval			0	(.)		
Black and Asian × Any disapproval			0.247*	(0.0981)		
Black and Asian × Any approval			0	(.)		
Black and Hispanic × Any disapproval			0.178	(0.109)		
Black and Hispanic × Any approval			0	(.)		
Asian and Hispanic × Any disapproval			−0.0728	(0.124)		
Asian and Hispanic × Any approval			0	(.)		
Asian and White × Any disapproval			0.0253	(0.121)		
Asian and White × Any approval			0	(.)		
Hispanic and White × Any disapproval			−0.0295	(0.119)		
Hispanic and White × Any approval			0	(.)		
Any disapproval					−0.0620	(0.107)
Any approval					0	(.)
White × Any disapproval					0.0860	(0.132)
White × Any approval					0	(.)
Black × Any disapproval					0.138	(0.194)
Black × Any approval					0	(.)

Asian × Any disapproval					0.101	(0.155)
Asian × Any approval					0	(.)
Hispanic × Any disapproval					0	(.)
Hispanic × Any approval					0	(.)
Black and White × Any disapproval					0.0315	(0.136)
Black and White × Any approval					0	(.)
Black and Asian × Any disapproval					0.220	(0.168)
Black and Asian × Any approval					0	(.)
Black and Hispanic × Any disapproval					0.203	(0.163)
Black and Hispanic × Any approval					0	(.)
Asian and Hispanic × Any disapproval					0.122	(0.174)
Asian and Hispanic × Any approval					0	(.)
Asian and White × Any disapproval					−0.0235	(0.119)
Asian and White × Any approval					0	(.)
Hispanic and White × Any disapproval					−0.0228	(0.165)
Hispanic and White × Any approval					0	(.)
Constant	0.478**	(0.0380)	0.585**	(0.0370)	0.609**	(0.0389)
Observations	4060		4060		4060	
r2	0.0949		0.0960		0.0948	

Standard errors in parentheses
$^{+}p < 0.10$, $^{*}p < 0.05$, $^{**}p < 0.001$

Table 5A.13: Hispanic Voters' Average Change in Probability of Selection of Candidates by Attitudes Toward Intermarriage with White, Black, and Asian People

	w/White people		w/Black people		w/Asian people	
Male	0	(.)	0	(.)	0	(.)
Female	0.0288^{+}	(0.0166)	0.0270	(0.0166)	0.0278^{+}	(0.0165)
White	0	(.)	0.0202	(0.0427)	−0.0444	(0.0388)
Black	−0.0245	(0.0410)	0	(.)	−0.0702*	(0.0354)
Asian	0.0374	(0.0388)	0.0535	(0.0367)	0	(.)
Hispanic	0.183**	(0.0366)	0.203**	(0.0404)	0.144**	(0.0367)
Black and White	0.0673	(0.0418)	0.0966*	(0.0411)	0.0293	(0.0389)
Black and Asian	0.0319	(0.0368)	0.0549	(0.0356)	−0.00385	(0.0375)
Black and Hispanic	0.134**	(0.0398)	0.160**	(0.0376)	0.0927*	(0.0349)
Asian and Hispanic	0.108*	(0.0406)	0.128*	(0.0391)	0.0671^{+}	(0.0358)
Asian and White	0.0599	(0.0366)	0.0883*	(0.0390)	0.0377	(0.0354)
Hispanic and White	0.150**	(0.0410)	0.151**	(0.0361)	0.110*	(0.0353)
Any disapproval	−0.00697	(0.0887)				
Any approval	0	(.)				
White × Any disapproval	0	(.)				
White × Any approval	0	(.)				
Black × Any disapproval	0.0171	(0.101)				
Black × Any approval	0	(.)				

Asian × Any disapproval	0.0767	(0.140)				
Asian × Any approval	0	(.)				
Hispanic × Any disapproval	−0.0594	(0.131)				
Hispanic × Any approval	0	(.)				
Black and White × Any disapproval	0.0519	(0.146)				
Black and White × Any approval	0	(.)				
Black and Asian × Any disapproval	−0.0142	(0.136)				
Black and Asian × Any approval	0	(.)				
Black and Hispanic × Any disapproval	−0.0689	(0.145)				
Black and Hispanic × Any approval	0	(.)				
Asian and Hispanic × Any disapproval	−0.0208	(0.111)				
Asian and Hispanic × Any approval	0	(.)				
Asian and White × Any disapproval	0.0998	(0.146)				
Asian and White × Any approval	0	(.)				
Hispanic and White × Any disapproval	−0.0532	(0.138)				
Hispanic and White × Any approval	0	(.)				
Born in the U.S.	0	(.)	0	(.)	0	(.)
Born Outside the U.S.	−0.125**	(0.0213)	−0.126**	(0.0213)	−0.126**	(0.0214)
Democrat	0	(.)	0	(.)	0	(.)
Republican	−0.0786*	(0.0260)	−0.0779*	(0.0259)	−0.0799*	(0.0259)

continued

Table 5A.13: *continued*

	w/White people		w/Black people		w/Asian people	
Independent	0.0586*	(0.0243)	0.0548*	(0.0244)	0.0541*	(0.0242)
Liberal	0	(.)	0	(.)	0	(.)
Moderate	−0.0170	(0.0222)	−0.0160	(0.0222)	−0.0179	(0.0221)
Conservative	−0.0712*	(0.0248)	−0.0707*	(0.0248)	−0.0723*	(0.0248)
Served in Congress	0	(.)	0	(.)	0	(.)
Served in City Council	−0.0784**	(0.0209)	−0.0753**	(0.0208)	−0.0753**	(0.0211)
Served in the State Legislature	−0.0161	(0.0196)	−0.0137	(0.0196)	−0.0141	(0.0197)
Not R's Party	0	(.)	0	(.)	0	(.)
R's Party	0.113**	(0.0216)	0.109**	(0.0218)	0.108**	(0.0218)
Any disapproval			−0.0343	(0.0578)		
Any approval			0	(.)		
White × Any disapproval			0.0215	(0.0827)		
White × Any approval			0	(.)		
Black × Any disapproval			0	(.)		
Black × Any approval			0	(.)		
Asian × Any disapproval			0.0783	(0.0798)		
Asian × Any approval			0	(.)		
Hispanic × Any disapproval			0.0153	(0.101)		
Hispanic × Any approval			0	(.)		

Black and White × Any disapproval	−0.00528	(0.0997)		
Black and White × Any approval	0	(.)		
Black and Asian × Any disapproval	−0.00266	(0.0848)		
Black and Asian × Any approval	0	(.)		
Black and Hispanic × Any disapproval	−0.0248	(0.0923)		
Black and Hispanic × Any approval	0	(.)		
Asian and Hispanic × Any disapproval	0.0229	(0.0823)		
Asian and Hispanic × Any approval	0	(.)		
Asian and White × Any disapproval	0.0623	(0.0970)		
Asian and White × Any approval	0	(.)		
Hispanic and White × Any disapproval	0.132	(0.0849)		
Hispanic and White × Any approval	0	(.)		
Any disapproval			0.0129	(0.0952)
Any approval			0	(.)
White × Any disapproval			0.0160	(0.132)
White × Any approval			0	(.)
Black × Any disapproval			0.0659	(0.0908)
Black × Any approval			0	(.)
Asian × Any disapproval			0	(.)
Asian × Any approval			0	(.)

continued

Table 5A.13: *continued*

	w/White people		w/Black people		w/Asian people	
Hispanic × Any disapproval					−0.0650	(0.144)
Hispanic × Any approval					0	(.)
Black and White × Any disapproval					0.0168	(0.157)
Black and White × Any approval					0	(.)
Black and Asian × Any disapproval					−0.0792	(0.118)
Black and Asian × Any approval					0	(.)
Black and Hispanic × Any disapproval					−0.0340	(0.110)
Black and Hispanic × Any approval					0	(.)
Asian and Hispanic × Any disapproval					−0.0190	(0.140)
Asian and Hispanic × Any approval					0	(.)
Asian and White × Any disapproval					−0.0699	(0.141)
Asian and White × Any approval					0	(.)
Hispanic and White × Any disapproval					−0.0674	(0.130)
Hispanic and White × Any approval					0	(.)
Constant	0.511**	(0.0439)	0.492**	(0.0417)	0.554**	(0.0386)
Observations	3688		3708		3708	
r2	0.0660		0.0655		0.0651	

Standard errors in parentheses
$^{+}p < 0.10$, $^{*}p < 0.05$, $^{**}p < 0.001$

Table 5A.14: Summary of Asian and Black Californians

	Asian Californians	Black Californians
Condition		
Mixed (1)	$N = 557$ 49.73%	$N = 191$ 53.06%
Not mixed (0)	563 50.27	169 46.94
Importance of Identity		
Important (1)	530 43.30	344 90.29
Not important (0)	694 56.70	37 9.71
Party ID		
Democrat	615 50.25	278 72.97
Republican	343 28.02	63 16.54
Independent	266 21.73	40 10.50

Table 5A.15: NAAS Balance Check

Asian Californians	0	[0,0]
Black Californians	0.0811	[−0.00495,0.167]
Race is not important	0	[0,0]
Race is important	−0.0570	[−0.135,0.0210]
Democrat	0	[0,0]
Republican	0.0670	[−0.0141,0.148]
Independent	0.0554	[−0.0398,0.151]
Constant	0.492***	[0.426,0.557]
Observations	1480	
r2	0.00807	

95% confidence intervals in brackets
$^{*}p < 0.05$, $^{**}p < 0.01$, $^{***}p < 0.001$

Table 5A.16: Figure 5.3: Testing the Electoral Support Gap for Harris in 2016 (OLS: Interaction Results with Original Identity Categories)

	Black Californians		Asian Californians	
Not mixed	0	(.)	0	(.)
Mixed	0.660*	(0.214)	0.0808	(0.202)
Not at all Important	0	(.)	0	(.)
Somewhat Important	0.445+	(0.252)	0.247	(0.224)
Very Important	0.494*	(0.227)	0.0952	(0.176)
Extremely Important	0.446*	(0.224)	0.313+	(0.175)
Don't Know	0.567*	(0.222)	0.331	(0.283)
Not mixed × Not at all Important	0	(.)	0	(.)
Not mixed × Somewhat Important	0	(.)	0	(.)
Not mixed × Very Important	0	(.)	0	(.)
Not mixed × Extremely Important	0	(.)	0	(.)
Not mixed × 88. Don't Know	0	(.)	0	(.)
Mixed × Not at all Important	0	(.)	0	(.)
Mixed × Somewhat Important	−0.686*	(0.283)	0.159	(0.276)
Mixed × Very Important	−0.930**	(0.257)	0.252	(0.239)
Mixed × Extremely Important	−0.569*	(0.223)	−0.0882	(0.264)
Mixed × Don't Know	−0.648*	(0.214)	0.0891	(0.332)
Not R's Party	0	(.)	0	(.)
R's Party	0.0928	(0.0735)	0.0543	(0.0828)
Constant	0.340	(0.214)	0.369*	(0.141)
Observations	206		205	
r2	0.162		0.124	

Standard errors in parentheses
$^{+}p < 0.10$, $^{*}p < 0.05$, $^{**}p < 0.001$

References

Abrams, Dominic, and Michael A. Hogg. 1990. "Social Identification, Self-Categorization and Social Influence." *European Journal of Social Psychology* 1(1): 195–228.

Abrajano, Marisa A., Christopher S. Elmendorf, and Kevin M. Quinn. 2018. "Labels vs. Pictures: Treatment-Mode Effects in Experiments About Discrimination." *Political Analysis* 26(1): 20–33.

Adida, Claire L., Lauren D. Davenport, and Gwyneth McClendon. 2016. "Ethnic Cueing Across Minorities." *Public Opinion Quarterly* 80(4): 815–836, Winter 2016. https://doi.org/10.1093/poq/nfw029.

Ahmed, Sara. 2007. "A Phenomenology of Whiteness." *Feminist Theory* 8(2): 149–168.

Ahmed, Sara. 2009. "Embodying Diversity: Problems and Paradoxes for Black feminists." *Race Ethnicity and Education* 12(1: Black Feminisms and Postcolonial Paradigms): 41–52. https://www.tandfonline.com/doi/abs/10.1080/13613320802650931

Ahuja, Amit, Susan L. Ostermann, and Aashish Mehta. 2016. "Is Only Fair Lovely in Indian Politics? Consequences of Skin Color in a Survey Experiment in Delhi." *Journal of Race, Ethnicity, and Politics* 1(2): 227–252.

Alamillo, Rudy and Loren Collingwood. 2016. "Chameleon politics: social identity and racial cross-over appeals." *Politics, Groups, and Identities* 5(4): 533–560. https://doi.org/10.1080/21565503.2015.1122641.

Anderson, Ben, Garrett Bird, Richard Kornrumpf, Maria Macaluso, Natasha Mundkur, Madison Swingholm, and Jason Gainous. 2020. "Ethnic Cues, Latino Skin Tone, and Voter Preferences: An Experimental Test." *Social Science Quarterly* 101(5): 1920–1935.

Banducci, Susan A., Jeffrey A. Karp, Michael Thrasher, and Colin Rallings. 2008. "Ballot Photographs as Cues in Low-Information Elections." *Political Psychology* 29(6): 903–917.

Bansak, Kirk, Jens Hainmueller, Daniel J. Hopkins, and Teppei Yamamoto. 2018. "The Number of Choice Tasks and Survey Satisficing in Conjoint Experiments." *Political Analysis* 26(1): 112–119.

Barari, Soubhik, Elissa Berwick, Jens Hainmueller, Daniel Hopkins, Sean Liu, Anton Strezhnev, and Teppei Yamamoto. 2023. "Package 'cjoint.'" https://cran.r-project.org/web/packages/cjoint/cjoint.pdf

Barber, John T. and Oscar H. Gandy Jr. 1990. "Press Portrayal of African American and White United States Representatives." *Howard Journal of Communications* 2(2): 213–225.

Barreto, Matt A. 2010. *Ethnic Cues: The Role of Shared Ethnicity in Latino Political Participation*. Ann Arbor: University of Michigan Press.

Beamer, Glenn. 2002. "Elite Interviews and State Politics Research." *State Politics & Policy Quarterly* 2: 86–96.

Bejarano, Christina E. 2013. *The Latina Advantage: Gender, Race, and Political Success*. Austin: University of Texas Press.

Benoit, Kenneth, Kohei Watanabe, Haiyan Wang, Paul Nulty, Adam Obeng, Stefan Müller, Akitaka Matsuo, William Lowe, Christian Müller, and European Research Council. 2022. "Package 'quanteda.'" Version 3.0.0. https://cran.r-project.org/web/packages/quanteda/quanteda.pdf.

Bernstein, Mary, and Marcie De la Cruz. 2009. "'What Are You?': Explaining Identity As A Goal of the Multiracial Hapa Movement." *Social Problems* 56(4): 722–745.

Bischof, Daniel (2017): "New Graphic Schemes for Stata: Plotplain & Plottig." *Stata Journal* 17(3): 748–759.

Blatt, Jessica. 2018. *Race and The Making of American Political Science.* University of Pennsylvania Press.

Bonilla-Silva, Eduardo. 2004. "From Bi-Racial to Tri-Racial: Towards a new system of racial stratification in the USA." *Ethnic and Racial Studies* 27(6): 931–950.

Bose, Purnima. 2020. "Kamala Harris's The Truths We Hold: An American Journey." *American Literary History* 32(2): e25–e32.

Bratter, Jenifer L. and Mary E. Campbell. 2023. "Mixing Races, Maintaining Racism? Considering the Connection Between Interracial Families, Social Distance, and Racial Inequality." *Journal of Family Theory & Review.* https://doi.org/10.1111/jftr.12504.

Bratter, Jenifer, and Holly E. Heard. 2009. "Mother's, Father's, or Both? Parental Gender and Parent-Child Interactions in the Racial Classification of Adolescents." *Sociological Forum* 24(3): 658–688.

Bratter, Jenifer L. and Ellen M. Whitehead. 2018. "Ties that Bind? Comparing Kin Support Available For Mothers Of Mixed-Race And Monoracial Infants." *Journal of Marriage and Family* 80(4): 951–962.

Bridges, Khiara M. 2013. "The Dangerous Law of Biological Race." *Fordham Law Review* 82: 21–80.

Broockman, David E. 2013. "Black Politicians are More Intrinsically Motivated to Advance Blacks' Interests: A Field Experiment Manipulating Political Incentives." *American Journal of Political Science* 57(3): 521–536.

Brown, Nadia E. 2012. "Negotiating the Insider/Outsider Status: Black Feminist Ethnography and Legislative Studies." *Journal of Feminist Scholarship* 3: 19–34.

Brown, Nadia. 2014a. *Sisters in the Statehouse: Black women and legislative decision making.* Oxford University Press.

Brown, Nadia. 2014b. "'It's More Than Hair ... That's why you Should Care': The Politics of Appearance for Black Women State Legislators." *Politics, Groups, and Identities* 2: 295–312.

Brown, Nadia and Danielle Casarez Lemi. 2021. *Sister Style: The Politics of Appearance for Black Women Political Elites.* Oxford University Press.

Brunsma, David L. 2006. "Public Categories, Private Identities: Exploring Regional Differences in the Biracial Experience." *Social Science Research* 35: 555–576.

Buggs, Shantel Gabrieal. 2020. "Understanding Kamala Harris, The Great Multiracial (Black) Hope." *Bitch Media.* November 2. https://shantelgbuggs.com/2023/04/09/understanding-kamala-harris-the-great-multiracial-black-hope/

Buggs. Shantel Gabrieal. 2020. 95: A convo about (mixed) race with Dr. Buggs (Part 1 of 2) in Lovett, April and Darryl Lovett, *Success in Black and White.* Podcast. https://www.successinblackandwhite.com/episodes/episode/af42b7e0/95-a-convo-about-mixed-race-with-dr-buggs-part-1-of-2. September 13.

Burge, Camille D., Julian J. Wamble and Rachel R. Cuomo. "A Certain Type of Descriptive Representative? Understanding How the Skin Tone and Gender of Candidates Influences Black Politics." *The Journal of Politics* 82(2020): 1596–1601.

Canon, David T. 1999. *Race, Redistricting, and Representation.* University of Chicago Press.

Carter, Niambi M., and Pearl Ford Dowe. 2015. "The Racial Exceptionalism of Barack Obama." *Journal of African American Studies* 19(2): 105–119.

Casellas, Jason P. 2010. *Latino Representation in State Houses and Congress.* Cambridge: Cambridge University Press. Google Play Books.

Caygle, Heather. 2017. Black caucus chafes at Latino who wants to join. *Politico*. February 3. http://www.politico.com/story/2017/02/congressional-black-caucus-hispanic-adriano-espaillat-234575.

Chang, Sharon. 2016. *Raising Mixed Race: Multiracial Asian Children in a Post-Racial World*. Routledge.

Chen, Jacqueline M., Nour S. Kteily, and Arnold K. Ho. 2019. "Whose Side Are You On? Asian Americans' Mistrust of Asian-White Biracials Predicts More Exclusion From the Ingroup." *Personality and Social Psychology Bulletin* 45(6): 827–841.

Cheng, Emily. 2014. "Pearl S. Buck's 'American Children': US democracy, Adoption of the Amerasian Child, and the Occupation of Japan in *The Hidden Flower*." *Frontiers: A Journal of Women Studies* 35(1): 181–210.

Chirco, Patrizia and Tonya M. Buchanan. 2022. "Dark Faces in White Spaces: The Effects of Skin Tone, Race, Ethnicity, and Intergorup Preferences on Interpersonal Judgments and Voting Behavior." *Analyses of Social Issues and Public Policy* 22(1): 427–447.

Citrin, Jack, Morris Levy, and Robert P, Van Howeling. 2014. "Americans Fill Out President Obama's Census Form: What is his Race?" *Social Science Quarterly* 95(4): 1121–1136.

Clark, Emily. 2016. "The Tragic Mulatto and Passing," in Street, S.C. and Crow, C.L. (Eds). *The Palgrave Handbook of the Southern Gothic*, 259–270. London: Palgrave Macmillan.

Clayton, Kristen A. 2020. "Biracial Identity Development at Historically White and Historically Black Colleges and Universities." *Sociology of Education* 93(3): 238–255.

Collet, Christian. 2008. "Minority Candidates, Alternative Media and Multiethnic America: Deracialization or Toggling?" *Perspectives on Politics* 6(4): 707–728.

Coppock, Alexander. 2019. "Avoiding post-treatment bias in audit experiments." *Journal of Experimental Political Science* 6(1): 1–4.

Coppock, Alexander and Oliver A. McClellan. 2019. "Validating the Demographic, Political, Psychological, and Experimental Results Obtained From a New Source of Online Survey Respondents." *Research & Politics*. https://doi.org/10.1177/2053168018822174

Cott, Nancy F. 1998. "Marriage and Women's Citizenship in the United States, 1830–1934." *The American Historical Review* 103(5): 1440–1474.

Crenshaw, Kimberlé. 1991. "Mapping the Margins: Intersectionality, Identity Politics, and Violence against Women of Color." *Stanford Law Review* 43(6): 1241–1299.

Creswell, John W. and Vicki L. Plano Clark. 2017. *Designing and Conducting Mixed Methods Research: Edition 3*. SAGE Publications. Google Play Books.

Creswell, John W., and Vicki L. Plano Clark. 2018. Designing and Conducting Mixed Methods Research. Third Edition. Thousand Oaks, CA: Sage. Google Play Books.

Csizmadia, Annamaria and Annabell L. Atkin. 2022. "Supporting Children and Youth in Multiracial Families in the United States: Racial-Ethnic Socialization and Familial Support of Multiracial Experiences." *Journal of Family Studies* 31: 664–674.

Cuizon Villazor, Rose. 2008. "Blood Quantum Land Laws and the Race Versus Political Dilemma." *California Law Review* 96: 801–837.

Curington, Celeste Vaughan. 2016. Rethinking Multiracial Formation in the United States: An Intersectional Approach. *Sociology of Race and Ethnicity* 2(1): 27–41.

Curington, Celeste Vaughan. 2020. "'We're the Show at the Circus': Racially Dissecting the Multiracial Body". *Symbolic Interaction* 44(32): 269–291.

Curington, Celeste Vaughan, Ken-Hou Lin, Jennifer Hickes Lundquist. 2015. "Positioning Multiraciality in Cyberspace: Treatment of Multiracial Daters in an Online Dating Website." *American Sociological Review* 80(4): 764–788.

DaCosta, Kimberly. 2007. *Making Multiracials: State, Family, and Market in the Redrawing of the Color Line*. Stanford University Press.

Dahlerup, Drude. 1988. "When Tokens Matter." *Legislative Studies Quarterly* 29(1): 109–136.

Dalmage, Heather M. 2000. *Tripping on the Color Line: Black-White Multiracial Families in a Racially Divided World*. New Jersey: Rutgers University Press.

Dancey, Logan and Jasmine Masand. 2019. "Race and Representation on Twitter: Members of Congress' Response to the Deaths of Michael Brown and Eric Garner." *Politics, Groups, and Identities* 7(2): 267–286.

Daniel, G. Reginald. 2001. *More Than Black? Multiracial Identity and the New Racial Order*. Philadelphia, PA: Temple University Press.

Daniel, G. Reginald. 2021. "Sociology of Multiracial Identity in the Late 1980s and Early 1990s: The Failure of a Perspective." *Journal of Ethnic and Cultural Studies* 8(2): 106–125.

Daniel, G. Reginald, Laura Kina, Wei Ming Dariotis, and Camilla Fojas. 2014. "Emerging Paradigms in Critical Mixed Race Studies." *Journal of Critical Mixed Race Studies* 1(1): 6–65.

Davenport, Lauren D. 2016a. "The Role of Gender, Class, and Religion in Biracial Americans' Racial Labeling Decisions." *American Sociological Review* 81(1): 57–84.

Davenport, Lauren D. 2016b. "Beyond Black and white: Biracial attitudes in contemporary US Politics." *American Political Science Review* 110(1): 52–67.

Davenport, Lauren D. 2018. *Politics Beyond Black & White: Biracial Identity and Attitudes in America*. New York: Cambridge University Press. Kindle.

Davenport, Lauren D. 2020. "The Fluidity of Racial Classifications." *Annual Review of Political Science* 23: 221–240.

Davenport, Lauren, Annie Franco, and Shanto Iyengar. 2022. "Multiracial identity and political preferences." *The Journal of Politics* 84(1): 620–624.

Davis, Angelique M. 2006. "Multiracialism and Reparations: The Intersection of the Multiracial Category and Reparations Movements." *Thomas Jefferson Law Review* 29: 161–187.

Davis, F. James. 1991. *Who is Black? One Nation's Definition*. University Park, PA: Penn State University Press.

Dawson, Michael C. 1995. *Behind the Mule: Race and Class in African-American Politics*. Princeton University Press.

Deeb, Alexander and Adam Love. 2018. "Media Representations of Multiracial Athletes." *Journal of Sport and Social Issues* 42(2): 95–114. https://journals.sagepub.com/doi/abs/10.1177/0193723517749598

Deo, Meera E. 2013. "Two Sides of a Coin: Safe Space & Segregation in Race/Ethnic-Specific Law Student Organizations." *Washington University Journal of Law & Policy* 42: 83–129.

Deterding, Nicole M. and Mary C. Waters. 2021. "Flexible Coding of In-Depth Interviews: A Twenty-First-Century Approach." *Sociological Methods and Research* 50(2): 708–739.

Devarajan, Kumari. 2020. "Claim us if you're famous." *National Public Radio, Code Switch*. November 10. https://www.npr.org/2020/11/10/933631207/claim-us-if-youre-famous

Dovi, Suzanne. 2002. "Will Just Any Woman, Black, or Latino Do?" *American Political Science Review* 96(4): 729–743.

Dowe, Pearl K. 2020. "Resisting Marginalization: Black Women's Political Ambition and Agency." *PS: Political Science & Politics* 53(4): 697–702.

Downey, Brant. 2015. "The Looking Glass Self and Deliberation Bias in Qualitative Interviews." *Sociological Spectrum* 35(6): 534–551.

Doyle, Jamie Mihoko and Grace Kao. 2007. "Friendship Choices of Multiracial Adolescents: Racial Homophily, Blending, or Amalgamation?" *Social Science Research* 36(2): 633–653.

Ensign, John. 2009. "SEN. ENSIGN COMMEMORATES ASIAN/PACIFIC AMERICAN HERITAGE MONTH." *US Fed News Service, Including US State News*, Jul 31.

Feagin, Joe R. 2013. *The White Racial Frame: Centuries of Racial Framing and Counter-framing*. Routledge. 2nd Edition. Google Play Books.

Feinerer, Ingo, Kurt Hornik, and David Meyer (2008). "Text Mining Infrastructure in R." *Journal of Statistical Software* 25(5): 1–54. URL: https://www.jstatsoft.org/v25/i05/.

Feinerer, Ingo, Kurt Hornik, and Artifex Software, Inc. (2020). tm: Text Mining Package. R package version 0.7-8. https://cran.r-project.org/web/packages/tm/tm.pdf

Feliciano, Cynthia. 2016. "Shades of Race: How Phenotype and Observer Characteristics Shape Racial Classification." *American Behavioral Scientist* 60(4): 390–419.

Feliciano, Cynthia and Jessica M. Kizer. 2021. "Reinforcing the Racial Structure: Observed Race and Multiracial Internet Daters' Racial Preferences." *Social Forces* 99(4): 1457–1486.

Fenno, Richard F. 2003. *Going Home: Black Representatives and their Constituents.* University of Chicago Press.

Fenno, Jr., Richard F. 1978. *Home Style: House Members in Their Districts.* 2003. New York: Pearson, Addison-Wesley Publishers, Inc., Longman Classics in Political Science.

Ferguson, Kennan. 2016. "Why Does Political Science Hate American Indians?" *Perspectives on Politics* 14(4): 1029–1038.

Fielder, Brigitte. 2020. *Relative Races: Genealogies of Interracial Kinship in Nineteenth Century America.* Duke University Press.

Fields, Barbara. 1990. "Slavery, Race, and Ideology in the United States of America." *New Left Review* 181: 95–118.

Fields, Karen E. and Barbara J. Fields. 2014. *Racecraft: The Soul of Inequality in American Life.* Verso.

Fine, Rachel D., Nour S. Kteily, Jacqueline M. Chen, Steven O. Roberts, and Arnold K. Ho. 2022. "United We Stand? Perceived Loyalty of Dual Nationals, Multiracial People, and Dual State Residents." *Group Processes & Intergroup Relations.* https://doi.org/10.1177/13684302221096322

Flores, René D. 2020. ""A Little More Ghetto, A Little Less Cultured": Are There Racial Stereotypes About Interracial Daters in the United States?" *Sociology of Race and Ethnicity* 6(2): 269–286.

Fraga, Bernard. 2016. "Candidates or Districts? Reevaluating the Role of Race in Voter Turnout." *American Journal of Political Science* 60(1): 97–122.

Fraga, Bernard L., Eric Gonzalez Juenke, Paru Shah. 2019. "Candidate Characteristics Cooperative Database, 2018 State Legislative Elections." Version 2; Published on 9/12/2019.

Fraga, Luis Ricardo, Linda Lopez, Valerie Martinez-Ebers, and Ricardo Ramirez. 2006. "Gender and Ethnicity: Patterns of Electoral Success and Legislative Advocacy among Latina and Latino State Officials in Four States." *Journal of Women, Politics & Policy* 28(3): 3–4, 121–145.

Fuchs, Chris. 2019. "In Kamala Harris' Presidential Campaign, Indian Americans Want More Opportunities to Connect." *NBC News.* February 12. https://www.nbcnews.com/news/asian-america/kamala-harris-presidential-campaign-indian-americans-want-more-opportunities-connect-n965436

Gage, Sue-Je Lee. 2007. "The Amerasian Problem: Blood, Duty, and Race." *International Relations* 21(1): 86–102. https://journals.sagepub.com/doi/abs/10.1177/0047117807073769

Garay, Maria M., Chanel Meyers, Jessica D. Remedios, and Kristin Pauker. 2019. "Looking Like vs. Acting Like Your Race: Social Activism Shapes Perceptions of Multiracial Individuals." *Self and Identity* 20(Issue 5: Unconventional Identities): 594–619.

Garcia Bedolla, Lisa. 2014. *Latino Politics*, 2nd Edition. John Wiley & Sons, Inc.

Gardner, Sheena K. and Matthew W. Hughey. 2019. "Still the Tragic Mulatto? Manufacturing Multiracialization in Magzine Media, 1961 2011." *Ethnic and Racial Studies* 42(4): 645–665.

Gay, Claudine, Jennifer Hochschild and Ariel White. 2016. "Americans' Belief in Linked Fate: Does the Measure Capture the Concept?" *Journal of Race, Ethnicity, and Politics* 1: 117–144.

Gerring, John. 2007. *Case Study Research: Principles and Practices.* Cambridge University Press.

Geron, Kim. 2005. *Latino Political Power.* Boulder, CO: Lynne Rienner.

Gillespie, Andra. 2012. *The New Black Politician: Cory Booker, Newark, and Post-Racial America.* NYU Press. Google Play Books.

Gillespie, Andra. 2020. *Race and the Obama Administration: Substance, Symbols, and Hope.* Manchester University Press.

Gomila, Robin. 2021. "Logistic or Linear? Estimating Causal Effects of Experimental Treatments on Binary Outcomes in Regression Analysis." *Journal of Experimental Psychology: General* 150(4): 700–709.

Graves, Kori A. 2019. "Amerasian Children, Hybrid Superiority, and Pearl S. Buck's Transracial and Transnational Adoption Activism." *The Pennsylvania Magazine of History and Biography* 143(2): 177–209.

Green, Keneisha M. 2006. "Who's Who: Exploring the Discrepancy Between The Methods of Defining African Americans and Native Americans." *American Indian Law Review* 31(1): 93–110.

Grose, Christian R. 2006. "Bridging the Divide: Interethnic Cooperation; Minority Media Outlets; and the Coverage of Latino, African-American, and Asian-American Members of Congress." *Harvard International Journal of Press/Politics* 11(4): 115–130.

Grose, Christian R. 2011. *Congress in Black and White: Race and Representation in Washington and at Home.* Cambridge: Cambridge University Press. Kindle.

Gruber J. 2021. "LexisNexisTools. An R package for working with newspaper data from 'LexisNexis'. " R package version 0.3.5, https://github.com/JBGruber/LexisNexisTools.

Grün, Bettina, Kurt Hornik, David M Blei, John D Lafferty, Xuan-Hieu Phan, Makoto Matsumoto, Takuji Nishimura, Shawn Cokus. 2021. "Package 'Topicmodels.' R Package Version 0.2-12." https://cran.r-project.org/web/packages/topicmodels/topicmodels.pdf

Guevarra, Rudy P. 2012. *Becoming Mexipino: Multiethnic identities and communities in San Diego.* Rutgers University Press.

Guinier, Lani and Gerald Torres. 2003. *The Miner's Canary: Enlisting Race, Resisting Power, Transforming Democracy.* Harvard University Press.

Hainmueller, Jens, Daniel J. Hopkins, and Teppei Yamamoto. 2014. "Causal Inference in Conjoint Analysis: Understanding Multidimensional Choices via Stated Preference Experiments." *Political Analysis* 22(1): 1–30.

Hancock, Ange-Marie. 2007. "When Multiplication Doesn't Equal Quick Addition: Examining Intersectionality As A Research Paradigm." *Perspectives on Politics* 5(1): 63–79.

Harbin, M. Brielle. 2020. "Who's Able to do Political Science Work? My Experience With Exit Polling and What It Reveals About Issues of Race and Equity." *PS: Political Science & Politics* 54(1): 144–146.

Hardy, Cynthia, Bill Harley, and Nelson Phillips. 2004. Discourse analysis and content analysis: Two solitudes? *Qualitative Methods, Spring 2004 Newsletter.*

Hardy-Fanta, Carol, Pei-te Lien, Dianne M. Pinderhughes, and Christine Marie Sierra. 2013. "Racial and Ethnic Identity of Elected Officials of Color: A Closer Look at a Complex Matter." Presented at the 2013 annual meeting of the American Political Science Association, Chicago, IL, August 29–September 1.

Harris, Adam S. 2020. "At the Borders of Identity: Identity Construction and Racial Bloc Voting." *The Journal of Race, Ethnicity, and Politics* 5(2): 326–355. https://doi.org/10.1017/rep.2019.35.

Harris, Adam S. and Michael G. Findley. 2012. "Is Ethnicity Identifiable? Lessons from an Experiment in South Africa." *Journal of Conflict Resolution* 58(1): 4–33.

Harris, Cheryl I. 1993. "Whiteness as Property." *Harvard Law Review* 106(8): 1707–1791.

Harris, David R., and Jeremiah J. Sim. 2002. "Who is Multiracial? Assessing the Complexity of Lived Race." *American Sociological Review* 67(4): 614–627.

Harris, Kamala. 2019. *The Truths We Hold, An American Journey*. Penguin Books.

Harrison, Robert L., Kevin D. Thomas, and Samantha N. N. Cross. 2017. Restricted visions of multiracial identity in advertising. *Journal of Advertising* 46(4): 503–520.

Haynie, Kerry L. 2001. *African American Legislators in the American States*. Columbia University Press.

Hearn, Josephine. 2007. "Rep. Butterfield is Black." *Politico*, May 1. http://www.politico.com/blogs/politico-now/2007/05/rep-butterfield-is-black-001235.

Hedge, David, James Button, and Mary Spear. 1996. "Accounting for the Quality of Black Legislative Life: The View from the States." *American Journal of Political Science* 40(1): 82–98.

Heilman, Monica. 2022. "The Racial Elevator Speech: How Multiracial Individuals Respond to Racial Identity Inquiries." *Sociology of Race and Ethnicity* 8(3): 370–385.

Henderson, Nia-Malika. 2015. "Is Kamala Harris the next Barack Obama?" *The Washington Post*. January 15. https://www.washingtonpost.com/news/the-fix/wp/2015/01/14/kamala-harris-democrats-next-big-thing/

Herman, Melissa. 2004. "Forced to Choose: Some Determinants of Racial Identification in Multiracial Adolescents." *Child Development* 75(3): 730–748.

Herman, Melissa R. 2010. "Do You See What I Am? How observers' Backgrounds Affect Their Perceptions of Multiracial Faces." *Social Psychology Quarterly* 73(1): 58–78.

Hernández, Tanya Katerí. 1998. "Multiracial Discourse: Racial Classifications in an Era of Color-Blind Jurisprudence." *Maryland Law Review* 57: 97–173.

Hernández, Tanya Katerí. 2018. *Multiracials and Civil Rights: Mixed Race Stories of Discrimination*. NYU Press.

Hero, Rodney E. and Robert R. Preuhs. 2013. *Black-Latino Relations in U.S. National Politics: Beyond Conflict of Cooperation*. Cambridge University Press. Kindle.

Hill Collins, Patricia. 2000. *Black Feminist Thought: Knowledge, Consciousness, and the Politics of Empowerment*. Routledge. 2nd edition. eBook.

Hill Collins, Patricia and Sirma Bilge. 2020. *Intersectionality Key Concepts*. Polity Press.

Hobbs, Allyson. 2016. *A Chosen Exile: A History of Racial Passing in American Life*. Harvard University Press.

Ho, Arnold K., Jim Sidanius, Daniel T. Levin, and Mahzarin R. Banaji. 2011. "Evidence for Hypodescent and Racial Hierarchy in the Categorization and Perception of Biracial Individuals." *Journal of Personality and Social Psychology* 100(3): 492–506.

Ho, Arnold K., Nour S. Kteily, and Jacqueline M. Chen. 2017. "'You're One of us': Black Americans' Use of Hypodescent and its Association with Egalitarianism." *Journal of Personality and Social Psychology* 113(5): 753–768.

Ho, Jennifer. 2020. "With Kamala Harris, Americans Yet Again Have Trouble Understanding What Multiracial Means." *The Conversation*. September 1. https://theconversation.com/with-kamala-harris-americans-yet-again-have-trouble-understanding-what-multiracial-means-145233

Hochschild, Jennifer and Vesla Mae Weaver. 2010. "'There's no One as Irish as Barack O'Bama': The Policy and Politics of Multiracialism." *Perspectives on Politics* 8(3): 737–759.

Hochschild, Jennifer L. and Maya Sen. 2015. "To Test or Not? Singular or Multiple Heritage? Genomic Ancestry Testing and Americans' Racial Identity." *Du Bois Review* 12(2): 321–347.

Hochschild, Jennifer L., Vesla Mae Weaver, and Traci R. Burch. 2012. *Creating a New Racial Order: How Immigration, Multiracialism, Genomics, and the Young can Remake Race in America*. Princeton University Press.

Hochschild, Jennifer L. and Vesla Weaver. 2007. "The Skin Color Paradox and the American Racial Order." *Social Forces* 86(2): 643–670.

Hogg, Michael A. 2001. "A Social Identity Theory of Leadership." *Personality and Social Psychology Review* 5(3): 184–200.

Hogg, Michael A., and Scott A. Reid. 2006. "Social Identity, Self-Categorization, and Communication of Group Norms." *Communication Theory* 16(1): 7–30.

Hogg, Michael A., Deborah J. Terry, and Katherine M. White. 1995. "A Tale of Two Theories: A Critical Comparison of Identity Theory With Social Identity Theory." *Social Psychology Quarterly* 58(4): 255–269.

Hogg, Michael A., Daan van Knippenberg, and David E. Rast III. 2012. "The Social Identity Theory of Leadership: Theoretical Origins, Research Findings, and Conceptual Development." *European Review of Social Psychology* 23(1): 258–304.

Hollinger, David A. 2005. "The One Drop Rule & the One Hate Rule." *Daedalus* 134(1): 18–28. http://www.jstor.org/stable/20027957.

Holman, M.R., Merolla, J.L. and Zechmeister, E.J., 2016. "Terrorist Threat, Male Stereotypes, and Candidate Evaluations." *Political Research Quarterly* 69(1): 134–147.

Huang, Leslie, Patrick O. Perry, Finn Årup Nielsen, Martin Porter, Richard Boulton, The Regents of the University of California, Carlo Strapparava and Alessandro Valitutti, Unicode, Inc. 2021. Package 'corpus.' R version 0.10.2. https://cran.r-project.org/web/packages/corpus/corpus.pdf

Hunter, Margaret. 2005. "The Persistent Problem of Colorism: Skin Tone, Status, and Inequality." *Sociology Compass* 1(1): 237–254.

Ifatunji, Mosi Adesina. 2024. "Toward an Ethnoracial Ontology for the Study of Race and Ethnicity: The Case of African Americans and Black Immigrants in the United States." *Sociology of Race and Ethnicity*. https://doi.org/10.1177/23326492241252917.

Inman, Arpana G., Howard, Erin E., Beaumont, Robin L., & Walker, Jessica A. 2007. "Cultural Transmission: Influence of Contextual Factors in Asian Indian Immigrant Parents' Experiences." *Journal of Counseling Psychology* 54(1): 93–100. https://doi.org/10.1037/0022-0167.54.1.93

Iverson, Sarah, Ann Morning, Aliya Saperstein, and Janet Xu. 2022. "Regimes beyond the One-Drop Rule: New Models of Multiracial Identity." *Genealogy* 6(2): 57. https://doi.org/10.3390/genealogy6020057

Jackson, Jenn M. 2020. "Kamala Harris as the VP Pick Challenges What We Know About Representation." *Teen Vogue*, August 13. https://www.teenvogue.com/story/kamala-harris-vp-pick-challenges-representation-identity-politics.

Jann, Ben. 2005. "Making Regression Tables from Stored Estimates." *The Stata Journal* 5(3): 288–308.

Jann, Ben. 2007. "Making Regression Tables Simplified." *The Stata Journal* 7(2): 227–244.

Janusz, Andrew. 2023. "The electoral consequences of racial fluidity." *Electoral Studies* 82: 102597.

Jardina, Ashley. 2019. *White Identity Politics*. Cambridge University Press.

Jardina, Ashley. 2021. In-group love and out-group hate: White racial attitudes in contemporary U.S. elections. *Political Behavior* 43: 1535–1559. https://doi.org/10.1007/s11109-020-09600-x

Jones-Correa, Michael, Sophia Jordan Wallace, Chris Zepeda-Millán. 2016. "The Impact of Large-Scale Collective Action on Latino Perceptions of Commonality and Competition with African Americans." *Social Science Quarterly* 97(2): 458–475.

Jordan, Winthrop D. 2014. "Historical Origins of the One-Drop Racial Rule in the United States." *Journal of Critical Mixed Race Studies* 1(1): 98–132. https://escholarship.org/uc/item/91g761b3

Joseph, Ralina L. 2013. *Transcending Blackness: From the New Millennium Mulatta to the Exceptional Multiracial.* Duke University Press.

Junn, Jane and Natalie Masuoka. 2008. "Asian American Identity: Shared Racial Status and Political Context." *Perspectives on Politics* 6(4): 729–740. https://doi.org/10.1017/S1537592708081887.

Kanter, Rosabeth Moss. 1977. "Some Effects of Proportions on Group Life: Skewed Sex Ratios and Responses to Token Women." *American Journal of Sociology* 82(5): 965–990.

Khaleghy, Julian, and Contributors. 2015–2016. Wayback Machine Downloader.https://github.com/hartator/wayback-machine-downloader

Khanna, Nikki. 2004. "The Role of Reflected Appraisals in Racial Identity: The Case of Multiracial Asians." *Social Psychology Quarterly* 67(2): 115–131.

Khanna, Nikki. 2010. "If You're Half Black, You're Just Black": Reflected appraisals and the Persistence of the One-Drop Rule." *The Sociological Quarterly* 51: 96–121.

Khanna, Nikki and Cathryn Johnson. 2010. "Passing as Black: Racial Identity Work among Biracial Americans." *Social Psychology Quarterly* 73(4): 380–397.

Kim, Claire J. 1999. "The Racial Triangulation of Asian Americans." *Politics & Society* 27(1): 105–138.

Kim, Jae Yeon (2020). tidyethnicnews: Tidying Ethnic NewsWatch Search Results. R package version 0.2.0. https://github.com/jaeyk/tidyethnicnews

King, Katrina Quisumbing. 2019. "Recentering U.S. Empire: A Structural Perspective on the Color Line." *Sociology of Race and Ethnicity* 5(1): 11–25.

King, Desmond S. and Rogers M. Smith. 2005. "Racial Orders in American Political Development." *American Political Science Review* 99(1): 75–92.

Kinder, Donald R. and Corrine M. McConnaughy. 2006. "Military Triumph, Racial Transcendence, and Colin Powell." *Public Opinion Quarterly* 70(2): 139–165.

Klarner, Carl, 2018, "State Legislative Election Returns, 1967–2016", https://doi.org/10.7910/DVN/3WZFK9, Harvard Dataverse, V: 2018 update, UNF:6:pV4h1CP/B8pHthjjQThTTw== [fileUNF]

Lavariega Monforti, Jessica, Melissa Michelson, and Annie Franco. 2013. "'Por Quien Votara?' Experimental Evidence About Language, Ethnicity, and Vote Choice (Among Republicans)." *Politics, Groups, and Identities* 1(4): 475–487.

Law, Anna O. 2015. "The Historical Amnesia of Contemporary Immigration Federalism Debates." *Polity* 47(3): 302–319.

Lee, Taeku. 2008. "Race, Immigration, and the Identity-to-Politics Link." *Annual Review of Political Science* 11: 457–478.

Lee, Jennifer and Frank D. Bean. 2010. *The Diversity Paradox: Immigration and the Color Line in 21st Century America.* New York: Russell Sage Foundation.

Leeper, Thomas, Sara B. Hobolt, and James Tilley. 2020. "Measuing Subgroup Preferences in Conjoint Experiments." *Political Analysis* 28(2): 207–221.

Lemi, Danielle Casarez. 2018. "Identity and Coalitions in a Multiracial Era: How State Legislators Navigate Race and Ethnicity." *Politics, Groups, and Identities* 6(4): 725–742.

Lemi, Danielle Casarez, and Nadia E. Brown. 2019. "Melanin and curls: Evaluation of Black women candidates." *Journal of Race, Ethnicity, and Politics* 4(2): 259–296.

Lemi, Danielle Casarez, Maneesh Arora, and Sara Sadhwani. 2022. "Black and Desi: Indian American Perceptions of Kamala Harris." *Journal of Women, Politics & Policy* 43(3): 376–89. https://doi.org/10.1080/1554477X.2022.2075678.

Lemi, Danielle Casarez, Sarah Virginia Hayes, Maricruz Ariana Osorio. 2023. "Theorizing Kamala Harris," in Nadia E. Brown and Sarah Allen Gerson (Eds). *Distinct Identities: Minority Women in U.S. Politics*, 214–226. Routledge.

Lenhardt, Robin A. 2008. "The Story of Perez v. Sharp: Forgotten Lessons on Race, Law, and Marriage," in Devon W. Carbado and Rachel F. Moran (Eds). *Chapter 10.* Foundation Press, Thompson/West.

Leong, Nancy. 2013. "Racial Capitalism." *Harvard Law Review* 126(8): 2151–2226.

Lerman, Amy E., Katherine T. McCabe, and Meredith L. Sadin. 2015. "Political Ideology, Skin Tone, and The Psychology of Candidate Evaluations." *Public Opinion Quarterly*, 79(1): 53–90.

Leslie, Gregory J. and David O. Sears. 2022. "The Heaviest Drop of Blood: Black Exceptionalism Among Multiracials." *Political Psychology* 43(6): 1123–1145. https://doi.org/10.1111/pops.12806

Liebler, Carolyn A. 2016. "On the Boundaries of Race: Identification of Mixed-Heritage Children in the United States, 1960–2010." *Sociology of Race and Ethnicity* 2(4): 548–568.

Lien, Pei-te and Nicole Filler. 2022. *Contesting the Last Frontier: Race, Gender, Ethnicity, and Political Representation of Asian Americans.* Oxford University Press.

Locke, Thomas and Ralina L. Joseph. 2021. "All Intersectionality is not the Same: Why Kamala Harris is Our Vice President and not Stacey Abrams." *Quarterly Journal of Speech* 107(4): 451–456.

López, Ian Haney. 1994. "The Social Construction of Race: Some Observations on Illusion, Fabrication, and Choice." 29 Harv C.R.-C.L. L. Rev. 1. 1–62.

López, Ian Haney. 1996. *White by Law: The Legal Construction of Race.* New York: University Press.

López, Nancy, Edward Vargas, Melina Juarez, Lisa Cacari-Stone, Sonia Bettez. 2018. "What's Your "Street Race"? Leveraging Multidimensional Measures of Race and Intersectionality for Examining Physical and Mental Health Status among Latinxs." *Sociology of Race and Ethnicity* 4(1): 49–66.

Lu, Fan. 2020. "Forging Ties: The Effect of Discrimination on Asian Americans' Perceptions of Political Commonality with Latinos." *Politics, Groups, and Identities* 8(3): 595–614.

Lung, Shirley. 2019. "Criminalizing Work and Non-Work: The Disciplining of Immigrant and African American Workers." *University of Massachusetts Law Review* 14(2): 290–348.

Ma, Sheng-Mei. 2007. "The Necessity and Impossibility of Being Mixed-Race in Asian American literature," in Kuortti, Joel and Jopi Nyman (Eds). *Reconstructing Hybridity: Post-colonial Studies in Transition, Textxet: Studies in Comparative Literature*, 51, Leiden: Brill. 163–190.

Mael, Fred A., and Lois E. Tetrick. 1992. "Identifying Organizational Identification." *Educational and Psychological Measurement* 52(4): 813–824.

Major, Lesa Hatley and Renita Coleman. 2008. "The Intersection of Race and Gender in Election Coverage: What Happens When the Candidates Don't Fit the Stereotypes?" *Howard Journal of Communications* 19(4): 315–333.

Mansbridge, Jane. 1999. "Should Blacks Represent Blacks and Women Represent Women? A contingent 'Yes.'" *Journal of Politics* 61(3): 628–657.

Manzano, Sylvia and Gabriel R. Sanchez. 2010. "Take One for the Team? The Limits of Shared Ethnicity and Candidate Preferences." *Political Research Quarterly* 63(3): 568–580.

Marshall, Catherine, and Gretchen B. Rossman. 2010. *Designing Qualitative Research, 5th Edition.* SAGE Publications, Inc.

Marshall, Catherine, Gretchen B. Rossman, and Gerardo L. Blanco. 2022. *Designing Qualitative Research, Seventh edition.* SAGE Publishing, Inc.

Masuoka, Natalie. 2017. *Multiracial Identity and Racial Politics in the United States.* Oxford University Press.

Masuoka, Natalie. 2008. "Political Attitudes and Ideologies of Multiracial Americans: The Implications of Mixed Race in the United States." *Political Research Quarterly* 61(2): 253–267.

Masuoka, Natalie. 2011. "The 'Multiracial' Option: Social Group Identity and Changing Patterns of Racial Categorization." *American Politics Research* 39(1): 176–204.

Masuoka, Natalie. 2015. "Racial Identification in a Post Obama Era: Multiracialism, Identity Choice, and Candidate Evaluation," In Amilcar Antonio Barreto and Richard L. O'Bryant, Editors, *American Identity in the Age of Obama*, chapter 2, pages 42–69. New York, NY: Routledge.

Masuoka, Natalie and Jane Junn. 2013. *The Politics of Belonging: Race, Public Opinion, and Immigration.* University of Chicago Press.

Matos, Yalidy, Stacey Greene, and Kira Sanbonmatsu. 2020. "Do Women Seek "Women of Color" for Public Office? Exploring Women's Support For Electing Women of Color." *Political Research Quarterly* 72(2): 259–273.

McClain, Paula D.,Jessica D. Johnson Carew, Eugene Walton, $1 Candis S. Watts. 2009. "Group Membership, Group Identity, and Group Consciousness: Measures of Racial Identity in American Politics?" *Annual Review of Political Science* 12: 471–485.

McClain, Paula D., Gloria Y. A. Ayee, Taneisha N. Means, Alicia M. Reyes-Barrientes, and Nura A. Sedique. 2016. "Race, Power, and Knowledge: Tracing the Roots of Exclusion in the Development of Political Science." *Politics, Groups, and Identities* 4(3): 467–482.

McConnaughy, Corrine M., Ismail K. White, David L. Leal, and Jason P. Casellas. 2010. "A Latino on the Ballot: Explaining Coethnic Voting Among Latinos and the Response of White Americans." *Journal of Politics* 72(4): 1199–1211.

McCormick, Joseph P. and Charles E. Jones. 1993. "The Conceptualization of Deracialization: Thinking Through the Dilemma." In Georgia A. Persons, (Ed.), *Dilemmas of Black Politics: Issues of leadership and strategy*, Chapter 4, pages 66–84. New York, NY: Harper Collins.

McIlwain, Charlton. 2013. "From Deracialization to Racial Distinction: Interpreting Obama's Successful Racial Narrative." *Social Semiotics* 23(1): 119–145.

McIlwain, Charlton D. and Stephen M. Caliendo. 2011. *Race Appeal: How Candidates/Invoke Race in U.S. Political Campaigns.* Temple University Press.

McRae, Elizabeth Gillespie. 2018. *Mothers of Massive Resistance: White Women and the Politics of White Supremacy.* Oxford University Press.

McRae, Elizabeth Gillespie. 2020. "Threatening Property: Race, Class, and Campaigns to Legislate Jim Crow Neighborhoods." *Journal of American History* 107(3): 774–775. https://doi.org/10.1093/jahist/jaaa414.

Merolla, Jennifer L., Abbylin H. Sellers, and Danielle Casarez Lemi. 2017. "Does the Presence of Women on the Ballot Increase Female Empowerment?" American Political Science Association Annual Meeting. San Francisco, CA. August 31–September 2.

Mills, Brandale. 2019. "Old Stereotypes Made New: A Textual Analysis on the Tragic Mulatto Stereotype in Contemporary Hollywood." *Howard Journal of Communications* 30(5): 411–429.

Minta, Michael D. 2020. "Diversity and Minority Interest Group Advocacy in Congress." *Political Research Quarterly* 73(1): 208–220.

Minta, Michael D. and Valeria Sinclair-Chapman. 2013. "Diversity in Political Institutions and Congressional Responsiveness to Minority Interests." *Political Research Quarterly* 66(1): 127–140.

Minta, Michael D. and Nadia E. Brown. 2014. "Intersecting Interests: Gender, Race, and Congressional Attention to Women's Issues." *Du Bois Review* 11(2): 253–272.

Miratrix, Luke. (2018). textreg: n-Gram Text Regression, aka Concise Comparative Summarization. Version 0.1.5. https://cran.r-project.org/web/packages/textreg/textreg.pdf

Mohan, Erica and Terah T. Venzant Chambers. 2010. "Two Researchers Reflect on Navigating Multiracial Identities in the Research Situation." *International Journal of Qualitative Studies in Education* 23(3): 259–281. https://www.tandfonline.com/doi/abs/10.1080/09518390903196609

Monk, Ellis P. 2022. "Inequality without Groups: Contemporary Theories of Categories, Intersectional Typicality, and the Disaggregation of Difference." *Sociological Theory* 40(1): 3–27. https://doi.org/10.1177/07352751221076863.

Morning, Ann, and Aliya Saperstein. 2018. "The Generational Locus of Multiraciality and its Implications for Self-Identification." *The ANNALS of the American Academy of Political and Social Science* 677(1): 57–68.

Moya, Paula M.L. and Hazel Rose Markus. 2010. "Doing Race: An Introduction," in Markus, Hazel Rose and Paula M.L. Moya (Eds). *Doing Race: Essays for the 21st Century*. New York, NY: W.W. Norton & Company: 1–102.

Mullinix, Kevin J., Thomas J. Leeper, James N Druckman, and Jeremy Freese. 2015. "The Generalizability of Survey Experiments." *Journal of Experimental Political Science* 2(2): 109–138.

Muro, Jazmin A. and Lisa M. Martinez. 2018. "Is Love Color-Blind? Racial Blind Spots' and Latinas' Romantic Relationships." *Sociology of Race and Ethnicity* 4(4): 527–540.

Nadal, Kevin L., Julie Sriken, Kristin C. Davidoff, Yinglee Wong, and Kathryn McLean. 2013. "Microaggressions Within Families: Experiences of Multiracial People." *Family Relations: An Interdisciplinary Journal of Applied Family Studies* 62: 190–201.

Nagai, Tyrone. 2016. "Multiracial Americans Throughout the History of the US." In Kathleen Odell Korgen (Ed.). *Race policy and multiracial Americans*. Bristol, UK: 13–28.

NALEO. 2019. "National Directory of Latino Elected Officials." https://naleo.org/wp-content/uploads/2019/12/2019_National_Directory_of_Latino_Elected_Offcials.pdf

National Conference of State Legislatures. 2015. "Legislators' Race and Ethnicity 2015."

Newman, Alyssa. 2021. "Revisiting the Marginal Man: Bridging Immigration Scholarship and Mixed-Race Studies." *Sociology of Race and Ethnicity* 7(1): 26–40.

Ngai, Mae. 2014. *Impossible Subjects: Illegal Aliens and the Making of Modern America*. Princeton University Press.

Nicholson Jr., Harvey L., J. Scott Carter, and Arjee Restar. 2020. "Strength in Numbers: Perceptions of political commonality with African Americans among Asians and Asian Americans in the United States." *Sociology of Race and Ethnicity* 6(1): 107–122.

Nobles, Melissa. 2000. *Shades of Citizenship: Race and the Census in Modern Politics*. Stanford University Press.

Norman, Jasmine B. and Jacqueline M. Chen. 2020. "I Am Multiracial: Predictors of Multiracial Identification Strength Among Mixed Ancestry Individuals." *Self and Identity* 19(5): 501–520.

Norwood, Candice. 2020. "Amid Historic Race, Voters Of Color Wrestle With Harris' Personal and Political Identities." *PBS News Hour*. October 7. https://www.pbs.org/newshour/politics/amid-historic-race-voters-of-color-wrestle-with-harris-personal-and-political-identities

Nunn, Tessa Ashlin. 2021. "Meghan Markle's Healthy Lifestyle in the Media: Multiracial Exceptionalism and the Cult of Slimness." *Women's Studies International Forum* 86 (May-June): https://www.sciencedirect.com/science/article/abs/pii/S0277539521000236

Ocampo, Anthony. 2014. "Are Second-Generation Filipinos 'Becoming' Asian American or Latino? Historical Colonialism, Culture and Panethnicity." *Ethnic and Racial Studies* 37(3), Issue 3: Race, Migration and Identity: Shifting Boundaries in the USA: 425–445.

Ocampo, Anthony. 2016. *The Latinos of Asia: How Filipino Americans Break the Rules of Race.* Stanford University Press.

O'Connor, Cliodhna and Helene Joffe. 2020. "Intercoder Reliability in Qualitative Research: Debates and Practical Guidelines." *International Journal of Qualitative Methods*, 19. https://journals.sagepub.com/doi/epub/10.1177/1609406919899220

Omi, Michael and Howard Winant. 1994. *Racial Formation in the United States: From the 1960s to the 1990s*, 2nd Edition. Routledge.

Onwuegbuzie, Anthony J. and Nancy L. Leech. 2007. "Sampling Designs in Qualitative Research: Making The Sampling Process More Public." *The Qualitative Report* 12(2): 238–254.

Ooms, Jeroen 2022. "Package 'Pdftools.'" Version 3.0.1. https://CRAN.R-project.org/package=pdftools

Orme, Bryan K. 2010. *Getting Started With Conjoint Analysis: Strategies for Product Design and Pricing Research.* Second. Glendale, CA: Research Publishers LLC.

Orey, Byron D. 2006. "Deracialization or Racialization: The Making of a Black Mayor in Jackson, Mississippi." *Politics & Policy* 34(4): 814–836.

Orey, Byron D. and Yu Zhang. 2019. "Melanated Millennials and the Politics of Black Hair." *Social Science Quarterly* 100(6): 2458–2476.

Ostfeld, Mara. 2017. "The Backyard Politics of Attitudes Toward Immigration." *Political Psychology* 38(1): 21–37.

Osuji, Chinyere K. 2019. *Boundaries of love: Interracial marriage the meaning of race.* New York: New York University Press.

Pascoe, Peggy. 2009. *What Comes Naturally: Miscegenation Law and the Making of Race in America.* Oxford University Press.

Pauker, Kristin, Colleen M. Carpinella, David J. Lick, Diana T. Sanchez, and Kerri L. Johnson. 2018. "Malleability in Biracial Categorizations: The Impact of Geographic Context and Targets' Racial Heritage." *Social Cognition* 36(5): 461–480.

Pena-Vasquez, Andrea and Maryann H. Kwakwa. 2020. "Barack Obama and Kamala Harris Both Identify as Black. The News Media Doesn't Describe Both That Way." *Washington Post.* September 16. https://www.washingtonpost.com/politics/2020/09/16/barack-obama-kamala-harris-both-identify-black-news-media-doesnt-describe-both-that-way/

Perry, Huey L. 1991. "Deracialization as an Analytical Construct in American Urban Politics." *Urban Affairs Review* 27(2): 181–191.

Perry, Samuel L. 2013. "Are Interracial Daters More Supportive of Same-Sex Unions?" *The Social Science Journal* 50(2): 252–256.

Pew Research Center. 2015. "Multiracial in America: Proud, Diverse and Growing in Numbers." Washington, D.C.: June.

Philpot, Tasha. 2007. *Race, Republicans, and the Return of the Party of Lincoln.* University of Michigan Press.

Pilgrim, Haley. 2020. "'I Wish I Didn't Look So White': Examining Contested Racial Identities in Second-Generation Black-White Multiracials." *Ethnic and Racial Studies* 44(14): 2551–2573.

Pitkin, Hannah. 1967. *The Concept of Representation.* Berkeley: University of California Press.

Poulsen, Melissa Eirko. 2012. "American Orientalism & Cosmopolitan Mixed Race: Reading Onoto Watanna and Han Suyin's Asian Mixed Race." *Asian American Literature: Discourses and Pedagogies* 3: 5–13.

Powell Jr., Adam Clayton. 1971. *Adam by Adam: The Autobiography of Adam Clayton Powell, Jr.* New York, NY: Kensington Publishing Corp. First Kensington Trade Paperback Printing: January, 2002.

Price, Melanye T. 2016. *The Race Whisperer: Barack Obama and the Political Uses of Race.* New York University Press.

Purdie-Vaughns, Valerie and Richard P. Eibach. 2008. "Intersectional Invisibility: The Distinctive Advantages and Disadvantages of Multiple Subordinate-Group Identities." *Sex Roles* 57: 377–391.

Ramakrishnan, Karthick, Jennifer Lee, Taeku Lee, and Janelle Wong. "National Asian American Survey (NAAS) 2016 Pre-Election Survey." Riverside, CA: National Asian American Survey. 2017-12-05.

Renn, Kristen A. 2012. *Mixed Race Students in College: The Ecology of Race, Identity, and Community On Campus.* State University of New York Press.

Robinson-Wood, Tracy, Chantal Muse, Ruthann Hewett, Oyenike Balogun-Mwangi, Jaylan Elrahman, Ava Nordling, Noora Abdulkerim, and Atushi Matsumoto. 2021. "Regular White People Things: The Presence of White Fragility in Interracial Families." *Family Relations: Interdisciplinary Journal of Applied Family Science* 70(4): 973–992. https://onlinelibrary.wiley.com/doi/abs/10.1111/fare.12549

Rockquemore, Kerry Ann. 2002. "Negotiating the Color Line: The Gendered Process of Racial Identity Construction among Black/White Biracial Women." *Gender & Society* 16(4): 485–503.

Rockquemore, Kerry Ann and David L. Brunsma. 2002. "Socially Embedded Identities: Theories, Typologies, and Processes of Racial Identity among Black/White Biracials." *The Sociological Quarterly* 43(3): 335–356.

Roth, Wendy D. 2016. "The Multiple Dimensions of Race." *Ethnic and Racial Studies* 39(8): 1310–1338.

Roth, Wendy D. and Biorn Ivemark. 2018. "Genetic Options: The Impact of Genetic Ancestry Testing on Consumers' Racial and Ethnic Identities." *American Journal of Sociology* 124(1): 150–184.

Roth, Wendy D. Rochelle Côté, Jasmyne Eastmond. 2024. "Bridging Boundaries? The Effect of Genetic Ancestry Testing on Ties across Racial Groups." *Social Problems* 71(1): 180–202. https://doi.org/10.1093/socpro/spab082

Roth, Wendy D., Şule Yaylacı, Kaitlyn Jaffe, and Lindsey Richardson. 2020. "Do Genetic Ancestry Tests Increase Racial Essentialism? Findings From a Randomized Controlled Trial." *PLoS ONE* 15(1): e0227399. https://doi.org/10.1371/journal.pone.0227399

Rouse, Stella. 2013. *Latinos in the Legislative Process: Interests and Influences.* Cambridge: Cambridge University Press.

Rousseau Anderson, Celia. 2015. "What are you? A CRT Perspective on the Experiences of Mixed Race Persons in 'Post-racial'" *America, Race Ethnicity and Education* 18(1): 1–19.

Sanchez, Gabriel R. and Edward D. Vargas. 2016. "Measurement of Group Consciousness and Linked Fate." *Political Research Quarterly* 69(1): 160–174.

Saward, Michael. 2014. "Shape-shifting representation." *American Political Science Review* 108(4): 723–736.

Schmidt, Ryan W. 2011. "American Indian Identity and Blood Quantum in the 21st Century: A Critical Review." *Journal of Anthropology*. https://doi.org/10.1155/2011/549521

Schuman, Howard, Charlotte Steeh, and Lawrence Bobo. 1985. *Racial attitudes in America: Trends and interpretations.* Harvard University Press.

Schwartz-Shea, Peregrine, and Dvora Yanow. 2011. *Interpretive Research Design: Concepts and Processes.* Taylor & Francis Group.

Sen, Maya and Omar Wasow. 2016. "Race as A Bundle of Sticks: Designs That Estimate Effects of Seemingly Immutable Characteristics." *Annual Review of Political Science* 19: 499–522.

Seto, Atsuko, Kent Becker, and Jared Lau. 2021. "'When You Take This Jump and Cross Racial Boundaries': Parents' Experiences of Raising Multiracial Children." *The Family Journal* 29(1): 86–94.

Shah, Paru R. and Nicholas R. Davis. 2017. "Comparing Three Methods of Measuring Race/Ethnicity." *Journal of Race, Ethnicity and Politics* 2(1): 124–139.

Sharfstein, Daniel J. 2007. "Crossing the Color Line: Racial Migration and the One-Drop Rule, 1600–1860." *Minnesota Law Review* 91: 592–656.

Shih, Margaret. and Sanchez, Diana T. 2005. "Perspectives and Research on the Positive and Negative Implications of Racial Identities." *Psychological Bulletin* 131(4): 569–591.

Shropshire, Terry. 2019. "The Rock sets the record straight about his racial identity." *Rollingout.* March 22. https://rollingout.com/2019/03/22/the-rock-sets-the-record-straight-about-his-racial-identity/

Sims, Jennifer Patrice. 2025. *The Inequality of Racial Perception: Theorizing the Patterns of How We See Race.* Oxford University Press.

Sigelman, Carol K., Lee Sigelman, Barbara J. Walkosz, and Michael Nitz. 1995. "Black Candidates, White Voters: Understanding Racial Bias in Political Perceptions." *American Journal of Political Science* 39(1): 243–265.

Silva, Andrea and Carrie Skulley. 2019. "Always Running: Candidate Emergence Among Women of Color Over Time." *Political Research Quarterly* 72(2): 342–359.

Sims, Jennifer Patrice. 2012. "Beautiful Stereotypes: the Relationship Between Physical Attractiveness and Race Identity." *Identities: Global Studies in Culture and Power* 19(1): 61–80.

Sims, Jennifer Patrice. 2016. "Reevaluation of the Influence of Appearance and Reflected Appraisals for Mixed-Race Identity: The Role of Consistent Inconsistent Racial Perception." *Sociology of Race and Ethnicity* 2(4): 569–583.

Sims, Jennifer Patrice and Remi Joseph-Salisbury. 2019. "'We were all just the Black kids': Black Mixed-Race Men and the Importance of Adolescent Peer Groups for Identity Development." *Social Currents* 6(1): 51–66.

Sims, Jennifer Patrice and Chinelo L. Njaka. 2019. *Mixed-Race in the US and UK: Comparing the Past, Present, and Future.* Emerald Publishing Limited.

Sims, Jennifer Patrice, Whitney Laster Pirtle, and Iris Johnson-Arnold. 2020. "Doing Hair, Doing Race: The Influence on Racial Perception Across the US." *Ethnic and Racial Studies* 43(12): 2099–2119.

Small, Mario Luis and Jessica McCrory Calarco. 2022. *Qualitative Literacy: A Guide to Evaluating Ethnographic and Interview Research.* University of California Press.

Snow, David A., and Leon Anderson. 1987. "Identity Work Among the Homeless: The Verbal Construction and Avowal of Personal Identities." *American Journal of Sociology* 6(92): 1336–1371. http://www.jstor.org/stable/2779840.

Song, Miri. 2020. "Rethinking Minority Status and 'Visibility.'" *Comparative Migration Studies* 8(5): https://doi.org/10.1186/s40878-019-0162-2

Song, Miri. 2009. "Is Intermarriage a Good Indicator of Integration?" *Journal of Ethnic and Migration Studies* 35(2): 331–348.

Spencer, Rainier. 1999. *Spurious Issues: Race and Multiracial Identity Politics in the United States.* Westview Press.

Squires, Catherine R. 2007. *Dispatches from the Color Line: The Press and Multiracial America.* State University of New York Press.

Sriram, Shyam Krishnan and Stonegarden Grindlife. 2017. "The Politics of Deracialisation: South Asian American Candidates, Nicknames, and Campaign Strategies." *South Asian Diaspora* 7(1): 17–31.

Starr, Paul and Christina Pao. 2024. "The Multiracial Complication: The 2020 Census and the Fictitious Multiracial Boom." *Sociological Science* 11(40): 2330–6696.

Stout, Christopher T. 2015. *Bringing Race Back in: Black Politicians, Deracialization, and Voting in the Age of Obama*. University of Virginia Press.

Streeter, Caroline A. 2002. "The Hazards of Visibility: 'Biracial' Women, Media Images, and Narratives of Identity," in Winters, L. I., and DeBose, H. L. (Eds.). *New faces in a changing America Multiracial identity in the 21st century*. Thousand Oaks, CA: SAGE Publications, Incorporated. 301–322.

Strezhnev, Anton, Jens Hainmueller, Daniel J. Hopkins, and Teppei Yamamoto. 2014. "Conjoint Survey Design Tool: Software Manual." https://scholar.harvard.edu/files/astrezhnev/files/conjoint_sdt_manual.pdf

Stephens-Dougan, LaFleur. 2020. *Race to the Bottom: How Racial Appeals Work in American Politics*. University of Chicago Press.

strmic-pawl, hephzibah virginia. 2016. *Multiracialism and its Discontents*. Lexington Books.

strmic-Pawl, hephzibah. 2014. "The Influences Affecting and the Influential Effects of Multiracials: Multiracialism and Stratification." *Sociology Compass* 8(1): 63–77.

Strolovitch, Dara Z., Janelle S. Wong, and Andrew Proctor. 2017. "A Possessive Investment in White Heteropatriarchy? The 2016 Election and the Politics of Race, Gender, and Sexuality." *Politics, Groups, and Identities* 5(2): 353–363.

Sui, Mingxiao, Newly Paul, Paru Shah, Brook Spurlock, Brooksie Chastant, and Johanna Dunaway. 2018. "The Role of Minority Journalists, Candidates, and Audiences In Shaping Race-Related Campaign News Coverage." *Journalism & Mass Communication Quarterly* 95(4): 1079–1102.

Sullivan, Kevin. 2019. "'I am Who I am': Kamala Harris, Daughter of Indian and Jamaican Immigrants, Defines Herself Simply as 'American.'" *The Washington Post*. February 2. https://www.washingtonpost.com/politics/i-am-who-i-am-kamala-harris-daughter-of-indian-and-jamaican-immigrants-defines-herself-simply-as-american/2019/02/02/0b278536-24b7-11e9-ad53-824486280311_story.html

Swain, Carol M. 1993. *Black Faces, Black Interests: The Representation of African Americans in Congress*. Harvard University Press.

Tajfel, Henri, and John C. Turner. 1986. "The Social Identity Theory of Intergroup Behavior," In *Psychology of Intergroup Relations*, in William G. Austin and Stephen Worchel, (Eds.). 7–24. Chicago, IL: Nelson-Hall Publishers.

TallBear, Kim. 2013. *Native American DNA: Tribal Belonging and the False Promise of Genetic Science*. University of Minnesota Press.

Tate, Katherine. 1997. *Black Faces in the Mirror: African Americans and Their Representatives in the U.S. Congress*. Princeton University Press.

Taylor, Keeanga-Yamahtta. 2017. *How We Get Free: Black feminism and the Combahee River Collective*. Haymarket Books.

Terkildsen, Nayda. 1993. "When White Voters Evaluate Black Candidates: The Processing Implications of Candidate Skin Color, Prejudice, and Self-Monitoring." *American Journal of Political Science* 37(4): 1032–1053.

Tesler, Michael. 2013. "The Return of Old-Fashioned Racism to White Americans' Partisan Preferences in the Early Obama Era." *Journal of Politics* 75(1): 110–123.

Thomas, David R. 2006. "A General Inductive Approach for Analyzing Qualitative Evaluation Data." *American Journal of Evaluation* 27(2): 237–246.

Thornton, Michael C. 2009. "Policing the Borderlands: White- and Black-American Newspaper Perceptions of Multiracial Heritage and the Idea of Race, 1996–2006." *Journal of Social Issues*, 65(1): 105–127.

Tormos, Fernando. 2017. "Intersectional Solidarity." *Politics, Groups, and Identities* 5(4): 707–720.

Torres, Mo. 2023. "Against Race, Toward the Abolition of Racism." *Sociology of Race and Ethnicity* 9(1): 124–127. https://doi.org/10.1177/23326492221136168.

Torres, Mo and Jared Clemons. 2022. "Racism without Races: Sociology beyond the 'Social Construction of Race.'" Working paper.

Townsend, Sarah S.M., Hazel R. Markus, and Hilary B Bergsieker. 2009. "My Choice, Your Categories: The Denial of Multiracial Identities." *Journal of Social Issues* 65(1): 185–204.

Turner, Jessie D. 2014. Reconsidering the relationship between New Mestizaje and New Multiraciality as Mixed-Race Identity models. *Journal of Critical Mixed Race Studies* 1(1): 133–148. http://dx.doi.org/10.5070/C811021378

Tyson, Vanessa C. 2016. *Twists of Fate: Multiracial Coalitions and Minority Representation in the U.S. House of Representatives.* New York, NY: Oxford University Press. Kindle.

U.S. Bureau of the Census. 1994. 1960, 1970, and 1980 Subject Reports on Marital Status and 1991 and 1992 Current Population Reports, P20, nos. 461 and 468. https://www2.census.gov/programs-surveys/demo/tables/marriage-and-divorce/time-series/interractab1.txt

U.S. Census Bureau. 2021. "Race and Ethnicity in the United States: 2010 Census and 2020 Census." https://www.census.gov/library/visualizations/interactive/race-and-ethnicity-in-the-united-state-2010-and-2020-census.html. August 12. Date accessed: June 14, 2022.

Vargas, Nicholas and Jard Kingsbury. 2016. "Racial Identity Contestation: Mapping and Measuring Boundaries." *Sociology Compass* 10(8): 718–729.

Vargas, Nicholas, and Kevin Stainback. 2016. "Documenting Contested Racial Identities among Latina/os, Asians, Blacks, and Whites." *American Behavioral Scientist* 60(4): 442–464.

Vaughan, Davis, Matt Dancho, and RStudio. 2022. Package 'furrr.' Version .0.2.3. https://cran.r-project.org/web/packages/furrr/furrr.pdf

Visalvanich, Neil. 2017. "Asian Candidates in America: The Surprising Effects of Positive Racial Stereotyping." *Political Research Quarterly* 70(1): 68–81.

Viser, Matt. 2019. "Sen. Kamala Harris Formally Opens Her Presidential Campaign With a Mix of Unity and Blunt Talk About Race." *The Washington Post.* January 27. https://www.washingtonpost.com/politics/sen-kamala-harris-formally-opens-her-presidential-campaign-with-a-mix-of-unity-and-blunt-talk-about-race/2019/01/27/059be682-20f9-11e9-8e21-59a09ff1e2a1_story.html

Wamble, Julian J. and Chryl N. Laird. 2020. "The Power of Post-Racial: An Exploration of Post-Racial Rhetoric's Influence on Candidate Influence." *Politics, Groups, and Identities* 8(3): 515–534.

Waring, Chandra D. L. 2013. "'They See Me As Exotic…That Intrigues Them': Gender, Sexuality, and the Racially Ambiguous Body." *Race, Gender & Class* 20(3/4): 299–317.

Waring, Chandra D.L. and Samit D. Bordoloi. 2019. "'I don't look like her': Race, Resemblance, and Relationships in Multiracial Families." *Sociological Perspectives* 62(2): 149–166.

Waring, Chandra D.L. and Bandana Purkayastha. 2017. "'I'm a Different Kind of Biracial': How Black/White Biracial Americans with Immigrant Parents Negotiate Race." *Social Identities* 23(5): 614–630.

Washington, Myra. 2017. *Blasian Invasion: Racial Mixing in the Celebrity Industrial Complex.* University Press of Mississippi. Google Play books.

Washington, Myra. 2020. "'Draw Your Own Box': Deciphering Meghan Markle's Mixed-Race Identity." *Women's Studies in Communication* 43(4: Rhetoric and the Temporal Turn: Race, Gender, Temporalities): 348–353.

Weaver, Vesla M. 2012. "The Electoral Consequences of Skin Color: The "Hidden" Side of Race in Politics." *Political Behavior* 34: 159–192.

Welbers, Kasper, Wouter Van Atteveldt, and Kenneth Benoit. 2017. "Text Analysis in R." *Communication Methods and Measures* 11(4): 245–265.

Wells-Barnett, Ida B. 2005. *Southern Horrors: Lynch Law in All Its Phases.* https://www.gutenberg.org/ebooks/14975

West, Candace, and Sarah Fenstermaker. 1995. "Doing Difference." *Gender and Society* 9(1): 8–37.

White, Walter Francis. 1995. *A Man Called White: The Autobiography of Walter White.* University of Georgia Press.

White, Ismail K., Chryl N. Laird, and Troy D. Allen. 2014. "Selling Out: The Politics of Navigating Conflicts between Racial Group Interest and Self-Interest." *American Political Science Review* 108(4): 783–800.

Williams, Kim M. 2017. "The Recursive Outcomes of The Multiracial Movement and The End of American Racial Categories." *Studies in American Political Development* 31(1): 88–107.

Williams, Kim M. 2005. "Multiracialism & the Civil Rights Future." *Daedalus* 131(1): 53–60.

Williams, Kim M. 2006. *Mark One or More: Civil Rights in Multiracial America.* Ann Arbor: University of Michigan Press.

Wilkinson, Betina Cutaia. 2014. "Perceptions of Commonality and Latino-Black, Latino-White Relations in a Multiethnic United States." *Political Research Quarterly* 67(4): 905–916.

Woldemikael, Eve and Olivia Woldemikael. 2021. "From Suits to Royals: The Politics of Meghan Markle's Racial Ambiguity." *Women's Studies International Forum* 85, 102439.

Wolfe, Patrick. 2006. "Settler Colonialism and the Elimination of the Native." *Journal of Genocide Research* 8(4): 387–409.

Wu, H. Denis and Tien-Tsung Lee. 2005. "The Submissive, the Calculated, and the American Dream: Coverage of Asian American Political Candidates in the 1990s." *Howard Journal of Communications* 16(3): 225–241.

Yancey, George. 2003. *Who is white? Latinos, Asians, and the new Black/Nonblack Divide.* Lynne Rienner Publishers.

Young, Iris Marion. 1997. "Difference as a Resource for Democratic Communication," in James Bohman and William Rehg (Eds.). *Deliberative Democracy: Essays on Reason and Politics*, Cambridge, Massachusetts: The MIT Press, 383–404.

Zuberi, Tukufu and Eduardo Bonilla-Silva. 2008. (Eds.). *White Logic, White Methods: Racism and Methodology.* Rowman & Littlefield Publishers.

Index

For the benefit of digital users, indexed terms that span two pages (e.g., 52–53) may, on occasion, appear on only one of those pages.

Tables and figures are indicated by an italic *t* and *f*, following the paragraph number.